Praise for Lean AI

Every now and then there is a new super-hyped technology. Most of the hype ends up in the graveyard, right next to companies that used them as their main line of business. AI isn't just hype. AI is defining software, processes, work environments, and decision making in every aspect of our lives. I have no doubt that AI will continue to drive tremendous transformation in digital marketing. Lean AI *enables companies to view these dramatic changes as real opportunities.*

Oren Kaniel, CEO, AppsFlyer

Lean AI *gives companies a pragmatic road map for growth in the new age of learning machines. It's an indispensable, modern guide for any marketing team to know how to measure and manage marketing in the era of big data.*

Jim Calhoun, CEO, Nectar9

The modern growth team started with changes to people and process: full-stack teams using experimentation to drive metrics. The next shift includes predictive analytics to better understand causal relationships between user actions and business results, and make product and marketing decisions accordingly. Lean AI *helps bring this potential into focus with practical steps for embracing the power of data.*

Naomi Pilosof Ionita, Partner, Menlo Ventures

The Fourth Industrial Revolution is here, and it's changing the nature of marketing as we know it. Lean AI *is required reading for any marketing professional looking to turbocharge growth in an age of artificial intelligence and big data.*

Erik Qualman, #1 Bestselling Author of *Socialnomics*

Lean AI is a must read for any growth team that's mastered the iterative approach of the Lean Startup and wants to drive further growth with AI.

Momchil Kyurkchiev, CEO and Cofounder, Leanplum

Lomit has written a great guide to the online marketing concepts your startup needs for successful growth.

Dan Olsen, Author of *The Lean Product Playbook*

This book does a great job explaining how the next wave of innovative startups will use AI and automation to scale up significantly faster, and why incumbents should be worried.

Grant Lee, COO, ClearBrain

Lean AI is a manifesto for growth in the artificial intelligence age. Lomit expertly guides us through the relevant topics and provides a blueprint for successfully leveraging AI in the world of data-driven growth.

Andy Carvell, Cofounder, Phiture

Stopping short of calling this a Bible for startups, I will say that Lean AI *indeed is excellent reference material to have in your collection.*

Akbar Lalani, CEO, Corelead Interactive

We've been impressed with how Lomit embraced AI to transform our user acquisition efforts into a hyper-efficient machine, delivering record growth rates over the past two years. Everyone charged with acquiring customers and driving revenue should give this book a serious read. It's an indispensable road map for today and well into the future.

Kevin Hendshaw, COO, IMVU

Lomit Patel has adopted and championed the power of autonomous marketing from the very earliest of days, and his practical, no-nonsense approach to outperforming against your growth goals will be indispensable reading for anyone looking to make their mark in the world of digital marketing.

Sal Arora, Chief Data Scientist, Nectar9

Companies are spending millions of dollars without understanding the true ROI of their marketing investments. With the advent of machine learning and artificial intelligence, marketers will be able to deepen their understanding of the customer journey and serve them in new, exciting ways. Lean AI *provides a solid foundation for the next generation of marketing automation in the age of intelligent machines.*

Shamanth Rao, CEO and Founder, RocketShip HQ

Companies that embrace Lean AI *will be able to test, learn, and iterate radically faster, raising the competitive bar for learning.*

Claus Enevoldsen, Vice President, Growth, Flipboard

AI is changing the rules of growth: those who can adapt will thrive, those who fail to ride the AI wave will perish. This book provides a blueprint of how to apply AI to growth in your business.

Jessica Osorio, Lead, Mobile Growth, Mozilla

Lean AI *defines the difference between old-fashioned practices in customer acquisition and how the times have changed in taking a much faster approach to acquiring users in an automated fashion.*

Arpit Patel, Head of User Acquisition, PSafe Technology

Millions of campaigns are ignored every hour by consumers, and evidence is mounting that people crave meaningful experiences, not marketing speak. However, the work required for companies to deliver personalization at scale—sifting through billions of data points (trillions if you count the input from the sensor networks that make up the Internet of Things)—has moved beyond human capacity. This hard truth is driving a seismic shift in marketing and mindset—and the realization that CEOs must learn to collaborate and cocreate with AI to reimagine customer acquisition and the complete customer experience. Lean AI *is a seminal work that brings the full potential of this intelligence into focus like no other, providing a must-read road map and a critical foundation for companies to master the building blocks that will allow them to embrace the future today.*

Peggy Anne Salz, Chief Analyst and Founder, MobileGroove

Lean AI *is a comprehensive guide for tackling a startup's toughest challenge: growth! Read how Lomit transformed the growth projections for IMVU with* Lean AI.

Fausto Gortaire, Sr. Growth Manager, IMVU

Many effects of AI are unknown, but one thing is certain—that the best growth teams will fully embrace Lean AI in some way, shape, or form to crush the competition.

Etienne de Guébriant, Head of UA at Gazeus Games

Lean AI

How Innovative Startups Use Artificial Intelligence to Grow

Lomit Patel

Beijing · Boston · Farnham · Sebastopol · Tokyo

Lean AI

by Lomit Patel

Copyright © 2020 Lomit Patel. All rights reserved.

Printed in the United States of America.

Published by O'Reilly Media, Inc., 1005 Gravenstein Highway North, Sebastopol, CA 95472.

O'Reilly books may be purchased for educational, business, or sales promotional use. Online editions are also available for most titles (*http://oreilly.com*). For more information, contact our corporate/institutional sales department: 800-998-9938 or *corporate@oreilly.com*.

Acquisitions Editor: Melissa Duffield
Development Editors: Alicia Young and Virginia Wilson
Production Editor: Katherine Tozer
Copyeditor: Jasmine Kwityn
Proofreader: Charles Roumeliotis
Indexer: Judith McConville
Interior Designer: Monica Kamsvaag
Cover Designer: Randy Comer
Illustrator: Rebecca Demarest

March 2020: First Edition

Revision History for the First Edition
2020-01-31: First Release

See *http://oreilly.com/catalog/errata.csp?isbn=9781492059318* for release details.

The O'Reilly logo is a registered trademark of O'Reilly Media, Inc. *Lean AI*, the cover image, and related trade dress are trademarks of O'Reilly Media, Inc.

The views expressed in this work are those of the author, and do not represent the publisher's views. While the publisher and the author have used good faith efforts to ensure that the information and instructions contained in this work are accurate, the publisher and the author disclaim all responsibility for errors or omissions, including without limitation responsibility for damages resulting from the use of or reliance on this work. Use of the information and instructions contained in this work is at your own risk. If any code samples or other technology this work contains or describes is subject to open source licenses or the intellectual property rights of others, it is your responsibility to ensure that your use thereof complies with such licenses and/or rights.

978-1-492-05931-8

[LSCH]

Contents

Foreword. XI

Preface. XIII

PART I: AI + GROWTH MARKETING = SMART MARKETING

Chapter 1
Introduction to Growth Marketing 3

Chapter 2
Why Lean AI? 11

PART II: CUSTOMER ACQUISITION 3.0

Chapter 3
What Is Customer Acquisition 3.0? 25

Chapter 4
Manual Versus Automation 31

Chapter 5
Framework of an "Intelligent Machine" 45

VII

Chapter 6
Build Versus Buy 63

PART III: WHAT METRICS MATTER TO YOU?

Chapter 7
Key Metrics for Startup Growth 73

Chapter 8
Creative Performance 81

Chapter 9
Cross-Channel Attribution 91

PART IV: SELECTING THE RIGHT APPROACH TO USER ACQUISITION

Chapter 10
Different User Acquisition Strategies 111

Chapter 11
The Growth Stack 119

PART V: MANAGING INCREASED COMPLEXITY AND RISK

Chapter 12
How to Manage Complexity 157

Chapter 13
How to Reduce Risk 165

Chapter 14
Human Versus Machine 173

PART VI: THE NEXT FRONTIER

Chapter 15
Planning for Success 181

Chapter 16
Ongoing Challenges 193

Chapter 17
How to Win Together with AI 201

Index 207

Foreword

What you have in front of you is not just one book, but two. It's a comprehensive look at the elements of building and scaling a successful startup, written with clarity by someone with deep experience. It's also a guide to the future of what that process will look like as companies add more and more artificial intelligence and automation to all of their practices—a transformation that has already begun and will evolve quickly in the coming years.

These two aspects of *Lean AI* work together for a number of reasons, but the most crucial one is that no matter what new technologies come along, the basic goals of growth teams aren't going to change. They'll remain the acquisition, retention, and monetization of customers. Some portions of this book cover how that process works, including discussions and examples of key metrics—like customer acquisition cost, retention rate, customer lifetime value, return on advertising spending, and conversion rate—and a deep dive into the elements that make up the optimal growth stack.

What will change going forward is how growth teams achieve their goals. This is where the other parts of the book come in, like the fundamentals of AI, its relationship to automation, what a basic framework looks like, and how to approach the decision about whether to build or buy the solution that fits your organization. It's optimistic while also being realistic, and it doesn't shy away from the risks and challenges inherent in adopting this new way of working (among them matters of transparency and privacy as well as the human cost of handing over some of our tasks to machines).

Artificial intelligence promises many things for the future of how Lean Startup works in organizations: savings in time and money, the ability to perform (by orders of magnitude) many more experiments to gather data faster and more efficiently, and a more multidimensional understanding of what customers are looking for and how to give it to them. As companies grow, these capabilities and others will add to their power. As Patel writes,

> scale will create value in new ways across multiple dimensions: scale in the amount of relevant data companies can generate and access, scale in the quantity of learning that can be extracted from this data, scale to diminish the risks of experimentation, scale in the size and value of collaborative ecosystems, scale in the quantity of new ideas they can generate as a result of these factors, and scale in buffering the risks of unanticipated shocks.

Finally, this is a book about the opportunity that awaits in human–machine partnership. It's full of information about how to prepare to take advantage of it so your organization can grow far into the future.

—*Eric Ries*

Preface

Launching and growing a new startup has always been a challenging endeavor. It requires most entrepreneurs and leaders to be open to trying new and innovative approaches to increase the odds of success—and that involves risk.

You can increase your chances for success by simply taking a rational and methodical approach to finding the best strategy for running the business. The Lean Startup movement has been one of the most successful systematic approaches to date. It has been widely adopted across the globe, changing the way startups are built and new products are launched.

The best growth teams in the world use the same approach to iterative learning by continuously running experiments for customer acquisition. They take the same logical approach to testing and tweaking their efforts to make the business grow as fast as possible.

Today, artificial intelligence, sensors, and digital platforms have created enormous opportunity for learning faster than ever before. Competing on the *rate of learning* will become the key difference between the startups that succeed and those that fail. Companies that embrace Lean AI will be able to test, learn, and iterate radically faster, raising the competitive bar for learning. By taking the wisdom outlined by Eric Ries in *The Lean Startup* into the golden dawn of artificial intelligence, we can radically improve our chances of successful outcomes.

This book provides practical advice on how you can scale up growth significantly faster when your company combines a Lean, nimble team with the judicious use of artificial intelligence and automation. It provides a pragmatic road map for growth in the age of intelligent machines. It's an essential, modern guide any business can use to better understand how to measure and manage marketing in the era of big data. I wrote this book based on my personal experience on what it takes to build and leverage an "intelligent machine" to turbocharge your business growth and outsmart your competitors.

Who This Book Is For

This book is for any business entrepreneur, leader, executive, or investor who wants the competitive edge to scale up their customer acquisition growth better, smarter, and faster than the incumbents. Likewise, aspiring or experienced founders, CEOs, marketing executives, venture capitalists, and heads of growth and user acquisition, as well as key members on their teams, will benefit from reading it.

How This Book Is Organized

The book consists of six parts:

- Part I focuses on growth marketing with an overview of the current startup landscape and the biggest challenges currently facing new companies around customer acquisition. It provides an overview of the main components of Lean AI and takes a look at industry trends for leveraging AI for smart marketing.

- Part II looks at Customer Acquisition 3.0, providing you an overview of how to effectively leverage your customer data using "intelligent machines" powered by artificial intelligence. The chapters in this part explain how to identify tasks to automate, offer an overview of the intelligent machine framework, and provide information that will help you decide whether to build it or buy it based on your resource constraints.

- Part III provides guidance on how to select the right metrics for success that align on driving long-term growth. It explores the importance of creative assets and the area of cross-channel attribution to help optimize your intelligent machine.

- Part IV outlines five proven keys to user acquisition strategies and how to choose the right one for your business. It also dives deep into the "growth stack"—a set of tools that all work together to help you get the specific results you're looking for, given your situation.

- Part V explores how to manage increased complexity and risk with the data needed for artificial intelligence to work. It also examines how the future growth team would coexist with humans and machines working together in ways that take advantage of the intelligent machine framework we share in the book.

- Part VI moves into how humans and machines can work symbiotically to produce the best work. We'll take a look at that "next frontier," including its potential for triumphs and the challenges it presents to your growth efforts.

Acknowledgments

I owe a tremendous debt of gratitude to the many people who have made this book possible.

First, I'm grateful to my amazing wife, Sophia Daryanani-Patel. She is my best friend, biggest cheerleader, and the love of my life. I really appreciate her giving me the time needed to focus on writing this book and being supportive throughout the process, as always with great insight, patience, and love.

This book took six months to write, but the concept for Lean AI took over two years to learn and perfect at IMVU. Kevin Henshaw was responsible for both recruiting me and always being my biggest advocate while supporting me with the resources needed to fully embrace Lean AI. I'm grateful to him and all the different people at IMVU who have always supported me in making Lean AI successful.

I thank Eric Ries for all his encouragement in helping to make this book idea come to life. His steadfast support for Lean AI from the start and belief in me in writing this book has been priceless. I couldn't ask for a better mentor.

I'm grateful to the amazing people at O'Reilly Media for the extraordinary task of transforming the Lean AI story from an idea into this amazing book before you. Thank you to my editors, Melissa Duffield and Alicia Young, for seeing the vision through from the start, offering insightful editing, and expertly managing it throughout the entire process. Katie Tozer, Virginia Wilson, Monica Kamsvaag, Karen Montgomery, Rebecca Demarest, Jasmine Kwityn, and others helped to make this book a reality. They are all extremely talented and I'm so lucky to have the opportunity to work with them in writing this book.

I'd also like to thank the co-founders of Nectar9, Inc.—Jim Calhoun, CEO, and Sal Arora, the company's chief data scientist—for their continued support, dedication, and the contributions they've made to the development of this book. We've enjoyed a close partnership built on a shared vision for marketing automation in the age of intelligent machines, pushing the envelope of possibility. I hope that spirit comes through in the pages of this book.

Thanks to all of the following incredible experts and peers for their patience in crowd-editing *Lean AI*: Abril McCloud, Aemee Doherty, Akbar Lalani, Andy Carvell, Claus Enevoldsen, Dan Olsen, Donnie Kajikawa, Etienne Guebriant,

Fausto Gortaire, Grant Lee, Jasper Radeke, Jim Calhoun, Kevin Hendshaw, Marjaneh Ravai, Naomi Pilosof Ionita, Rajeev Raman, Sal Arora, and Sergey Grytsuk. Their insights and suggestions were extremely important in making this book what it is.

To my mother, Kusum Patel, who has guided me, loved me, and consoled me through it all: I love you more than words can say.

I have no doubt neglected to include some very important people, which is an oversight on my part. I hope you can forgive the oversight and accept my sincere thanks!

Finally, and most importantly, I'd like to thank you, the reader. That you spent your precious time and attention reading this book means the world to me. Feel free to contact me at *LomitPatel.com/Contact* if there are any questions or concerns I can help you with.

PART I

AI + GROWTH MARKETING = SMART MARKETING

Part I of this book consists of Chapter 1 and Chapter 2. Chapter 1, "Introduction to Growth Marketing," provides an overview of the current startup landscape and the biggest challenges currently facing new companies—chief among them is customer acquisition, with the need to acquire customers widely and effectively in a crowded field. This is where Lean AI comes in, which is the focus of Chapter 2. In this chapter, you'll learn about the main components of Lean AI (artificial intelligence and machine learning applied to the function of growth marketing) and we'll take a look at industry trends for leveraging AI for smart marketing, which will prepare you for Part II's dive into what we call "Customer Acquisition 3.0."

CHAPTER 1

Introduction to Growth Marketing

At its core, this is a book about growth marketing and how advances in technology can help achieve your company's goals faster—at a lower cost and with less risk—than ever before. In the last 10 years, "growth marketing" functions have sprung up inside Silicon Valley startups and yielded incredibly valuable companies like Facebook, Pinterest, Uber, and others that have institutionalized their growth marketing approach. As our experience with growth marketing has matured, we're in a good place to document the best practices and modern approaches any company can understand and adopt to help them unlock their full growth potential.

For most companies, growth marketing is the way of the future for leveraging data and agility to scale revenue and increase customer lifetime value. As campaigns continue to shift more toward digital, it's easier to track and monitor every move. Designing strategies around the entire customer journey and funnel, and constantly being ready to iterate and improve, will deliver clarity around attribution sources and fuel revenue growth. The days of guessing about how to invest your user acquisition budget are over. With a well-thought-out growth marketing strategy, you can now use real-time data to validate which efforts are working and which are not.

 With a well-thought-out growth marketing strategy, you can now use real-time data to validate which efforts are working and which are not.

Entrepreneurs flock to Silicon Valley, affectionately called the "Valley of Dreams," to build fast-growing startup companies fueled by venture capital.

3

These startups aim to scale their growth to hundreds of millions of users and guide their company to a successful exit, whether that be an acquisition by a larger entity or through an IPO. For the venture capitalists funding these endeavors, the risks and the rewards are high; most venture capital funds have a fund life of approximately 10 years, in which they seek a liquidity event for their portfolio companies.[1]

With this additional pressure on venture-backed startups, companies know that they must accelerate growth at all costs. The reality, however, is that most venture-backed startups fail spectacularly. As discussed in "How VCs Deploy Operating Talent to Build Better Startups," research estimates that between 30% to 40% of high-potential start-ups end up liquidating all assets within the first five years. If failure is defined as failing to see the projected return on investment—say, a specific revenue growth rate or date to break even on cash flow—then more than 95% of startups fail.[2]

Considering the risk of failure, startups have to come to market prepared to address the three biggest challenges to success: hiring the right people, acquiring and keeping customers, and optimizing for revenue growth.[3] While every startup purports itself to be the next unicorn, it's only the ones who are prepared to overcome these key challenges that end up becoming successful. The financial pressure and constant state of resource constraint is also one of the startup's most significant advantages, because it fosters a creative, agile environment where teams are encouraged to experiment, learn, and outmaneuver incumbents and the competition. In this book, you'll learn how to take advantage of the Lean AI + Customer Acquisition strategy for leveraging data and automation to scale your user growth.

One of the most crucial stages that has the potential to make or break any startup beyond determining your basic product/market fit is *growth marketing*. Growth marketing looks at the entire customer funnel as a singular object with many working parts, where experimenting with messaging at the top of the funnel and down-funnel hypothesizing and testing work together to increase customer acquisition rates by any means possible. Understanding the intricacies of this approach to marketing is critical to figuring out how you can use a new class of software—artificial intelligence and machine learning capable of making sense of immense amounts of data and market feedback—so we'll

---

[1] A liquidity event is an event that allows founders and early investors in a company to cash out some or all of their ownership shares. The liquidity event is considered an exit strategy for an illiquid investment—that is, for equity that has little or no market to trade on.

[2] Drew Hansen, "How VCs Deploy Operating Talent To Build Better Startups," *Forbes*. *https://oreil.ly/ZNl9s*.

[3] "State of Startups 2018," First Round. *https://oreil.ly/UKk0A*.

spend plenty of time bringing clarity to the fundamental underpinnings of growth marketing.

In *The Lean Startup*, Eric Ries teaches entrepreneurs how to be hyper-efficient with resources in order to make the most viable business decisions. He argues that entrepreneurs should run small *experiments* all the time. Even though 9 out of 10 experiments may fail, the one that succeeds may make your business grow 100x faster. The growth marketer plays a crucial role in the Lean Startup process by constantly testing and tweaking to make the business grow as fast as possible. The key is to take action—to try, to fail, to learn, and, eventually, prevail.

Having a wide customer base is a key determining factor for revenue, and, consequently, the success of any startup. Acquiring this wide customer base is growth marketing's primary function, making it an essential part of any marketing strategy. But the fact stands, the procedure requires immense time and intelligence to make a startup stand out from the crowd. In this book you will learn how to take advantage of leveraging artificial intelligence (AI) in growth marketing to help you crush your goals to acquire customers and drive revenue growth once you have achieved product/market fit.

> **Thought Experiment: Autonomous Cars for Marketing**
>
> In many ways, the advent of cloud-based computing and powerful computational capabilities available on demand has ushered in a new era that has the capability to bring some of our most ambitious dreams to life. Case in point: autonomous vehicles, or "self-driving cars."
>
> The idea for self-driving vehicles followed closely behind the advent of the automobile itself. In 1925, New Yorkers witnessed the first radio-controlled vehicle—an empty touring car—as it sauntered up Broadway and down Fifth Avenue through congested streets. The inventor, Francis Houdina, operated the vehicle from a second car, as shown in Figure 1-1.
>
>
>
> **Figure 1-1.** *The first radio-controlled vehicle, demonstrated in New York*

> The ambitious project floundered after an altercation with Harry Houdini (who felt Houdina was using a play on his name to profit) and a few more demonstrations. Grand plans to sell and further develop the *Phantom Auto* in the greater Milwaukee area fell victim to the Great Depression.

Champions of growth marketing adopt a cross-functional approach with multiple stakeholders, including product, marketing, engineering, and data science. These teams enable an organization to "compete on the rate of learning" and create a path to hyper customer acquisition growth. In many ways, this book is an extension of the latter stages of a Lean Startup, after startups have reached product/market fit; the speed of learning needs to accelerate, and this book presents a framework for tackling that challenge. The emergence of growth as a function has changed people's expectations around velocity. This means that *learning* needs to happen faster, because decisions need to be made faster to compete.

Taking the wisdom of *The Lean Startup*'s approach into the golden dawn of artificial intelligence, we can radically improve our chances of successful outcomes. A properly instrumented approach to modern artificial intelligence, machine learning, and automation combine to offer companies large and small the ability to conduct far more experiments simultaneously. Conducting experiments at scale improves the likelihood of finding successful experiments, some of which you'd never have taken the time to test in a pre-AI world. Incremental experiments that otherwise would have been sidelined for cost or complexity are now valid for observation in the world of autonomous marketing.

 Taking the wisdom of The Lean Startup's *approach into the golden dawn of artificial intelligence, we can radically improve our chances of successful outcomes.*

The Attention Economy

> *Lean Startup isn't about being cheap [but it is about] being less wasteful and still doing things that are big.*
> Eric Ries

For any business, the goal is to create sustainable and systematic customer acquisition strategies that keep revenue and profits flowing while keeping up with industry trends. As more brands continue to increase ad spend across a myriad of channels to acquire new customers, the average cost of expanding your customer base continues to climb year over year.

The average consumer's attention is now literally worth billions of dollars, because that's how much money companies are spending on their user acquisition efforts across mobile, desktop, television, radio, and/or voice assistants. Every digital interaction is an opportunity for brands to bombard users with advertisements in an effort to turn your attention toward their product or service.

While we may not think about it through this lens often, the fact is that human attention is a *finite resource*. For every 24 hours, Americans spend on average only 5.9[4] online, which means that companies only have those six hours every day to get the right messaging in front of the right audience and convert them into customers. With endless demand and a finite supply, human attention is arguably one of the most valuable resources in the world—companies are constantly and quite literally competing for your attention and your wallet. And the race for your time and money has only gotten tighter thanks to the addition of the apps and channels we use to live, work, learn, and play like Google, Facebook, Instagram, YouTube, Amazon, Netflix, Pandora, and Fortnite among many others. If six hours per day are spent online, then taking time spent on social media, streaming, and gaming sites reduces "marketable" hours to a small fraction of each day. But that's where the challenge, and the opportunity, lies.

How you bring new consumers to your business is customer acquisition, which is also sometimes referred to as "user acquisition," depending on the type of products or services you're offering. Given the demand that exists to command human attention, one of the top challenges for any startup is acquiring and retaining new customers cost-effectively.

In the beginning, the vast majority of startups struggle to find users or customers. No wonder: if you've got a new product or service, very few people will be familiar with it or your brand. Regardless of the size of your business or startup, acquiring customers profitably is a critical aspect of running a business. It also acts as evidence of traction for your startup to customers, partners, investors, influencers, and prospects. All future startup growth depends on two things: acquire customers fast and acquire customers sustainably.

Most startups generally work with contractors or marketing agencies in the early days to help with growth marketing. The general approach is to broadly test many different paid and organic user acquisition channels to figure out what works and doesn't. There is no generic growth playbook guaranteed to

---

4 The average adult spends 5.9 hours per day with digital media, up from 3 hours a day in 2009, according to Mary Meeker's 2018 Internet Trends Report.

CHAPTER 1: INTRODUCTION TO GROWTH MARKETING

work across all different startups because every business is unique. I can confidently say there is no silver bullet to drive growth.

The real secret to scaling customer growth in a startup is to run as many A/B tests as possible. A/B testing, as it's commonly referred to, involves testing a set of independent variables (offer, copy, pricing, etc.) to find statistically significant improvements toward reaching your business goals.

This approach would lead you to test, learn, and iterate as quickly as possible by finding small wins that end up compounding into massive growth in the long term. Obviously, the A/B testing and hypothesis development have to be scientifically based on some best practices, observable evidence, and statistical significance. But as an organization the big takeaway here is not to sit back and suffer from "analysis paralysis" where overthinking gets in the way of making decisions, working against your ultimate objective.

Your biggest leverage is to figure out how to increase the volume and velocity of experiments and tests you can run across the entire customer journey from different prospecting and retargeting channels as well as product features and experiences to help you better engage, retain, and monetize customers. The lifeblood of any startup is cash in the bank because you need to pay your expenses. The biggest expense for most startups—second only to payroll—is their user acquisition budget that the head of growth manages.

But there's a problem with this conventional approach to scaling user growth in startups. Successful businesses following this paradigm can become highly dependent on people to help execute all the different A/B tests, which is both time and labor intensive. When I think about the next generation of growth teams they're going to have to be much quicker in execution with the increasing pace of change in today's world. Everything happens much faster now with even more pressure to produce results that are being tracked in real time. It's hard for any startup to build a successful growth team quickly. The future will involve leveraging AI in growth marketing, as the only way any startup can survive and thrive in a highly competitive world is by getting A/B testing ideas quicker and implementing them faster than anyone else, because global competition means the time frame you have is shorter and shorter.

There is a smarter approach on the horizon, and becoming familiar with the pros and cons of this new way of thinking presents a major opportunity to businesses and leaders as well as employees. Today, we can leverage artificial intelligence and machine learning to enhance and manage your user acquisition channels, radically accelerate the velocity of A/B testing all the key variables (like audiences, geographic markets, creatives), and process all your user data faster to uncover better insights and make smarter decisions on where to invest your user acquisition budget to get the best return on investment (ROI).[5]

All of these major marketing platforms have application programming interface (API)[6] connections, which make it much easier to capture and share data to automate the key levers for optimizing campaigns without being dependent on humans. This book will show you how to leverage these ideas, strategies, tools, and technologies to scale up your startup growth and stack the odds for success in your favor. To start, let's move on to Chapter 2, where we will explore some of the building blocks and the possibilities you can unlock with Lean AI.

---

[5] ROI measures the gain or loss generated on an investment relative to the amount of money invested. ROI is usually expressed as a percentage and is typically used for personal financial decisions, to compare a company's profitability or to compare the efficiency of different investments.

[6] In basic terms, an API allows applications to communicate with one another. An API is not a database. It is an access point to an app that can access a database.

CHAPTER 2

Why Lean AI?

The hype around AI and machine learning (ML) has continued to gain momentum as every major industry, from marketing to healthcare to manufacturing to transportation to finance to retail and beyond, has started to leverage advances in AI and AI-based applications to improve productivity and performance. Economists have hailed AI as a core enabling technology of the "Fourth Industrial Revolution."[1] With all of this excitement, executives have started thinking about how their businesses will use AI to not only survive this revolution, but excel among their cohorts. According to PwC,[2] AI will contribute $15.7 trillion to the global economy by 2030. Clearly, there is a huge opportunity for businesses to benefit from investing in AI. The MIT Sloan Management Review 2017 Artificial Intelligence Global Executive Study and Research Project (*https://oreil.ly/YuZuy*) found that 85% of executives believe that AI will help their businesses gain or sustain competitive advantage.

As with any technology that fuels the public and business imagination, there is a lot of confusion around the terms "machine learning" and "artificial intelligence." Many people use AI and ML interchangeably, while others utilize them as discrete, parallel advancements. This confusion ripples into the common understanding of AI and ML, where much of the public discussing these advancements are unaware of the distinctions between the two. For some, this

---

1 Professor Klaus Schwab, Founder and Executive Chairman of the World Economic Forum, characterized the Fourth Industrial Revolution by a range of new technologies that are fusing the physical, digital, and biological worlds, impacting all disciplines, economies, and industries, and even challenging ideas about what it means to be human.
2 "Sizing the Prize," PwC, 2017. *https://oreil.ly/vf7dj*.

dilution of the terms is overlooked in favor of creating hyper-excitement for advertising and sales purposes. Machine learning is simply one of the most common and approachable applications of AI.

This chapter will provide you with working definitions for AI and ML that we'll carry through the rest of the book, and we'll also explore how these concepts support the framework of a Lean Startup.

What Is Artificial Intelligence?

Artificial intelligence is often used as an umbrella term to describe types of technology that can simulate human intelligence. It's the ability of a computer program or a machine to think and learn. It is also a field of study that tries to make computers "smart," where computers work on their own without being encoded with commands.

John McCarthy came up with the term "artificial intelligence" in 1955. Artificial intelligence is essentially building a machine or computer program to parse data to learn from different signals to make smart decisions on predictive actions to achieve a given goal or desired outcome. Artificial intelligence is the science and engineering of making computers behave in ways that, until recently, we thought required human intelligence.

The term "artificial intelligence" has a broader meaning. It's the idea that machines and computers can complete tasks normally requiring human intelligence. AI as we know it today is manifested in human–AI interaction gadgets and services such as Google Home, Siri, and Alexa; the ML–powered video prediction systems that power Netflix, Amazon Prime, and YouTube; and the algorithms hedge funds use to make micro-trades that rake in millions of dollars every year. These technology advancements are progressively becoming important in our daily lives. In fact, they are intelligent assistants that enhance our abilities, making us more productive.

What Is Machine Learning?

Let's define *machine learning* since it is such a ubiquitous term these days but has many meanings. Machine learning is a type of artificial intelligence developed around allowing computer systems to progressively improve performance on a task by "learning" through a range of statistical approaches. Put another way, machine learning is the development of algorithms that allow for more and more accurate predictions based on the incremental collection of data.

The machine learning concept is about giving machines access to data to enable them to learn from it themselves. In contrast to ML, AI is a moving target, and its definition changes as its related technological advancements are further developed. AI incorporates a bunch of technologies that include ML, deep learning, inference algorithms, natural language processing, neural networks, and computer vision. These technologies are starting to show real promise, despite the hype and confusion in the marketplace. Artificial intelligence is at a critical point in its evolution, especially as it relates to marketing automation.

Machine learning usually works best with large data sets by examining and comparing the data to find common patterns and explore nuances. It automates model building for data analysis. The concept behind machine learning is that a computer can learn from the data it analyzes by identifying patterns. Ultimately, this technology can make decisions without humans. Essentially, it gives machines the ability to learn and adapt through experience. Here's how it works: the system uses probability to make decisions or predictions based on the available data. It then uses feedback loops to find out if its prediction was right or wrong. Predictions get more and more accurate—and the system gets smarter.

An example of a startup that has successfully leveraged ML is IMVU, which is the world's largest avatar-based social network. They work with third-party customer relationship management (CRM)[3] engagement platforms like Leanplum to collect a huge amount of real-time customer data—from user profiles, location, revenue and usage stats, which features users are interacting with, and much more. But on its own, this data only tells us what happened in the past. Machine learning, on the other hand, uses this information to predict the future—for example, which users are most likely to churn so that critical attention can be offered to keep them engaged to experience the value in the product. Data is useless if it doesn't help you make better decisions in the future to achieve your desired business goals to scale growth.

What Is the Lean Startup?

Launching and growing a new startup has always been a challenging endeavor—which is why you need to be open to trying new and innovative approaches to increase your odds for success. The chances of being successful can be significantly increased simply by taking a rational and systematic approach to finding the best strategy for running the business. The Lean Startup movement has been one of the most successful systematic approaches to date and has been widely adopted across the globe, changing the way startups are built and new products are launched.

---

3 CRM is an approach to managing a company's interaction with current and potential customers. It uses data analysis about customers' history with a company to improve business relationships with customers, specifically focusing on customer retention and ultimately driving sales growth.

The Lean Startup is a methodology for developing businesses and products that aims to shorten product development cycles and rapidly discover if a proposed business model is viable; this is achieved by adopting a combination of business-hypothesis-driven experimentation, iterative product releases, and validated learning. The Lean Startup method teaches you how to drive a startup—how to steer, when to turn, and when to persevere—and grow a business with maximum acceleration. It is a principled approach to get a desired product into customers' hands faster.

Central to the Lean Startup methodology is the assumption that when startup companies invest their time into iteratively building products or services to meet the needs of early customers, the company can reduce market risks and sidestep the need for large amounts of initial project funding and expensive product launches and failures.

The same approach to iterative learning by continuously running experiments is practiced by the best growth teams, who take the same systematic testing and tweaking approach to make the business grow as fast as possible. The key is to take action—to try, to fail, to learn, and to win by learning faster than anyone else.

Taking the wisdom of the Lean Startup approach into the golden dawn of artificial intelligence, we can radically improve our chances of successful outcomes. It's basically running experiments on steroids. A properly instrumented approach to modern artificial intelligence, machine learning, and automation offers companies large and small the ability to conduct far more experiments simultaneously. This speeds up the process of finding successful experiments—some of which you'd never have taken the time to test in a pre-AI world. Incremental experiments that otherwise would have been sidelined for cost or complexity are now valid for observation in the world of autonomous marketing.

Three Key Drivers of Artificial Intelligence

Here are three key factors that have helped accelerate recent advances in AI, which is leading to more major demand-side and supply-side partners adopting AI to offer more robust paid advertising options for growth teams to get better performance on their paid user acquisition budget.

Computing Power

The price performance of computing power has grown exponentially in alignment with Moore's law.[4] Exponential means that, year over year, the computing speed doubles and/or the price drops by half. In recent years, machine learning as one of the key drivers of AI advances has greatly benefited from graphics processing units (GPUs). GPUs are very performant for conducting the vectorized numerical operations needed for all machine learning calculations. Google's Tensor Processing Unit (TPU) is another example where (co)processors are optimized for machine learning problems. With great advances in quantum computing it is very likely that this trend will continue and accelerate. They give us the ability to solve complex problems that are beyond the capabilities of classical computers like encryption, optimization, and other similar tasks.

Quantum computers can analyze large quantities of data to provide artificial intelligence machines the feedback required to improve performance. In addition, they are much more efficient than traditional computers and therefore accelerate the learning curve for artificial intelligence machines. Just like humans, artificial intelligence machines powered by the insights from quantum computers can learn from experience and self-correct. Quantum computers will help artificial intelligence expand to more areas of growth marketing and also help technology become much more intuitive.

Availability of Data

Data is the fuel for AI and your own customer data is the most precious asset. There is an accelerated generation and availability of data powered by the increased use of connected devices like mobile technology and social media. In fact, the number of internet users has grown by over a billion in the last five years; more than half of the world's web traffic now comes from mobile phones. Large amounts of data are essential to successfully utilize machine learning and therefore achieve a high accuracy for predictions for growth marketing questions like which of your customers are most likely to purchase or churn in the near future. More user behavior and activity is being tracked and shared than ever before, flooding out of the dozens of connected devices we use every day, and it shows no signs of slowing down. Knowledge is power and there's a lot of knowledge trapped in your internal data as well as external sources. To best unlock that knowledge, you have to consider the type of data

---

4 Moore's law (*http://www.mooreslaw.org*) is a computing term which originated around 1970; the simplified version of this law states that processor speeds, or overall processing power for computers, will double every two years. A quick check among technicians in different computer companies shows that the term is not very popular but the rule is still accepted.

you need, where to look for it, how to get it, and how to build the right data models to analyze your business questions. And just as importantly, you need to continually update your data to retrain and enhance the algorithms. There's certainly a lot that goes into data collection, but it's worth it. As the lifeblood of AI, data is critical to helping you get the business insights you need to move your business forward.

 Data is the fuel for AI and your own customer data is the most precious asset.

Algorithms

Algorithms are used for calculation, data processing, and automated reasoning. We have witnessed algorithms become a ubiquitous part of our lives, to the extent that we may not even always know where they lurk; the biggest focus in the machine learning space is on data mining and pattern recognition. Algorithms can make systems smarter; for example, movie recommendations from Netflix. However, there is a common principle that underlies all supervised machine learning[5] algorithms for predictive modeling. Machine learning algorithms are described as learning a target function (f) that best maps input variables (X) to an output variable (Y): Y = f(X). The most common type of machine learning is to learn the mapping Y = f(X) to make predictions of Y for new X. This is called predictive modeling (or predictive analytics) and the goal is to make the most accurate predictions possible. The questions being raised about algorithms at the moment are not about algorithms per se, but about the way society is structured with regard to data use and data privacy with data breaches becoming more prevalent. It's also about how models are being used to predict the future. Algorithms embedded into the technology through which we access so much information could be shaping what information we receive, how we receive it, even how we react to it. And AI might be shaping our behavior, not as an unintended consequence of its use, but by design. Technology, often aided by AI, is exploiting human psychology to shape how we behave.

---

5 Supervised learning is the machine learning task of learning a function that maps an input to an output based on example input-output pairs.

Industry Trends for AI Marketing

Today, artificial intelligence, sensors, and digital platforms have already increased the opportunity for learning more effectively—but competing on the rate of learning (*https://oreil.ly/b38mY*) will become the key difference between the startups that succeed and those that fail. Companies that embrace AI will be able to test, learn, and iterate much faster, raising the competitive bar for learning.

The benefits will generate a "data flywheel" effect,[6] which is the idea that more users get you more data, which lets you build better algorithms and ultimately a better product to get more users. Rinse and repeat—companies that learn faster will have better offerings, attracting more customers and more data, further increasing their ability to learn. This is similar to the Lean Startup premise where every startup is in a constant flux of running experiments to create a feedback loop around "build-measure-learn" using data to answer key questions on whether to preserve or pivot. But when it comes to concrete tasks or goals such as a product release or acquiring new users, all that matters is: do we have a strong hypothesis that will enable us to learn? If so, execute, iterate, and learn. We don't need the best possible hypothesis. We don't need the best possible plan. We need to get through the build-measure-learn feedback loop with maximum speed. The same applies with customer acquisition, where the goal is to leverage AI to speed up the velocity of experiments at different stages of the customer marketing funnel to enable startups to learn or fail fast with minimum impact on cash burn rate. The end goal is to figure out how to move new customers further down the funnel faster powered by AI + data to get smarter with optimizing the right levers.

According to the eMarketer report "Artificial Intelligence for Marketers 2018,"[7] the advent of new algorithms, faster processing, and massive, cloud-based data sets is making it possible for companies in all industries to experiment with AI. Here are the key takeaways from the eMarketer report on AI industry trends for marketers:

- Investment and interest in AI remains high, though large-scale adoption is happening more slowly. Still, many companies have ambitious plans for AI systems and are looking to them to improve their business operations.

---

[6] "The Data Flywheel," CB Insights, June 2017. *https://oreil.ly/rdOvC*.

[7] Victoria Petrock, "Artificial Intelligence for Marketers 2018," eMarketer, October 2017. *https://oreil.ly/IkzVU*.

- AI technologies—including machine learning, deep learning, natural language processing, and computer vision—are starting to show real promise, despite a significant amount of confusion in the marketplace.
- A robust ecosystem of prepackaged APIs, open source software, and cloud-based platforms is helping accelerate AI adoption, bringing new capabilities to speed up, scale, and personalize marketing campaigns in more economical ways.
- Agencies and other consultants are stepping up to the plate, beefing up their technical resources and forging technology partnerships in an effort to help their clients navigate the dizzying array of AI and marketing-tech solutions.
- Best practices for marketers include clearly defining business goals, thoroughly understanding the technology, planning for the future, having the right data, and using AI ethically.

The 2018 AI in Marketing report (*https://oreil.ly/W6bLm*) from BI Intelligence shared the following insights on the key challenges and opportunities on leveraging AI in marketing:

- The digital marketing industry is already focused on streamlining operations and reducing costs; integrating AI takes it even further. Common current uses and applications of AI in digital marketing are cost and ROI analysis for performance advertising on search, social media sentiment analysis, and chatbots for customer service.
- Marketers are increasingly incorporating AI tools into their strategies. Over half (51%) of marketers currently use AI, and an additional 27% are expected to incorporate the technology by 2019. This represents the highest anticipated year-over-year (YoY) growth of any leading technology that marketers expect to adopt.
- But the rapid pace of innovation is contributing to marketers' sense of unpreparedness for AI implementation and future use cases. When asked to choose which trending technology they felt most unprepared for, 34% of global marketing executives chose AI, the most of any option, according to Conductor.
- AI is advancing beyond data analysis and moving rapidly into data generation, as machines get better at automating two basic human senses: sight and hearing. AI technology has now developed to the point where gleaning insights from data-rich media like voice and video is possible, and humans no longer have to manually categorize or describe various types of media.
- AI will transform marketers from reactive to proactive planners. The enhanced analytics that AI provides will help marketers more efficiently

plan and execute campaigns in three main areas: segmentation, tracking, and keyword tagging.
- Programmatic advertising will become smarter and more automated. Implementing AI and getting the most valuable insights depends on a reliable, consistent flow of data to train algorithms and help them learn and improve over time. Programmatic ad buying generates billions of data points, and over the next few years, AI will reduce the manual oversight of programmatic ad campaigns, and help optimize ad parameters in real time.
- AI will aid in content creation, but human marketers are still necessary. It's still early days for marketers to use AI to automatically create editorial content or stitch together the right image with the right messaging for display ads. Machines will help cut down on production time, but humans are needed for their creative juices and ability to inform strategy.

Both of these reports clearly articulate that AI is at a critical point in its evolution. The future of marketing trends in the world of AI looks extremely bright if you can start to figure out now how to fully leverage it to drive more growth in your business. There is no denying that things will get even more exciting with the adoption of 5G to introduce marketers to retail apps that take into account foldable displays, better-timed and longer ads, and tighter integration between mobile and store experiences. However, the reality is that it will take 5G another five years before it reaches critical mass among consumers in most countries. The user data you can capture across many different touch points on a daily basis is limitless. It's only going to get faster, cheaper, and bigger. And if you're not leveraging AI to make sense of all the data coming at your organization at such a high velocity, you're likely to be left behind your competition.

The question is this: how are you going to best leverage AI to give your startup a competitive advantage to take better actions to scale up your user growth efforts to hit your success goals? Today, artificial intelligence, sensors, and digital platforms—and a proliferation of data—have already increased the opportunity for learning more effectively; but competing on the rate of learning will become a necessity in the 2020s. The dynamic, uncertain business environment will require startups to focus more on discovery and adaptation rather than only on forecasting and planning.

The startups that move fast to adopt and expand their use of AI will raise the competitive bar for learning. And the benefits will generate a "data flywheel" effect—startups learning faster by attracting more customers and more data, further increasing their ability to learn and scale up growth at a faster pace than their competitors. For example, Netflix's algorithms take in behavioral data from its video streaming platform and automatically provide dynamic, personalized recommendations for each user; this improves the product, keeping more users on the platform for longer and generating more data to further fuel the learning cycle to scale user growth.

AI + Growth Marketing = Smart Marketing

There are many exciting ways you can apply the power of AI and ML to streamline marketing processes across the entire customer marketing funnel to help growth teams work smarter by automating in the following areas to help them stand apart from the competition:

- Segmentation
- Personalization
- Media buying
- Campaign optimization
- Predicting customer behavior
- Data analysis and reporting
- Customer support
- Better cross-platform attribution
- Fraud prevention
- Creative development and iteration

I've found plenty of examples of ways that AI is transforming growth marketing to allow us to achieve things that would never have been possible without it. With AI, you can work smarter and gain a holistic, real-time view of your customers and their relevant interactions throughout the entire journey. AI lets you act quickly on your data and makes it easier to focus on the higher value work by getting fast, actionable insights.

However, while the data to support AI is critical, data is nothing without a clearly defined business problem focused on cost reduction, risk reduction, and profit. Perhaps the most interesting thing about AI is that, while it can automate and do "work" at greater efficiency, it uses machine learning to "think" and "learn" over time, strategizing, designing, recognizing patterns, and making decisions. If that sounds a lot like a human brain, it's because deep learning, one of the most important methods of machine learning, is based on the idea of a neural network, modeling the structure and function of the human brain.

Assessing the Maturity of Autonomous Marketing (with Help from the Self-Driving Car Folks)

With ambitions to launch self-driving cars to the public in 2020, Tesla gets a lot of attention in the autonomous vehicle industry. But big automobile companies, startups, and tech giants are all working to deliver safe, self-driving vehicles to the masses.

To make sense of where artificial intelligence and automation is at and where it's going, the industry trade association the Society of Automobile Engineers (SAE) introduced its autonomy scale. It helps the industry determine and classify different levels of autonomous capabilities for vehicles (Table 2-1).

Table 2-1. SAE autonomy scale

Level 0	No automation. The driver controls steering and speed (both acceleration and deceleration) at all times, with no assistance at all. This includes systems that only provide warnings to the driver without taking any action.
Level 1	Limited driver assistance. This includes systems that can control steering and acceleration/deceleration under specific circumstances, but not both at the same time.
Level 2	Driver-assist systems that control both steering and acceleration/deceleration. These systems shift some of the workload away from the human driver, but still require that person to be attentive at all times.
Level 3	Vehicles that can drive themselves in certain situations, such as in traffic on divided highways. When in autonomous mode, human intervention is not needed. But a human driver must be ready to take over when the vehicle encounters a situation that exceeds its limits.
Level 4	Vehicles that can drive themselves most of the time, but may need a human driver to take over in certain situations.
Level 5	Fully autonomous. Level 5 vehicles can drive themselves at all times, under all circumstances. They have no need for manual controls.

I propose a similar scale for the purpose of evaluating autonomous marketing and marketing automation solutions (Table 2-2).

Table 2-2. The Lean AI autonomy scale

Level 0	No automation. Marketers manage all tasks with basic tools and CRM systems that provide no real automation, but act as storage repositories for marketing data and results reporting (dashboards or "business intelligence" systems).
Level 1	Recommendation automation. Marketers leverage systems capable of following business rules (defined by the marketer) to make business recommendations for optimizing marketing outcomes. Examples include dashboards with recommendation systems for adjusting marketing spend by channel. The user must take the final step of making the recommended adjustments.
Level 2	Rules-based automation. Building on business rules set by marketers in Level 1, Level 2 rules-based automation goes the next step and adjusts marketing campaigns automatically (generally via an application or API) without user intervention or approval. Such systems rely on the user to create the rules. Dynamic market conditions shift on a daily, hourly, or even minute-by-minute basis; rules-based systems are rigid and not very flexible to adapt to market changes.
Level 3	Computational autonomy. Systems that use machine learning to observe, learn, and improve outcomes based on statistical analysis combined with marketing automation. No intervention is required by the user, apart from setting goals or broad-based parameters such as campaign dates or geographies for digital campaigns.
Level 4	Insightful autonomy. Systems that understand the contextual meaning of user interactions, content, behavior, performance data, and more to personalize 1:1 marketing messages across various channels and drive optimal performance for operators.
Level 5	Fully autonomous. Level 5 systems build insightful autonomy capabilities but generate their own unsupervised tests, creative variations, targeting parameters, and more with no ongoing intervention from the marketing team.

The next chapter more fully details how this scale is being applied to autonomous marketing and marketing automation solutions. Most growth teams are in the process of figuring out how to reach a level of proficiency to move from Level 0 to Level 2. However, the biggest challenge and opportunity is to advance from Level 2 to Level 5, to completely reap the benefits of the full superpowers of artificial intelligence to scale up your efforts into the world of Customer Acquisition 3.0.

PART II

CUSTOMER ACQUISITION 3.0

Part II moves you into the world of Customer Acquisition 3.0. What is that you ask? Let's first quickly define Customer Acquisition 1.0 as the phase of siloed customer data living in different physical servers that resulted in running paid user acquisition efforts with poor data without full confidence into how well it was performing.

Customer Acquisition 2.0 is the ability to leverage cloud and data processioning capabilities to integrate all your customer data from multiple sources into one unified customer data platform. With this you can share good data to leverage the individual AI capabilities and automation of major advertising partners running in silos like Facebook, Google, Snapchat, and others to help you better optimize your budget to hit your performance goals.

This brings us to what I call Customer Acquisition 3.0. For starters, it's the focus of Chapter 3, which provides an overview of how to effectively leverage your customer data using "intelligent machines." With this, you will be able to holistically manage your entire paid user acquisition effort with real-time data to optimize your budget and drive great performance with a far more efficient Lean team, hands-off management approach powered by artificial intelligence.

The rest of the chapters focus on different components including how to identify tasks to automate (Chapter 4), an overview of the "intelligent machine" framework (Chapter 5), and whether to build and buy it based on your resource constraints (Chapter 6). This will prepare you for Part III's dive into how to determine which metrics to select for measuring success.

CHAPTER 3

What Is Customer Acquisition 3.0?

The advent of new algorithms, faster processing, and massive, cloud-based data sets is making it possible for all the major digital media providers who sell advertising to experiment with artificial intelligence to help drive better performance for their advertisers. And while all areas of marketing are particularly ripe for transformation, this chapter will focus on the areas of new customer acquisition and revenue growth, because that is where most startups usually spend the most discretionary money. These areas—which collectively we will call Customer Acquisition 3.0—have the biggest impact on scaling growth in your business and the power to unlock future rounds of funding.

New Dimensions for Scale and Learning

In the world of Customer Acquisition 3.0, no longer will scale represent only the traditional value of achieving cost leadership and optimizing the provision of a stable offering. Instead, scale will create value in new ways across multiple dimensions: scale in the amount of relevant data companies can generate and access, scale in the quantity of learning that can be extracted from this data, scale to diminish the risks of experimentation, scale in the size and value of collaborative ecosystems, scale in the quantity of new ideas they can generate as a result of these factors, and scale in buffering the risks of unanticipated shocks.

Learning has always been important in business. As Bruce Henderson observed more than 50 years ago (*https://oreil.ly/r7LLh*), companies can generally reduce their marginal production costs at a predictable rate as their cumulative experience grows. But in traditional models of learning, the knowledge that matters—learning how to make one product or execute one process more efficiently—is static and enduring. Going forward, it will instead be necessary to build organizational capabilities for *dynamic* learning—learning how to do new things, and "learning how to learn" leveraging new technology and vast data sets.

Today, artificial intelligence, sensors, and digital platforms have already increased the *opportunity* for learning more effectively—but according to BCG, competing on the rate of learning (*https://oreil.ly/itY7g*) will become a *necessity* by the 2020s. The dynamic, uncertain business environment will require companies to focus more on discovery and adaptation rather than only on forecasting and planning. Companies will therefore increasingly adopt and expand their use of AI, raising the competitive bar for learning. And the benefits will generate a "data flywheel" effect—companies that learn faster will have better offerings, attracting more customers and more data, further increasing their ability to learn.

However, there is an enormous gap between the traditional challenge of learning to improve a static process and the new imperative to continuously learn new things throughout the organization. Therefore, successfully competing on learning will require more than simply plugging AI into today's processes and structures. Instead, companies will need to:

- Pursue a digital agenda that embraces all modes of technology relevant to learning—including sensors, platforms, algorithms, data, and automated decision making
- Connect them together in integrated learning architectures that can learn at the speed of data, rather than being gated by slower hierarchical decision making
- Develop business models that are able to create and act on dynamic, personalized customer insights

Never before have marketers had access to more customer data. The first-party data companies collect with user profiles can go beyond basic name and demographic data and might include downstream rich data points on engagement, retention, monetization, and much more; companies can use this to build great user segments for running prospecting and retargeting campaigns for growth teams. Ingesting and processing all this first-party data from brands layered on top of the existing rich user data enables these media partners to perform sophisticated modeling and analysis with machine learning that wasn't possible even a few years ago. This results in better targeting with new insights and data analysis.

> *If you are still manually optimizing campaigns the same way it was done half a decade ago, you may find yourself among a quickly disappearing breed in the customer acquisition game.*

If you are still manually optimizing campaigns the same way it was done half a decade ago, you may find yourself among a quickly disappearing breed in the customer acquisition game. Any manual process is likely much less effective and far more prone to human error than the new solutions quickly emerging to attack inefficiencies.

AI and Customer Acquisition

The accelerated adoption of AI for customer acquisition by major media platforms like Google, Facebook, programmatic ad networks, and many others represents a fundamental and pivotal transition in the way that marketing dollars are invested in mobile marketing campaigns. No longer do growth marketers have the ability to choose where or how their ads are shown to users—instead, algorithms decide these logistics, guided by few inputs, such as bids and budget. While that may be good for most growth teams, some of the most intelligent growth marketers in the industry are looking beyond the obvious ways AI can improve results to focus on the cutting edge "out of the box" ways AI can turbocharge their paid user acquisition performance. Companies like IMVU, Netflix, Lyft, and others are pioneers leading the way on the AI frontier, both on their core offerings (entertainment, recommendations, efficient routing, etc.) and on the customer acquisition front. They're at the forefront of using intelligent machines to automate actionable insights to fully manage their paid acquisition campaigns with fewer human dependencies.[1]

It's Time to Turn on the Intelligent Machines

At the end of the day, the best way to evaluate any emerging technology is to figure out its practical use in your business or industry. Just like good user experiences are personalized for an individual's needs, the future of scaling customer acquisition will be won by startups who can adapt each platform's out-of-the-box artificial intelligence solutions to fit their needs, objectives, and goals. Successful startups have learned the importance of focusing on the right metrics and key performance indicators (KPIs), which are measurable value that demonstrates how effectively a company is achieving critical business

---

[1] *Actionable insight* is a term in data analytics and big data for information that can be acted upon or information that gives enough insight into the future that the actions that should be taken become clear for decision makers.

objectives. Examples of KPIs are customer acquisition costs (CAC), return on ad spend (ROAS), daily active users (DAU), monthly active users (MAU), retention, churn rate, and so on.

AI-powered machines (which we'll explore in Chapter 5) can help orchestrate acquisition campaigns that more efficiently move toward these goals compared to the relatively brittle process of manual campaign intervention. This requires a holistic cross-channel approach, which massively increases operational complexity—from data-driven targeting to creative proliferation to attribution and performance optimization. And with complexity comes exactly what you don't want: risk and uncertainty.

Sooner rather than later, your customer acquisition efforts will rely on artificial intelligence, machine learning, and automation (which you'll learn about in Chapter 4) to adapt, customize, and personalize cross-channel user journeys and deliver optimal results in ways that would be impossible using last-generation business intelligence and dashboards. Managing complex, cross-channel campaigns with multiple targets, creatives, and sequences will require an intelligent machine operational layer above the out-of-the-box solutions to deliver great results—or you may have to settle for being average.

Most companies find a comfort zone with one or two major channels and skip the rest. But each of the big platforms have different advantages:

- Snap skews younger.
- Pinterest has a higher composition of women in their audience.
- LinkedIn is where people conduct business activities.
- Instagram's core audiences are highly engaged and tend to interact on the platform, which is great for educating consumers and building audiences.
- Search is all about lower funnel intent.
- Demand-side platforms (DSPs)[2] to reach people outside of the all the other platforms listed here.

Taking these factors into account is important as you develop your strategy. I always recommend managing a broad, diversified mix of different platforms for your customer acquisition, to reduce your business risk of ever being highly dependent on any one single source like the duopoly of Google and Facebook.

---

2 A DSP is a system that allows buyers of digital advertising inventory to manage multiple ad exchange and data exchange accounts through one interface. Real-time bidding for displaying online advertising takes place within the ad exchanges, and by utilizing a DSP, marketers can manage their bids for the banners and the pricing for the data that they are layering on to target their audiences.

Too many startups spend their entire budget on the Google and Facebook black boxes with very limited visibility and poor understanding of how the algorithms work or how they change. Imagine what would happen if all your budget was going into only Facebook or Google and their algorithms changed without any notice in such a way that could significantly impact your ability to acquire new customers?

Always continue to invest at least 5% to 10% of your monthly user acquisition budget into testing new channels every month. By leveraging a portfolio of platforms for prospecting, you are able to get a varied mix of users into the system, which the artificial intelligence can then manage for retargeting—a funnel filled with much less effort across a variety of platforms.

It is also important to note that there will be distinct and shifting bid dynamics on different networks even within month-long campaigns (of course, they're all subject to seasonality). It's very hard to take full advantage of these shifts in bid pressures across the entire user journey from prospecting to retargeting without leveraging your own fully customized intelligent machine that can be trained to operate and automate budget orchestration a layer above each individual channel for truly dynamic cross-channel optimization. No human user acquisition managers and growth marketers can ever outperform a fully automated intelligent machine because the machines can process, analyze, and take the predictive actions 24-7 without ever needing to take a day off. Humans are prone to making mistakes, changing jobs, and/or needing to sleep, which always gives the advantage to the intelligent machines. The AI machines would only get better with more data to help perfect the training of their algorithms over time.

You must learn how to train the algorithms to control your key campaign optimization levers (Chapter 5), focus on creative and strategy (Chapter 8), and turn the drudgery and math over to the machines to get data-driven results far beyond manual capabilities. The rest of this book will show you how by drawing on examples from IMVU and other cutting-edge startups who are successfully doing this now and reaping the benefits.

For example, IMVU has strict KPIs around CAC and ROAS. By leveraging AI, we were able to take advantage of cross-channel efficiencies, and improve the KPIs dramatically across the board. While channels will vary in their CAC and ROAS every month, by leveraging smart machines to manage against our goals, we were able to effectively allocate our resources to take as much advantage of each channel while keeping performance within our key metric zones. By prospecting across the different channels, our retargeting rates for incremental in-app purchases has increased dramatically.

The future of Customer Acquisition 3.0 rests on the shoulder of intelligent machines, orchestrating complex campaigns across and among key marketing platforms—dynamically allocating budgets, pruning creatives, surfacing insights, and taking actions autonomously. These machines hold the potential to drive great performance with a far more efficient Lean team, hands-off management approach powered by artificial intelligence.

Now that you understand of Customer Acquisition 3.0, let's talk about one of the most fundamental aspects of Lean AI for marketing: automation.

CHAPTER 4

Manual Versus Automation

If you are still manually optimizing campaigns the same way it was done half a decade ago, you may be a quickly disappearing breed in the user acquisition space.

Let's remember that machine learning is a type of artificial intelligence developed around allowing computer system to progressively improve performance on a task by "learning" through statistical approaches. Put another way, machine learning is the development of algorithms that allow for more and more accurate prediction with incremental collection of data. That is why Facebook, Google, and all the major media platforms are perfectly ripe for automation—the bigger your paid customer acquisition budget, the more data you can deliver into these machines to enable them to train and learn faster to help you hit your desired success goals.

The key question to ask is: why are you looking to automate something? Let's remember that the two biggest challenges for startups are hiring people and acquiring new customers. The best way to tackle these challenges is to figure out how to run a Lean growth team without compromising on driving results.

Intelligent Machine Thinking in the World of Digital Marketing

Digital marketing has revolutionized advertising in the last three decades. From its humble beginnings in the early 1990s—fueled by hypertext, open source web servers, and crude browsers—digital media has grown into one of the top investment channels for marketers globally. The first commercial banner hit the web in 1994; by 1996 the industry had grown to $267 million in global media investment and showed no signs of slowing down. By 2017, global digital ad spend (*https://oreil.ly/fxgh0*) had reached more than $88 billion and grown at a 21% clip from the prior year.

Today, marketers can take advantage of search, display, video, and mobile advertising through advertising networks and related solution providers. Investment in these channels is fueled by increasing amounts of consumer data, sophistication, compute power, and more all aimed at improving results for advertisers and, ideally, creating a more personalized and relevant ad experiences in the consumer's digital life.

The amount of digital media investment options available to marketers is endless, but more options and more data have required marketers to adopt increasingly sophisticated approaches to the space. As digital spend grew, larger companies hired digital media agencies to handle media planning and buying and worked those efforts into their "offline" media spending; agencies and smaller advertisers alike adopted business intelligence tools—referred to as dashboards—to help them analyze and optimize their client's media spend across this growing swath of channels.

Advances in cloud computing, artificial intelligence, and machine learning present a new opportunity to digital marketers. They can now move past dashboards, reporting, and manual optimizations to improve the efficiency and effectiveness of their digital dollars, gain new insights based on behavioral patterns, and even generate new, personalized ads dynamically based on those evolving insights.

None of this is trivial, mind you. Major platform players like Google and Facebook have been working for years refining their own targeting algorithms, data-driven targeting capabilities, machine learning, and more to make their solutions more effective for advertisers. That's great for individual platforms, but not necessarily so great for marketers or agencies, who are left to perform manual analysis and reporting to optimize spend between major platforms to meet their various objectives.

By 2015, a wave of innovation around neuro-linguistic programming (NLP),[1] neural networks,[2] and machine learning advances coincided with cheap, robust cloud computing infrastructure available on demand from vendors like Amazon (Amazon Web Services or AWS), Google (Google Cloud), and Microsoft

---

[1] NLP is a psychological approach that involves analyzing strategies used by successful individuals and applying them to reach a personal goal. It relates thoughts, language, and patterns of behavior learned through experience to specific outcomes.

[2] A neural network is a series of algorithms that endeavors to recognize underlying relationships in a data set through a process that mimics the way the human brain operates.

(Azure). Meanwhile, digital media buying evolved from a transactional business into a highly scalable programmatic business designed to be interacted with through APIs.

The stage had now been set for the next transformation: to move digital media and marketing beyond the purely tactical into a world that's more intuitive, highly automated, and more strategic than ever before.

Given all the promise and possibilities, what can automation and artificial intelligence really accomplish when applied to digital marketing efforts? There are several areas ripe for innovation.

Automated Media Buying

Machine learning is particularly well suited to making predictions when given a large amount of data. Major marketing platform providers like Google and Facebook use machine learning to deliver more relevant ad experiences to consumers and improve the performance of their offerings in an effort to get advertisers to spend more.

Advances in machine learning have given rise to independent software providers building out packaged solutions to save time for media buyers. They help advertisers take advantage of machine learning algorithms to improve their media buying efficiency without the overhead of building and maintaining custom-developed software on their own (an expensive proposition). These systems can adjust bid strategies to shift budgets around to better performing creatives and different customer segments to make ongoing performance improvements without manual intervention.

These systems are classified as Level 3 in our Marketing AI Autonomy scale (Table 2-2)—a step up from manual budget optimization and rules-based automation. These systems can save you time on everyday gruntwork and free you up to work on strategy, creatives, segmentation, and more.

Cross-Channel Marketing Orchestration

The next step up from automated media buying involves more complex systems that can work across multiple digital marketing platforms. Each major marketing platform (Google, Facebook, Twitter, Snapchat, etc.) offers different capabilities, APIs, and relative strengths and weaknesses given your specific marketing objectives.

Orchestration is a key concept in this class of autonomous marketing solutions. It goes far beyond automated bid management to take into account your marketing funnel, customer journey, or life cycle. Certain marketing platforms, for example, may be better at driving awareness among prospective customers or users. Others may be better at driving app installs or generating revenue.

Systems that orchestrate marketing efforts with a more robust view of the customer journey encompass a host of benefits driven by AI and automation, particularly in the following areas:

- Segmenting and targeting customers
- Predicting behaviors across various channels with a unified view of the customer journey
- Fine-tuning and perfecting cross-sell and upsell opportunities
- Identifying the right channel to drive engagement based on reach and frequency modeling
- Improving attribution accuracy
- Fraud detection and protection

Cross-channel marketing orchestration capable of Level 3 and Level 4 Marketing AI Automation are emerging classes of software, but they're also increasingly within reach. Aspects of Level 3 and Level 4 Marketing AI Automation *within a single channel* are generally available and often offered as a feature of different major marketing platform providers.

Virtual Marketing Assistants

Voice-based interfaces to intelligent assistants like Amazon Alexa represent an area of growth and exploration in the marketing world. While most "assistants" are designed for consumer use or customer service applications, these intuitive voice interfaces hold promise in helping marketers better understand what's happening in their digital media efforts, uncover trends, make adjustments, and take advantage of opportunities in new ways that would have been too laborious or complex using traditional user interfaces (UIs) or reporting dashboards. These emerging capabilities are on the leading edge of Level 4 and Level 5 Marketing AI Automation on our scale.

Content Curation

The amount of digital content available today is absolutely staggering. On Instagram alone, consumers publish 95 million images per day according to statistics from the company in February 2019. More than 72,000 GB of global internet traffic is moving around every second.

So what kind of content do your customers like? What resonates with your prospective customers? Artificial intelligence can help marketers sift through huge amounts of content to help them find out what their customers are spending their time consuming or engaging with. This can lead to ideas around what types of media outlets might be fruitful places to advertise. These insights can also fuel your content development, content marketing, and advertising efforts from a creative perspective.

Customer Support and Service

Today, chatbots serve as a first line of contact for routine customer support requests. According to Gartner research, 85% of all customer interactions will be handled without a human agent. The increased adoption of chat-based interfaces for customer service, marketing, shopping, and more serves both business and consumer interests. The volume, structure, and repetitive nature of routine service requests make automation highly approachable with off-the-shelf solutions that plug into common chat interfaces ranging from text messaging, Facebook Messenger, and beyond.

There are many great benefits of AI-powered customer service for businesses and consumers alike. For consumers, chat-based interfaces are accessible, feel familiar, and provide immediate responses to most common queries. It saves consumers time compared to wading through support lines, phone trees, and support queues, or waiting for customer support emails to get addressed and answered by a support agent.

Similarly, offloading the lion's share of support requests to an AI-based agent can help improve the customer experience—and the company's bottom line. IBM estimates that companies spend $1.3 trillion annually handling 265 billion customer support requests. Chatbots can help businesses save on customer service costs by speeding up response times, freeing up agents for more challenging work, and answering up to 80% of routine questions autonomously.

Businesses can further improve the customer experience by integrating chat-based customer service and support channels with their CRM systems and data management platforms. This type of integration allows a company to escalate your most valuable customers to the top of the service queue, for example to present retention-based offers to customers on the verge of lapsing or poised for an upgrade or new purchase based on their behavioral patterns.

Chat-based service and support interfaces are great sources of customer data for the Lean AI marketing automation framework.

Segmentation Development and Management

The amount of data coursing through the global internet (*https://oreil.ly/k9yTa*) at any given moment is nearly unfathomable. The big four alone—Amazon, Microsoft, Google, and Facebook—store upwards of 1.2 petabytes of data between them. That's 1.2 million terabytes (a terabyte is 1,000 gigabytes). Trillions upon trillions of customer data points exist within this primordial data soup, ready to be accessed and pumped into the modern digital customer experience—personalized ads, offers, content, services, and more based on the newfound ability to anticipate customers' needs and desires.

Marketers can tap their vast data stores to create unlimited customer segmentation models powered by artificial intelligence. Companies can already tap third-party data sources to enhance their customer records with tens of thousands of attributes, like household income, zip code, behaviors, and more. AI allows companies to take this to the next level by combining these conventional data attributes to a live stream of customer interactions, transaction data, product usage data, support and service data, and beyond.

Segmentation vendors are using AI to generate and update ever-evolving dynamic customer segments to feed into their execution systems to run precisely targeted campaigns across the customer's user journey.

Insight Generation

Artificial intelligence can look through a mountain of behavioral data on a hyper-granular level to predict with great accuracy what a consumer will do next, based on their past behaviors and actions.

This is how ad platforms create lookalike audiences. Leveraging vast amounts of data and machine learning, these systems can easily cluster people based on behavioral attributes (or other factors) to anticipate their next move, motivations, and desires. If everyone in Cluster 1 takes actions A, B, and C then we can predict that customers who take actions A and B will likely follow that with action C.

By looking at audience behavior, AI systems find out the interests, context, and hedonistic activities around users and products. And the system automatically adapts with evolving consumer behaviors and interests. This can lead to new insights that can inform your strategy, creative approaches, offers, and much more. You can then take action on these insights and add them to your intelligent machine.

Creative Generation

Perhaps one of the most fascinating aspects of artificial intelligence today intersects with marketing technology in some potentially problematic (even dangerous) ways. Natural language generation—coding computers to write or generate written or spoken words in a way that can pass as human—has been a field of academic study for decades. Advances in recent years, particularly around recurring neural networks and their offshoots, have led to rapid improvements in natural language generation.

As it relates to marketing, applications around natural language generation could be used to analyze your marketing copy and create variations using your brand's "voice." This requires some training, but is well within the realm of possibility these days.

Natural language generation models have become so powerful that Open AI, a research company working on artificial general intelligence or AGI, refused to release the code related to its large-scale language model known as GPT2 (*https://oreil.ly/8Uk4s*). The company cited concerns over misuse and abuse related to the "fake news" problem.

Which brings us to "deepfakes"—AI-generated video content that is nearly indistinguishable from the original content. The technique uses human image synthesis to combine and superimpose existing images and video onto source images or videos using machine learning. Marketing applications for the technology revolve around creative generation, personalization, and more, but fears of misuse related to fake news and even "revenge porn" make deepfake technology concerning in its ability to be weaponized by rogue actors and nation states.

Given the breadth of applications for artificial intelligence in growth marketing, it's important to assess the ability for each to impact your most important outcomes. For example, training a neural network to generate copy variations based on a catalog of ads and customer service interactions might be interesting, but the cost, complexity, and time involved may outweigh any lift you might achieve with some fancy new AI-generated ad creatives.

> *Given the breadth of applications for artificial intelligence in growth marketing, it's important to assess the ability for each to impact your most important outcomes.*

When it comes to immediate impact with the AI-powered marketing technology just outlined, the following are your best bet:

- Segmentation development and management
- Automated media buying
- Cross-channel marketing orchestration
- Insight generation

These four interrelated disciplines all play a role in how you approach optimization today—with or without AI. They also fit nicely into a broader framework of a customer life cycle, which we will discuss next. And for any of the four disciplines just listed, AI offers a high enough "risk to reward" ratio to make the potential benefits of time and resources involved worth the cost and distraction factor.

Table Stakes: Customer Life Cycle Management

Many companies ignore customer life cycle management—much to their peril. They limit their focus on acquiring new customers, rather than retaining and "upselling" them over time. This approach to growth marketing is costly and unsustainable for a number of reasons:

- Acquiring a new customer costs anywhere between *5 and 25 times more* than retaining an existing customer (Harvard Business Review (*https://oreil.ly/2lgRU*)).
- According to Bain & Company's research (*https://oreil.ly/JtCK9*), your existing customers spend 67% more than new customers.
- You're much more likely to get an existing customer to make a purchase (60% to 70% chance) compared to a new customer (5% to 20% chance of converting to a sale), according to reporting by ClickZ (*https://oreil.ly/cXnY7*).

While a life cycle marketing approach can take a bit more thinking, the justification for orienting your growth team this way is clear. Not only is it more efficient, but your focus shifts from acquisition efforts to a more holistic view of your customer and their journey along the customer life cycle with your company. It's a better experience for the customer and a much more rewarding relationship for your company.

Let's think about a typical customer life cycle and how it lines up against the classic purchase funnel in Figure 4-1.

The purchase funnel is a great tool for developing a framework around the different types of content you're going to need to develop to inspire a prospective customer to take the plunge and "convert" into becoming a new customer. We'll dig deeper into the upper funnel later in Chapter 10 and Chapter 11, but for now, an overview in Figure 4-2 is helpful to set the stage for a life cycle marketing approach.

Awareness and Discovery
People are looking for general help or information about a topic

Consideration and Evaluation
People are seeking more information about a product or service

Conversion and Purchase
People want to learn how your product or service is superior to others, or they want to learn how to make a purchase on your site

Figure 4-1. *Classic customer purchase funnel*

Awareness → Engagement → Evaluation → Purchase → Post-purchase → Advocacy

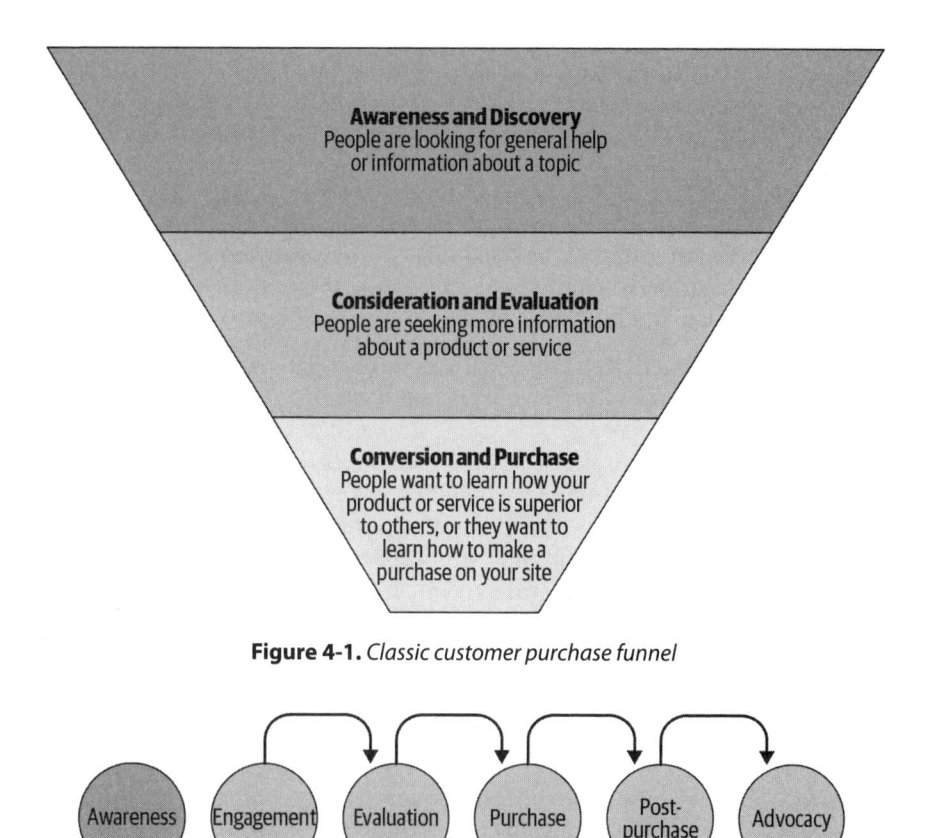

Figure 4-2. *The different stages for a life cycle marketing approach funnel*

Awareness

Awareness is the very top of the customer funnel: people can't buy something they don't know exists. Companies use mass media techniques like television, billboards, or social media to drive awareness. Editorial content, social posts, podcasts, and other types of engaging content work well for driving awareness and educating consumers on *why they should care* about what you're offering.

The trick here is not to focus on awareness to the exclusion of the rest of the customer journey, a risk that leaves potentially willing prospects to find their own way through the rest of the funnel—this leads to significant drop-off from awareness to conversion, higher marketing costs, and alienating otherwise promising prospective customers.

While it's clearly an important part of the marketing funnel, it's important to remember that it's just the beginning. You'll need to figure out ways to engage the audience you've developed in your awareness phase, to begin walking them down the conversion funnel to becoming customers.

Engagement

Once you've built an audience of potential customers aware of your offering, you'll need to keep them engaged. At this stage, the customer has a sense of what you're offering and how it might fit into their daily lives.

In the engagement phase, your job is to get more specific with the customer on a few key points. Approach your content and creative development to ensure that it gives your prospects a reason to dig deeper into consideration. What are your top features? How do they compare with alternative offerings out there in the market that a prospect may be evaluating? Why should someone buy your product or service right now? Offers and discounts can be a good tactic to drive engagement, but don't become over-reliant on them. It's more likely at this stage that an offer won't sway them one way or another, so the focus should be on educating prospects on the benefits you offer.

Evaluation

The evaluation stage sits at the bottom of your marketing funnel. It's where your prospective customer is comparing your product offering to other options available. They're reading reviews and comments to confirm that the choice they're making is the right one. It's important that your marketing content dives into great detail to ensure your prospects feel comfortable making a purchase commitment. Be sure to detail how your offering stacks up to competitive alternatives.

An offer or guarantee can help get someone over the final hurdle to making a purchase commitment. Test your calls to action and observe how they impact your customer lifetime value down the road.

Purchase

The purchase stage is self-evident. Making it easy to conduct a transaction is one critical point of optimization at this stage; the other is answering the question, "Why should I buy *now*?"

It's at the purchase phase that a customer enters the next and often trickier stage of their life cycle marketing journey.

Post-Purchase

The post-purchase phase of marketing can be a creative challenge. Determining what types of content your new customers will find useful once they've made a purchase isn't easy, particularly for certain types of products or services that have a limited life cycle or utility. Newsletters are the most common form of post-purchase marketing used today.

But AI holds tremendous potential in the post-purchase phase, thanks to the amount of transactional data that can be fed into our marketing engine. A few years back, triggered emails were the height of post-purchase CRM efforts. But today, companies aren't limited to email for digital customer relationship management. Advanced segmentation techniques can feed targeting information to media partners for retention and activation marketing efforts in apps, on social, around the web, and beyond.

Advocacy

Activating your best customers and turning them into advocates can be a powerful technique for both deepening your customer relationships and improving your product or service offering. Brands that engage in customer advocacy marketing look for vocal customers who hold (and share) strong opinions about their products or services. Successful brands find ways to empower these advocates to make them feel connected to the company through loyalty programs, rewards for customer feedback or participating in focus groups, and other opportunities.

IMVU's Strategy for Automating on the Growth Team

At IMVU, our growth team comprised several user acquisition managers, agencies, and consultants to help us manage our significant budget across different channels including mobile, paid search, SEO, mobile, display, affiliates, CRM, and retargeting. The biggest risk to our business was that our growth team was heavily dependent on humans and felt the impact of this especially with employee churn on the team. Most of the churn was related to the highly competitive job market in the San Francisco Bay Area where people working in user growth could easily job hop for more money.

A key insight that came from hiring and training new members on my team was that a lot of user acquisition tasks around managing and optimizing user acquisition campaigns were boring, repetitive tasks like changing bids, budgets, creative, running A/B testing, data analysis, and reporting. A lot of these tasks have logic and data as the central element, and as such machines could be trained to outperform humans in taking them on. That's when the big "a-ha moment" hit me to solve this challenge by trying to figure out automation, so we could run a Lean team while applying technology to accomplish a lot of the tasks that are better managed by technology to scale up growth more efficiently.

Our approach to figure out what to consider for automation was as follows:

- Identify all the human repetitive tasks being done to optimize our biggest paid channels
- Calculate how much time was allocated in hours dedicated to each task
- Order the tasks by time spent, budget, and impact on performance
- Add a rank to each task that takes into consideration the time, complexity, and impact
- Evaluate the ordered list to identify opportunities for automation and machine learning

When applying this approach to the growth team at IMVU, we initially decided to focus our automation efforts on our top two biggest paid channels—Facebook and Google—as those would have the biggest impact on the ROI of scaling up our user growth. The good news is that both of these partners are investing to provide more AI solutions and automation into their offerings for growth teams to make it easier to manage with less manual work.

Remember that machine learning is a type of artificial intelligence developed around allowing computer systems to progressively improve performance on a task by "learning" through statistical approaches. Put another way, machine learning is the development of algorithms that allow for more and more accurate prediction with incremental collection of data. That is why all these major media platforms are perfectly ripe for automation in user acquisition campaigns because the bigger your paid acquisition budget the more data you can deliver into these machines to enable them to train and learn faster to help you hit your desired success goals.

In 2018, both Facebook and Google Universal App Campaigns introduced ML algorithms that significantly improved the ability for advertisers to manage and scale up their campaigns based on success goals, with downstream optimizations becoming more easily managed using their native tools. The benefit is that now advertisers only have to focus on managing a few key levers like choosing the right optimization goals (CPI, CAC, ROAS), budgets, bids, and creative, leaving the time-consuming complex campaign optimization tasks in the hands of the powerful automated ML capabilities of Facebook and Google Universal App Campaigns.

I would envision Facebook and Google Universal App Campaigns algorithms getting even smarter with more accurate predictions for hitting KPIs (CPI,

CAC, ROAS, and lifetime value [LTV]) and serving better personalized creative formats from incremental collection of data. This virtuous cycle will result in shifting even more budget toward the duopoly, which would impact the competitor's ability to continue to invest significant R&D budget into further improving its own ML capabilities. What is still unknown is how much first-party data advertisers will need to continue to share with Facebook and Google Universal App Campaigns as these algorithms get better at predicting user intent with all the data signals they collect about users.

Building a Business Case for Automation

Most startups are resource-constrained and therefore need to develop a business case to determine which projects to prioritize based on their cost/benefit analysis compared to the success goals of the business. The challenge with new technology is always dealing with uncertainties to find the right data and costs to present in the business case. It's important to clearly articulate the problems that leveraging AI/ML to automation would help solve. For example at IMVU the problem was to figure out how to better optimize our paid user acquisition budget across our key paid channels by accelerating our A/B testing to test new audience segments, creative, bids, and budgets at scale with real-time optimization that wasn't possible with a Lean team. In our case at IMVU, we were able to project out the ROI of how much money we would save based on lowering the cost to acquire new users and hiring fewer user acquisition managers to manage these campaigns.

> *Most startups are resource-constrained and therefore need to develop a business case to determine which projects to prioritize.*

In growth teams, you can determine your costs/benefits ROI formula using the following variables in your business case. The costs include:

- In-house resources to support the project (engineering, data science, infrastructure, user acquisition managers, agencies, consultants, etc.). An example would be $100,000 per year on in-house resources to support the project.
- Third-party AI/ML technology platforms (attribution, media buying, CRM, etc.). An example would be $200,000 per year for leveraging a third-party tool to support the project.

And the benefits include:

- Efficiency improvement in CAC or ROAS. An example of projecting a 20% improvement in CAC on $20 would result in $4 savings per new payer, so if you project getting 100,000 new paying customers per year this would result in $400,000 savings in your acquisition budget.
- Cost saving in hiring less people like user acquisition managers, consultants, or agencies to manage all the different paid channels that would be automated to enable a Lean growth team to scale up better with AI/ML automation. An example would be cutting costs of around $70,000 per year (which is the median salary for a user acquisition manager in the United States according to LinkedIn in April 2019).

To calculate ROI, the benefit (or return) of an investment is divided by the cost of the investment. The result is expressed as a percentage or a ratio.

The return on investment formula is:

ROI = (Current value of investment – Cost of investment) / Cost of investment

In this formula, "Current value of investment" refers to the proceeds obtained from the benefits of the investment. Because ROI is measured as a percentage, it can be easily compared with the returns from other investments, allowing one to measure a variety of types of investments against one another. In the example we've been looking at, our ROI would be:

ROI = ($470,000 - $300,000) / $300,000 = 57%

It is highly recommended to determine longer-term ROI projections over a three- to five-year timeframe. The goal should be achieving an ROI that remains positive over time and compounds that value by continuing to enrich growth team efficiencies and results. Because AI and ML automation systems need to be continually recalibrated and trained, contingencies or risks should always be factored into the ROI formula. As a rule of thumb, add a 15% cushion to your projected costs as a margin for the unexpected.

Now that we've mapped out the basics as they relate to customer life cycle marketing and automation, let's start building out a framework for an autonomous marketing intelligent machine in the next chapter.

CHAPTER 5

Framework of an "Intelligent Machine"

While it's helpful to think of AI in terms of doing things differently within your existing business processes, it's also true that AI can help you explore and benefit from entirely new approaches and redefined processes. Gaining efficiency is of course a big, obvious win, but today's new breed of intelligent algorithms enable us to engage customers and prospects in new ways, create entirely new experiences, and even develop new business opportunities we have never considered before—if you can successfully get your company behind your AI-powered vision of the future.

When we were getting started with AI in the realm of marketing automation, we found it helpful to think in terms of a framework for building an "intelligent machine." The basic elements of this framework include:

- An understanding of your *customer journey*, experience, and life cycle.
- *Creatives or content* designed to impact the customer journey at different stages in their life cycle—the more variety, the better. Be sure to map multiple creatives, offers, etc. to different stages of the life cycle for optimal results.
- *Data* for understanding the customer journey and breaking behavioral cohorts into targeting segments.
- *API-based access* to your preferred marketing channels—Facebook, Instagram, Google, Snapchat, your email service provider, etc. to allow for campaign creation and orchestration.
- A *working feedback loop* for reporting and ongoing optimization, likely running through a third-party attribution provider or coming directly from the platforms themselves.

- *An approach to optimization*, which can be turned into one or more algorithms used to drive performance based on the feedback your system is getting.

This framework could be universally applied to any company considering building their own AI-powered intelligent machine to fully automate their customer acquisition efforts. It can also be used to help evaluate vendors to ensure they offer a comprehensive approach to autonomous marketing. Now, let's get a bit smarter about the types of artificial intelligence you can explore and apply to your specific business case or needs.

It also helps to remember that—for the most part—all of these functions are simply core marketing activities that are enabled in today's digitized world. This is about doing these things better, faster, smarter, and sometimes in entirely new ways.

Amazon founder and CEO Jeff Bezos often gets asked to predict what the future will be like in 10 years. While he's happy to indulge audiences with his thoughts and readily admits he really can't predict the future, Bezos often thinks about the things that *won't change* in the next 10 years, and how that can impact business decisions. That way, "you can work on those things with the confidence to know that all the energy you put into them today is still going to be paying you dividends 10 years from now," he said.

That's good news when it comes to applying AI and machine learning to marketing. These business activities, functions, and business processes aren't going away any time soon, but the days are numbered for the old ways of dealing with this familiar workload. Think about it this way: the work you do today to make your intelligent machine a reality will still be paying off dividends in 10 years.

Breaking Down Machine Learning for Marketing Purposes

While the study of machine learning and artificial intelligence is quite broad, there are a handful of approaches to developing effective "learning" algorithms and approaches. Consider this a primer to get you started with a good understanding of current approaches and how they apply to your AI-based marketing efforts:

Supervised learning algorithms
These use properly labeled data sets to train an algorithm to make predictions. They're great for classification, or labeling new data through a mapping function from input variables to discrete output variables. A classic use of supervised learning algorithms you can likely relate to is the

classifying of emails as "spam" or "not spam" based on input variables leading to a discrete output variable ("spam" or "not spam"). A second major use of supervised learning is for regression analysis, in which the training data is used to map input variables to a continuous output variable—a real number or value, often quantities like amounts or sizes, within certain error boundaries to indicate the accuracy of the prediction.

Unsupervised learning algorithms

This category takes unlabeled sets of data with no known outcomes or results and is useful for discovering the underlying structure of the data. They are typically used for clustering data within sets, detecting anomalies (like fraudulent transactions), mining for associations (understanding what types of goods are on a typical retail receipt to better merchandise products on retail shelves), reducing the number of features in a given data set, or breaking out a data set into multiple, smaller sets for further analysis.

Semi-supervised learning algorithms

These use a combination of labeled and unlabeled data for training. Generally speaking, they rely on smaller labeled data sets that include outcome information used in conjunction with much larger unlabeled data sets. They're used when you don't have enough labeled data to produce an accurate model. With this approach, you can increase the size of your training data by applying this technique.

Reinforcement learning

This one of the newest approaches to machine learning. As the name indicates, a reinforcement algorithm learns by trial and error to achieve its objective. The machine tries out lots of different things and gets rewarded or penalized based on the outcomes of its behaviors and how well they help or hinder it from reaching its objective. Google's AlphaGo used reinforcement learning algorithms to beat the best players in the world in the complex strategy game Go.

Deep learning

Architectures represent another, perhaps even more revolutionary, approach to AI-based application development—a field of data science that has also accelerated in recent years. They're based on artificial neural networks (ANNs) and support a variety of learning approaches, including supervised, unsupervised, and semi-supervised. "Deep" refers to the number of layers through which data is transformed; in certain models, the number of transformations is fixed, and in others, known as recurrent neural networks, the number of transformations is potentially infinite. These architectures are among the most exciting in data science today and have been applied successfully to drug design, bioinformatics, social network filtering, speech recognition, computer vision, natural language processing, machine translation, audio recognition, material inspection, medical image analysis, and board game programs. In many cases, they've produced results comparable to or even superior to human subject-matter experts.

As you can see in Figure 5-1, many of the different approaches to machine learning described here can be applied to different applications related to marketing automation. Each application represents an order of magnitude leap from the conventional, manual approaches of days gone by thanks to the availability and sheer volume of data that we can now feed into these algorithms.

The "x" factor is deep learning, which cuts across the four major approaches to machine learning. This approach can be incorporated where the benefits of this more computationally intensive method outweigh the more lightweight methods of classical machine learning approaches.

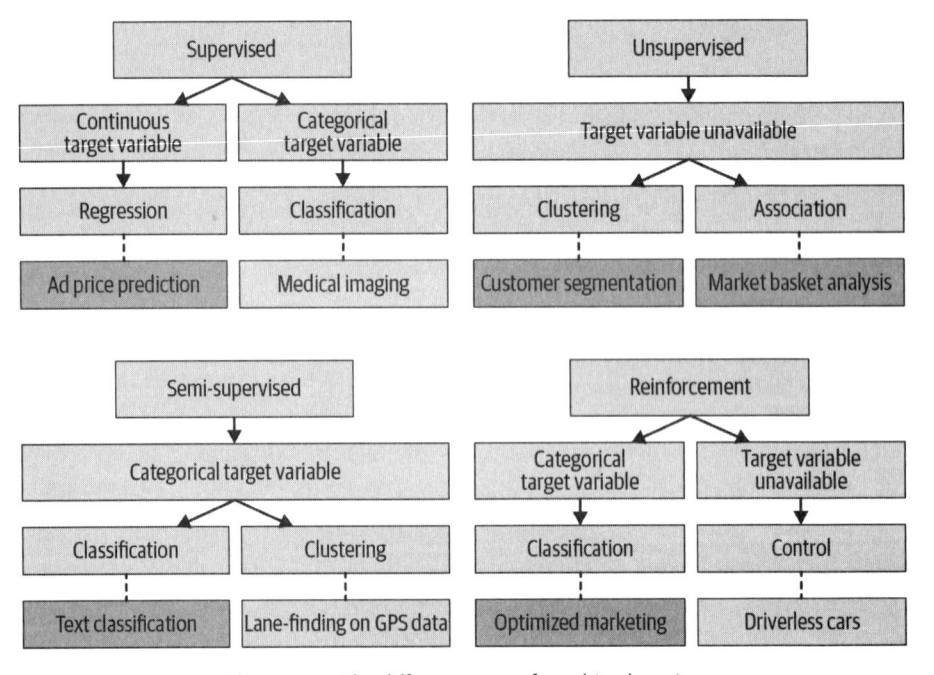

Figure 5-1. *The different types of machine learning*

Major Types of Supervised Learning Algorithms

As you can see in our handy chart, supervised learning algorithms can be useful in a marketing context for predicting things like ad prices in an auction, along with associated predicted yield. There are several approaches to these types of supervised learning algorithms and plenty more available online if you want to dive deeper into the math. The following sections present a primer on the four major types.

Linear Regression

Regression analysis shows the relationship between inputs and outputs in a given system. Linear regression is one of the most common types of regression analysis; in its simplest form, it uses a linear relationship to predict the value of Y for a given value of X using a straight (regression) line. It can allow us to see what factors in our marketing efforts relate to others. Exploring these relationships can help us with testing the actual cause or "causality" of certain outcomes—like what factors indicate or predict a higher probability of a click or a conversion.

One important note: linear regression requires some careful tuning to get reliable outcomes, so be careful when applying it to your modeling. You'll need to find a fairly strong correlation between the X and the Y to have confidence going forward with this approach. Perhaps the data fails to form a natural line; there is no need in trying to use a line to fit the data and make predictions.

Logistic Regression

Logistic regression is used primarily for classification, labeling, or sorting data sets. Although similar to regular linear regression, logistic regression is aimed at gaining insight into understanding the relationship between the dependent variable with one or more independent variables provided the dependent variable is binary, or "dichotomous."

Apart from the similarities stated before, logistic regression differs from a linear regression through the non-usage of regular least squares to plot the line of best fit, which is used in predicting the value of the dependent variable based on the information derived from the independent variable. In logistic regression, the value of y is usually set at 0 or 1 rather than being distributed along the line of best fit as seen in linear regression.

Logistic regression is an important market research tool that can be used to predict the response of a customer to a product based on certain factors. For instance, it can be used to predict if a customer will purchase a product if, say, we know their health status.

It's important to note that logistic regression may require a certain number of participants for each set of dependent variables before the results can be processed. Most people who have used logistic regression feel that interpreting logistic regressions can be time consuming and somewhat confusing. It is therefore highly recommended that you make use of important statistic analysis tools like Intellectus, which allows you to conduct analysis and interprets the results in plain English.

k-Nearest Neighbor

Often regarded as a non-parametric technique, *k-nearest neighbor* (k-NN) can be described as a simple algorithm that can store all available cases and also predict the numerical target based on a similar measure (e.g., distance). This predictive, non-parametric technique is capable of predicting the future outcome of a test based on reports on how people might have reacted to the same parameters in the past. For instance, you can easily determine which product a customer is likely to go for by considering what their nearest neighbors bought.

This method is often used by growth teams to determine the most effective customer acquisition strategy and how customers are likely to respond when approached with a new product by simply considering what their nearest neighbors are likely to purchase. It creates a chance to compare the reaction of old and new customers.

Support Vector Machines

Most growth marketing processes or challenges tend to require making the right predictions of a future state or system, and this is where support vector machines (SVMs) come into play. SVMs are a type of supervised learning model that makes use of algorithms for finding a hyperplane in an N-directional space (where N is the number of features) and classifying the data points distinctively. SVMs are very important in predicting the outcomes of emerging environments like data mining, intelligent software agents, mass-produced models, and automated modeling.

Major Type of Unsupervised Learning Algorithms

There's only one major variety of unsupervised learning algorithm that we're going to address here: *k*-means.

k-Means

Simply put, this type of unsupervised learning algorithm is useful whenever there is a need to divide *n* observations into *k* clusters. More often than not, these observations may belong to a cluster with the nearest mean and can serve as a prototype of the cluster leading to the partitioning of the data space into Voronoi cells. Clustering involves dividing data or population points into a certain number of groups where data points in the same group have similar appearances and are differentiated from those outside the group. The major goal of using this algorithm is to locate groups in the data with the number of groups represented by the k variables. The algorithm can assign each data point to one of the k groups by capitalizing on the features provided.

The k-means algorithm has been successfully used in the following aspects of marketing: classification of documents, optimization of delivery routes for stores, identifying crime localities, customer segmentation, statistical analysis of fantasy leagues, detection of insurance fraud, rideshare data analysis, cyberproofing criminals, analysis of call records, and automatic clustering of IT alerts.

Learning Algorithms That Can Be Supervised or Unsupervised

The learning algorithms can either be supervised or unsupervised using the following popular machine learning methods.

Decision Tree

Just as the name implies, a decision tree can be described as a support tool that uses a tree-like model (Figure 5-2) in reaching decisions and also determining their possible consequences such as outcomes, utility, and cost of resources. It serves as one of the most effective ways of displaying algorithms containing conditional control statements. A decision tree shares the same features as a flowchart where each internal (non-leaf) node is used to represent a test on a parameter, branches represent the test outcome, and leaves (or terminal) serve as a class label. These trees can serve as an integral part of operation research in decision analysis and play an important role in identifying a strategy that is most likely to reach a goal.

There is no denying the fact that businesses have to deal with lots of data obtained from market, competition, and customer analysis. Dealing with this data effectively to reach the right conclusion may take longer than expected, thus causing a delay. Since identifying and proffering solutions to business problems can be time consuming for most executives or managers, the use of decision trees can provide them with a simple abbreviated method of predicted outcomes for each of the split trees. A decision tree is a visual representation of the decision-making process and can be used to simplify problems as different as credit card attrition and currency exchange rates.

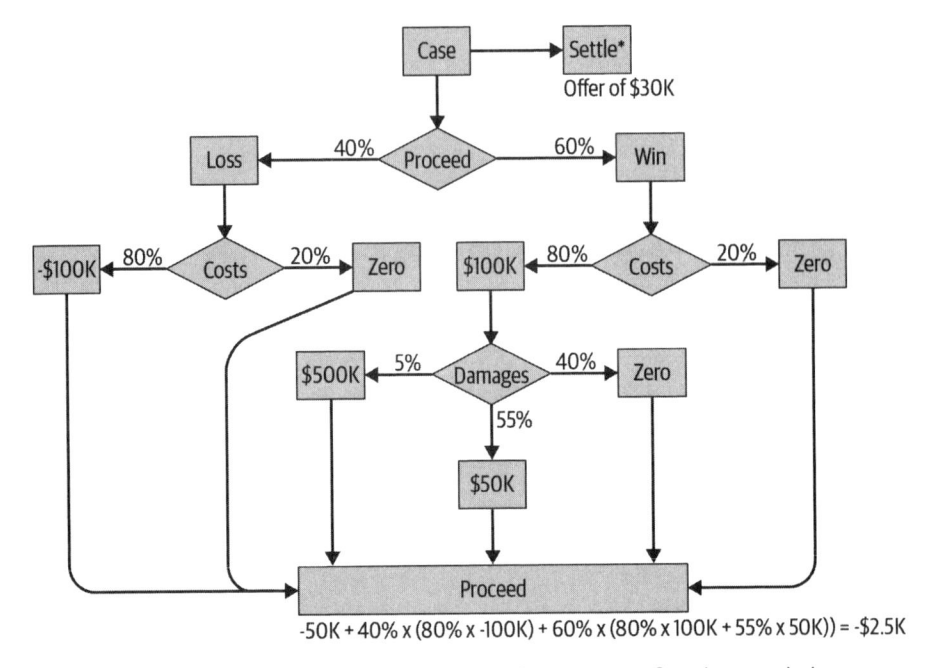

Figure 5-2. *An example of a decision tree diagram using flowchart symbols*

Naïve Bayes

Naïve Bayes can be described in a good number of ways depending on the area of use. In machine learning, it can be described as a family of simple probabilistic classifiers[1] that are based on the application of Bayes's theorem[2] containing naïve (strong) independent assumptions in the features. This is one of the most popular methods of text characterization and has been in existence since the 1960s. Text characterization is the problem of judging documents as either belonging to one category or not (e.g., legitimate or spam, politics or sports, old or new, single or married, etc.). Naïve Bayes utilizes word frequencies as features.

In a learning problem, naïve Bayes classifiers might require a specific number of parameters linear in the number of variables (predictors or features). Naïve Bayes classifiers can be used in classifying customers based on certain

---

1 In machine learning, a probabilistic classifier is a classifier that is able to predict, given an observation of an input, a probability distribution over a set of classes, rather than only outputting the most likely class to which the observation should belong.

2 In probability theory and statistics, Bayes's theorem describes the probability of an event, based on prior knowledge of conditions that might be related to the event.

parameters such as age, gender, nationality, and occupation, thus giving the company additional insights about their consumers.

Random Forest

Using several decision trees to determine the final result and predict possible outcomes can be better than using a single decision tree. A single tree cannot make a forest, and that's why random forest (random decision forest algorithm) is the preferred method for regression, classification, and other tasks that need to construct a lot of decision trees during training time and release the class mode or mean prediction of these trees.[3] (See Figure 5-3 for an illustration of how random forest works.)

Random forest is often used by many companies to make predictions with a process concerning machine learning. It uses multiple decision trees aimed at making a more holistic analysis of a given data set. During analysis, the random forest can build on the decision tree model and make the entire process more complicated. Most experts are of the view that these random forests represent "stochastic guessing" or "stochastic discrimination."

A random forest algorithm can be used to test the quality of a customer growth strategy or product quality; for example, it has been used by companies to determine the quality of wine through parameters like alcohol content, sulfur dioxide level, pH, acidity, and sugar content. It can also be utilized in taking various product properties and variables to indicate the interests of customers and how best to meet their needs.

In many business settings, a random forest algorithm takes note of the random subset features for each tree and determines the most probable outcome. In this way a multitude of evaluations can be performed and the most likely outcome used to predict success.

> **NOTE**
>
> Before using the random forest algorithm, I advise that you first isolate the predictive data utilized during production and apply it to the random forest model while using a certain set of training data.

---

[3] Random subsets of features: selecting a random set of the features when considering splits for each node in a decision tree. Random forest is an ensemble model made of many decision trees using bootstrapping, random subsets of features, and average voting to make predictions.

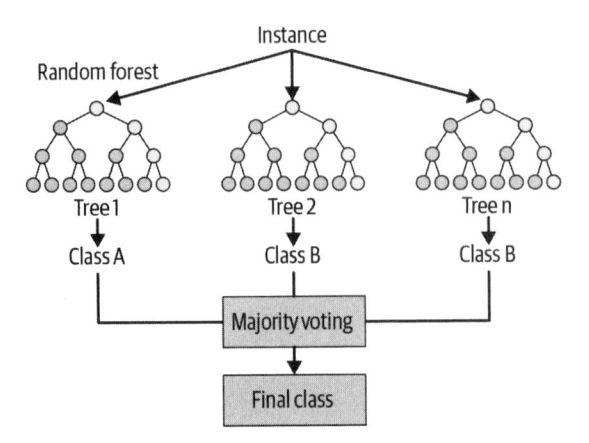

Figure 5-3. *An example (https://oreil.ly/E9rgx) of a random forest simplified diagram*

The Importance of Data

The most important rule to remember is that data is what powers algorithms—it's the fuel that fires up the AI machine. So what happens when the data used to train machines is flawed? Many data scientists and others building next generation AI solutions actually spend a good amount of time scrubbing the data, cleaning it up, and putting it into a format computers can actually use. If you put garbage in, then you'll get garbage out.

> *The most important rule to remember is that data is what powers algorithms—it's the fuel that fires up the AI machine.*

The best way to get clean data is to set up the right API connections from all of your key data sources and pipe them into your AI intelligent machine.[4] At IMVU, we have the following data sources that were connected via API to our AI intelligent machine called Athena Prime:

- AppsFlyer, which is our mobile attribution and marketing analytics platform. This is our source of truth for measuring success from our mobile user acquisition campaigns from different partners, including Google,

---

[4] An API is a set of routines, protocols, and tools for building software applications. Basically, an API specifies how software components should interact. Additionally, APIs are used when programming graphical user interface (GUI) components. A good API makes it easier to develop a program by providing all the building blocks. A programmer then puts the blocks together.

Facebook, Snapchat, Apple Search, Instagram, Liftoff, InMobi, and many more. AppsFlyer, like most other attribution solutions in the space, is integrated with all the major mobile ad networks and partners so it's seamless to track all these campaigns in one place. We also pass back all our key CRM downstream event data like new payers, revenue, and engagement. This enables AppsFlyer to pass all this valuable data back to all our advertising partners to enable them to build lookalike user segments for our systems to target on those different partner networks.

- Leanplum is our marketing automation and CRM platform. We pass our cross-platform data into Leanplum from our backend data warehouse to help us create customized on-boarding, retargeting, and reengagement campaigns to help us better engage, retain, and monetize our users. Our goal is to ensure all new users follow similar user journeys to replicate our best lifetime value customers by influencing them to take the same user actions and behaviors.

- All the paid user acquisition channels—Facebook, Google, Snapchat, Apple Search, Liftoff, InMobi, and many others—are connected to pass their data back to enable us to control the optimization levers like budgets, bids, and goals.

- Creative assets are developed by the marketing team in-house at IMVU, based on an ongoing analysis of what's working and what's creating the most value within any given market segment. Creatives are added to each marketing channel for automated distribution.

These elements are all feeders into Athena Prime (which is the "intelligent machine" used by IMVU); we can turn over customer segments for targeting, channels for promotion, and creative elements to Athena to drive our desired marketing outcomes with maximum efficiency.

Athena Prime starts with our base business needs for any given campaign, such as marketing objective, creatives to be used within a campaign, and any additional constraints (budget, campaign dates, etc.). These parameters are fed into Athena using the UI or through programmatic API calls, providing the instructions or marching orders for the system.

As a Software as a Service (SaaS) platform, Athena Prime abstracts key components of digital media campaigns:

- Business Needs (*campaign configuration*) from Audience Selection, Message Placement
- Performance Optimization (i.e., *campaign orchestration*, contained in the large box below)

- Reporting on Business Outcomes (meeting business goals, performance insights on aggregate audiences included in a campaign, and any insights into how content or ads performed)

In a generic framework sense, you can view an intelligent marketing machine in Figure 5-4, with the classes of machine learning algorithms written in white.

Business requirements	Audience selection	Message placement	Audience selection	Business outcomes

- Objectives
- Creatives
- Constraints
  - budget
  - dates
  - geographies
  - other
	- Behavioral
	- First party
	- Custom audiences
			- Budgets
			- Creatives
			- Audiences
				- Performance insights
				- Content insights
				- Audience insights

	Neural classifiers, RNN, clustering	Classifiers, reinforcement learning	Reinforcement learning	

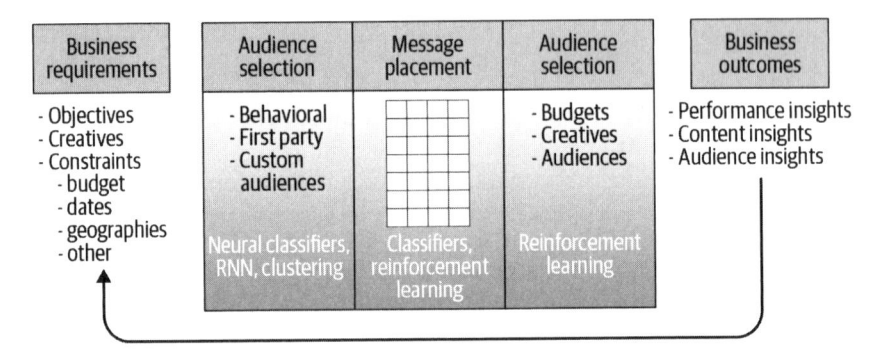

Figure 5-4. *The intelligent machine framework*

Audience Selection

In terms of Audience Selection, Athena Prime uses natural language processing, neural processing, and deep learning models to analyze ad copy and landing pages to extract interest-based targeting parameters to the extent they are made available by participating channels to improve ad relevance and performance. This feature, dubbed "Athena Sense," does not allow for targeting on an individual level, but instead adds a contextual or interest-based component to campaign targeting without any human intervention. Athena Sense may add hundreds of additional interest-based targeting parameters to any given targeting set—something that would require an inordinate amount of work by employees or agencies to attain that level of targeting detail.

These interest-based targeting parameters are provided by platform/channel partners via programmatic APIs. These interest-based, behavioral, or demographic targeting parameters are identical to those available directly within the corresponding platform's user interface.

For example, Athena Sense may identify that a particular ad in a campaign makes reference to *Game of Thrones*. Figure 5-5 shows how this targeting parameter is made available in the Facebook user interface.

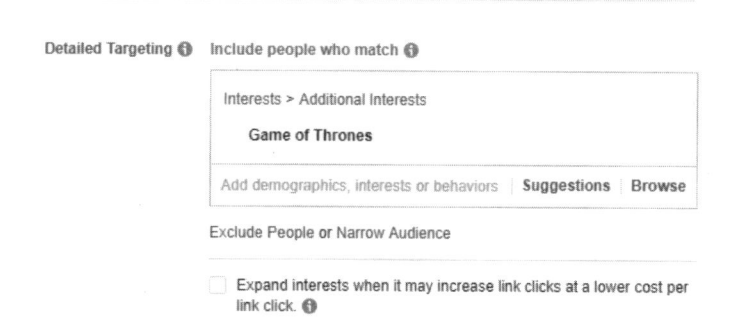

Figure 5-5. *A targeting parameter in the Facebook UI*

Instead of an agency or team member working through the UI of five or more marketing channels, Athena enhances targeting intelligently and automatically. This saves time, improves performance, and generates higher return on our marketing spend.

It's also interesting to note that features like Athena Sense—which extracts meaning and context from creatives and landing pages—add valuable targeting insights that are used by the marketing platform AI on the other side of the handshake. These clues are so valuable that platforms like Facebook and Google reward advertisers that add detailed targeting enhancements to their campaigns, further boosting performance and ROI.

First-Party/CRM Data

First-party or CRM data is data collected by the advertiser through its own data-gathering systems. At IMVU, we exercise the customer engagement platform Leanplum to organize all this data into segments for optimally efficient targeting. These audiences are uploaded periodically to various marketing platforms/channels, where they are then made available to systems like Athena Prime for inclusion or exclusion in campaign targeting, but only in aggregate and in ways that prevent marketing automation providers (like Nectar9) from "reverse engineering" audiences to reveal any personally identifiable information (PII).

Custom Audiences

Custom Audiences can be created on various platforms based on a variety of methods. They are typically generated as "lookalike audiences" based on first-party or CRM data uploaded to platforms (although they can also include demographic, behavioral, or interest-based parameters as well). Custom Audiences are created directly on platform/channel providers through their user interfaces or in some cases via API calls. Regardless, Custom Audiences are aggregated in such a way so as to prevent marketing automation providers from "reverse engineering" audiences to reveal PII.

Message Placement

This functionality includes features that take ad creatives or "content" and configure them for use on various channels, and as such, don't take into account audience targeting on any granular level beyond placement availability or relevance.

Exploration and Optimization

The final component of Athena Prime is an optimization engine that makes campaign adjustments based on performance. Athena Prime observes results being reported programmatically across channels to shift budgets to ensure maximum efficiency. This may involve shifting budgets away from certain audience segments or increasing budgets against others. It may also shift budget between different channels based on current performance against goals. But in no case does this optimization engine deal with performance on an individual user basis.

Applying Machine Learning and AI to the Customer Journey for IMVU

IMVU analyzed user journeys with our data team to explore what organic behaviors resulted in the most valuable users or purchasers. One key insight became very clear: if we can get someone to make an in-app purchase within the first seven days, this is a significant indicator of higher lifetime value. In addition, users interacting with different features and exhibiting certain behaviors within IMVU proved to be good indicators of what leads to a purchase. Our goal was to find ways to increase customer LTV and create incremental lift over organic purchases (LTV will explored in further depth in Chapter 7).

To put the insights from this study to work, we segmented our customers into three primary groupings:

- People who installed the app, but didn't register
- People who were on a "First Seven Days" journey
- Lapsed purchasers

Taking the insights from our user journey study, the marketing team then created a host of creatives for each segment grouped by where they appeared to be in their user journey. The "winners" for IMVU at each stage in the sequence are shown in Figure 5-6.

UA & MARKETING: BEAUTIFUL SCIENCE

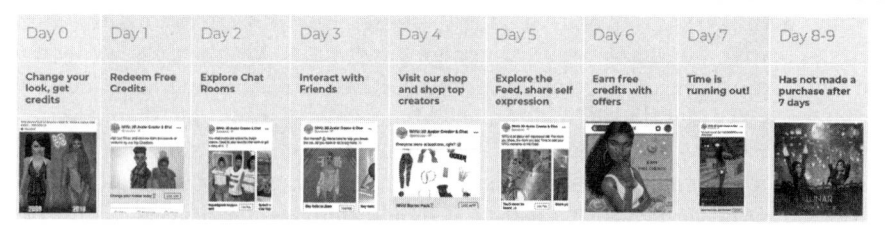

Figure 5-6. *IMVU user journey creative sequence for different segments by day*

Autonomous Marketing

We leveraged an AI intelligent machine platform to orchestrate and automate the delivery of sequenced ads on multiple channels in a synchronized way to get optimal results.

Typically, executing this type of sophisticated campaign with a complex array of audiences, channels, creatives, and dynamic sequencing using manual processes is challenging to say the least. But artificial intelligence is making it possible to identify the right sequencing for different cohorts of people at different stages of their life cycle.

The application of AI has allowed us to run full life cycle user acquisition and revenue generating campaigns benefiting from thousands of experiments across these cohorts. The reward of taking this approach has been an incredible 3.5X improvement in the new CAC and ROI.

Iterative Testing

The massive scale with which we can experiment, learn, and optimize messaging throughout the user journey simply isn't possible (or worth the time and effort) without an autonomous artificial intelligence marketing engine. We can test, learn, and iterate at a much faster pace to quickly identify what works and what doesn't across creatives, audiences, messaging, and more. It allows us to better target people with the right ads and messages based on where they are in the IMVU life cycle, encouraging them to take actions that naturally lead to higher lifetime value.

Specifically, all of this orchestration and automated learning drove a 46% lift in in-app purchases compared to the control group that was not exposed to this messaging and orchestration.

Artificial Intelligence

Let's review the business processes at play and how the application of AI drives meaningful optimizations and outcomes through large-scale experimentation.

Starting with IMVU's overall strategy, we set our objectives (desired outcomes), creatives, and any other campaign constraints. We then get segmentation data from our data warehouse and CRM sources, along with custom audiences we've developed over time. AI automates blending segmentation models with cross-channel message placement, which automatically explores, observes, and optimizes for the right business outcomes. From there, we seek further potential audience or creative insights, update our approach, and the cycle goes on. Figure 5-7 shows an example of an IMVU split test of thousands of different creative variables across different segments.

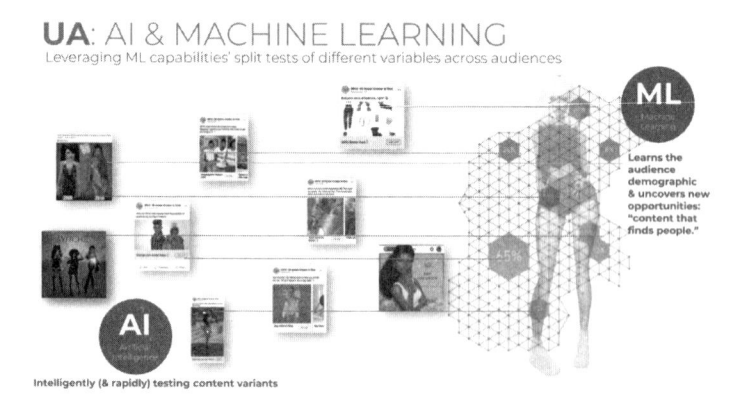

Figure 5-7. *IMVU example of testing different creative variables across different segments*

Rapid-Fire Experimentation

What's happening behind the scenes as artificial intelligence orchestrates cross-channel experimentation? You can think of it like split tests of different variables across multiple digital channels—but on steroids. You're intelligently running rapid-fire content and audience experimentation and learning in a way that uncovers new opportunities to present the right content to the right people at the right time, and taking action in the instant.

What did we take away from all this? Besides dramatically improved performance and efficiency, we gained insights into the best-performing creatives and segments.

Findings

For our lapsed purchasers segment—defined as anyone who made an in-app purchase in the last 180 days but not in the last 30 days—we learned that there were two kinds of content that worked best:

- As a user-generated platform, IMVU benefits from an evergreen pipeline of amazing content created by its members (similar to YouTube or Soundcloud). The firm found that highlighting content from IMVU's most influential creators delivered a showcase of novel products from the best of IMVU's creators.
- Weekly contests, in which users can participate to win free credits as you see in Figure 5-8, proved very popular and did a great job of attracting lapsed users back both to participate and purchase again.

We also learned that our Day 1 users were motivated by a simple message: reminding them that they can redeem free credits to get started, as you can see in Figure 5-9. This engaged them in the app and encouraged them into the flow of becoming a high lifetime value customer.

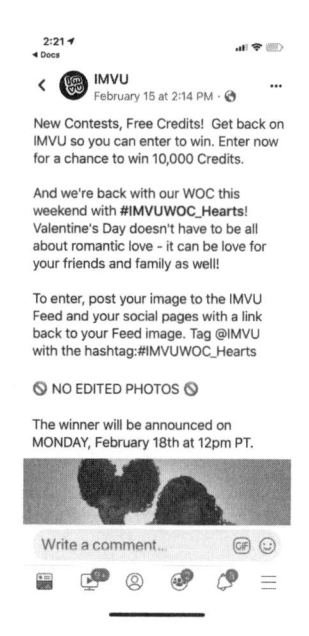

Figure 5-8. *An example of the IMVU weekly contest Facebook ad*

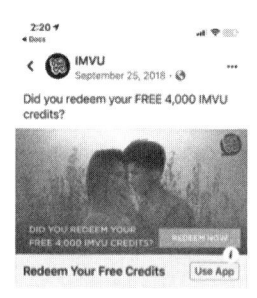

Figure 5-9. *IMVU example of a retargeting ad to remind users to redeem their free credits*

Bringing It All Together

Scaling growth doesn't come easy. Let this be your road map to maximizing your customer LTV by always running sequential tests for different cohorts at different stages throughout the entire user journey. To turbocharge your performance, consider working with (or building) an intelligent AI machine to help you automate key levers like blending segmentation models with cross-channel creative placements, achieving data-driven results far beyond manual capabilities.

Now that we've got the basics of AI as they're applied to marketing, and an understanding of customer life cycle marketing, we can explore options around building or buying a solution to help you turbocharge your startup's growth.

CHAPTER 6

Build Versus Buy

All startup growth teams are tasked with trying to acquire more new customers and growing revenues while consuming the least amount of resources. The benefit of being a startup today is that there are more robust off-the-shelf SaaS growth stack tools available to leverage to help successfully acquire, engage, retain, and monetize customers.

All startups will face the same dilemma around whether to build or buy an intelligent machine. This is an important decision for businesses of all sizes, but especially startups because they are by definition so very resource constrained. Making the wrong decision could have severe consequences to the long-term success—or even viability—of the business.

The first step is for the growth team to work with their product team to create a product requirements document—commonly referred to as a PRD—that clearly articulates all the requirements and provides a strong business case for their desire to integrate an "intelligent machine" into the product road map. This is an important document because it allows people to understand what the product should do and win internal support for the project to be prioritized. Here is a list of the typical components to include in your PRD:

- Purpose and scope of the project from a business and technical perspective
- Projected assumptions on the key metrics of the business (e.g., 10% lift in ROI)
- Typical use cases on how this would help the growth team
- Constraints (budget, time, development resource availability and expertise)
- Any dependencies

- High-level workflow plans, timelines, and milestones
- Evaluation plan and performance metrics
- Requirements would fall under:
  — Functional requirements (e.g., what the product should do)
  — Usability requirements (e.g., how the product would be used)
  — Technical requirements (e.g., data, security, network, integration, etc.)
  — Support requirements (e.g., what resources are needed to support the product)
  — Interaction requirements (e.g., how the product should work with other systems)

A PRD should be created by the growth team in close collaboration with the product team to ensure it has the right level of business and technical details. The key to success for any AI project is to get executive support early in the process and have them champion this from the top down to ensure all the teams are aligned and excited to support this cross-functionally.

Once a PRD is developed, then the next step is to share broadly with the different technical key stakeholders (e.g., data and engineering teams) who need to work together to determine the amount of time, money, skill sets, and research needed to make an educated recommendation to compare the options of whether to move forward with the build or buy. These teams are tasked with figuring out the right path that reconciles their company's immediate needs with their strategy for long-term scalability. Each startup has different strengths and weaknesses based on their internal resources and bandwidth, so there is no universal answer to this question that can apply to all startups. This chapter will introduce you to the framework for build versus buy as well as the pros and cons to bear in mind as you are making these decisions.

Build Versus Buy Analysis

In this section, we'll walk through the steps for analyzing whether building or buying is right for your startup.

The Problem

The first step is to clearly define the problem you are attempting to solve. Is this a common problem, or a unique one facing your company specifically?

For example, developing ways to get smarter in acquiring new customers is a common problem, but most startups don't currently leverage an AI intelligent machine to solve this problem. The most common approach is to hire more user acquisition managers, consultants, and/or agencies so more humans can analyze the data and optimize the campaigns. This can be an expensive, high-risk proposition.

It's always good to first look at how other startups are trying to solve the problem—are there any external third-party solutions you can leverage? If it's a problem specific to your startup, you may have trouble finding an existing workable solution. Even if the problem is already well addressed, it's possible your business needs fall closer to edge cases not encompassed by the products currently on the market, which could be an argument for the decision to build.

At most startups, building an AI intelligent machine isn't a good option because they don't have the dedicated resources available to build and support a complicated AI project of this magnitude. Most startups have a limited number of technical and data resources and need to focus on their own core products. The best viable option is to find a SaaS partner who has the solution and resources to solve this problem.

IMVU decided to partner with Nectar9 and their Athena Prime platform. Nectar9 is an AI-focused startup that was working on building an AI intelligent machine SaaS platform for growth teams, but it faced a common conundrum of startups in the AI field: Nectar9 didn't have access to the volumes of test data to perfect the potential for it to work at scale across all the main paid media channels.

This is where IMVU collaborating with Nectar9 became a win/win partnership. We had a significant user acquisition budget and were spending a lot of money across all the main media channels (Google, Facebook, Programmatic, Apple Search, and others) in our customer acquisition efforts. This generated the data at scale to experiment with and train the Athena Prime AI machine. By offering up our existing campaign data, we gained the ability to influence Nectar9's product road map and help them figure out how to tune Athena Prime to work for the IMVU growth team and their customers beyond IMVU.

The Budget

The next concern is budget. Do you have the necessary funds to see this project through to completion as well as extra resources in case you go over budget? Most startups do not have a big budget to invest into building their in-house AI capabilities. This is why it can often be easier to justify a monthly recurring payment or even an annual expense for a third-party SaaS product.

A good analogy to use is the decision to buy or rent a home. If you do not have the necessary funds to make a down payment on a house, then it becomes necessary to rent, even if the rental fee is equivalent to what the mortgage payment would be. When deciding if you should build a solution to your problem, the budget must include the long-term technical debt (mortgage) associated with hosting and maintaining your solution, in addition to the up-front costs (down payment).

The Timeline

The next consideration is the time horizon. Is your problem a threat to the survival of your startup or just a nagging annoyance that could be improved? What is the impact to your startup if this problem isn't solved soon? You must consider whether or not the problem will compromise the performance of the business. If you need a solution now, it can be an easy decision. Is there a solution in existence? If yes, buy it. If no, then, well…you're going to have to build it as soon as possible.

There are risks awaiting you at every turn as you navigate this framework and ultimately make the final decision to build or buy. Let's discuss some of these risks so you can make the most informed decision possible.

Risks of Building an AI Solution

The end goal in building an AI intelligent machine is to help your growth team to make smarter data-driven decisions on the right optimization levers to pull to efficiently spend your budgets and resources to help accelerate growth. Some of the risks of building your own software solutions boil down to opportunity cost, quality concerns, and technical debt, among others. Here are the main ones to keep in mind:

Is marketing AI your core competency?
   Most startups are not set up to have marketing AI as their core competency unless that is their main product focus. There are high costs to support AI—building teams of data scientists and machine learning engineers, building data infrastructures, and maintaining all of these resources. The reality is that you need your internal resources to focus on developing and supporting the unique product capabilities that you offer. Building an AI solution is a huge undertaking even with the right internal resources in place to support this project. Companies that build out of their circle of competence risk building inferior products compared to companies dedicated to solving the problem.

How often will it need to be updated?
   The ability to dedicate resources to maintain and manage your AI project is very important because the machine learning needs oversight to ensure the right data is going in. The algorithms need to be validated to confirm they are making the right decisions to help you acquire new customers cost effectively. This isn't going to be something you build once and never touch (as if that ever happens). It's going to need constant updating—

further taking time away from your core product development. Is it worth it? This is generally the big challenge with trying to prioritize in-house resources to maintain an AI project that isn't the top priority for the business and getting in-house technical resources excited about maintaining it. One thing you are guaranteed is that the AI space will continue to evolve rapidly with constant innovation that will require having a team of experts dedicated to staying on top of all the research and best practices to ensure you don't get left behind. Therefore, investing into resources in-house or externally to leverage all this knowledge to train and customize models to continue to give your startup the competitive edge is invaluable to getting the most value out of AI.

What is the opportunity cost?

The trade-off in any startup is the opportunity cost of resources being deployed to support Project A compared to Project B while considering the timeframe of either project being deployed. An example would be the costs in time and money of employees (data scientists, engineers, quality assurance, etc.) building and maintaining an AI project versus leveraging those resources to work on something else like improving your core product user experience (which is most likely the reason they joined your startup). Your decision to build may be *to the detriment of other projects* that will likely hurt morale and postpone any major technological breakthroughs with lost productivity. Another cost to factor in is any delays in the deployment of an AI solution (including the necessary machine learning training) that would result in your growth team not spending their budget as efficiently as possible. Taking time to think considerably about how the pricing structure of an off-the-shelf solution compares to a custom solution when considering organizational growth will allow the most effective, responsible, and successful decision making.

Technical debt

This is a common concept in programming that reflects the extra development work that arises when code that is easy to implement in the short run is used instead of applying the best overall solution. Technical debt can be taken on intentionally when a quick fix is not the ideal solution but necessary given the timeline and budget. Other times technical debt is the result of poor planning and architecture. The long-term costs associated with building and maintaining an AI solution internally can lead to expensive issues down the road with quality, performance, lost time, and money. This is bad because technical debt is one of the largest and most impactful issues affecting software development today with startups under pressure to deliver projects on time.

No economies of scale
> Are you disadvantaged when it comes to sourcing tools that contribute to the AI build? Unanticipated expenses such as server fees and monthly database charges as well as hiring talent like data scientists and engineers could be a huge risk of building. Companies that service many customers are able to distribute the costs of software operations and maintenance evenly across their clients. These economies of scale can allow them to charge less for a product or service than you would be able to achieve by building it yourself. If a third party's economies of scale and other factors put your build at a disadvantage you may strongly consider the option to buy, but not before evaluating the risks associated with buying. It's important to look at the long-term ROI on this project that factors in the economies of scale.

Risks of Buying an AI Solution

Most AI solution partners will offer a free-trial or proof-of-concept (POC) period to give you the ability to evaluate their capabilities with your data. Before moving forward with a trial, demo, or quote, review some of the surface-level risks of buying a software solution versus building one yourself (you need to do a thorough job on the due diligence process to mitigate these risks):

Forfeiture of data
> One important consideration to make when buying a software solution from a third party is data. In today's ecosystem of privacy concerns and regulations, it's more important than ever to ask: how will this third party use your proprietary data? Does this mean you lose access and oversight to important customer data and other business insights? It's important to be aware that any AI partner would need access to your first-party data to help the AI be successful and you want to ensure they are fully compliant with all data privacy regulations to avoid any major issues down the road.

Security risks
> Can this third party be trusted? Are they using cybersecurity best practices? Enterprise-level software companies are the targets (and often victims) of large-scale cyber-attacks leading to millions of compromised accounts. Even with security best practices, breaches do happen and it's worth extra consideration before willingly bringing the Trojan horse into your castle walls.

Not a thorough solution
> Another risk of buying software from an external supplier is whether or not their solution adequately solves your company's problem. Let's assume many companies face the same problem and the marketplace is saturated

with options to choose from. It's possible your particular use case has not been identified by these third parties. Some companies may be open to customer feedback about future features but if your problem is limited to your niche, it's unlikely the company will see your problem as a worthy addition.

Exposure to partner's market risk
It's important to fully vet any AI solution partner you consider working with on their ability to weather a market downturn or other external factors that may impact the health of their business. For example, if you work with an AI startup that isn't well funded then it faces a strong risk of going out of business and/or getting acquired, which could negatively impact your business.

Machine Learning as a Service

Another option to consider is what's become known as Machine Learning as a Service (MLaaS).[1] This is an umbrella definition encompassing various cloud-based platforms that cover most infrastructure issues such as data pre-processing, model training, and model evaluation, with further prediction. Amazon Machine Learning services, Azure Machine Learning, Google Cloud AI, and IBM Watson are four leading cloud MLaaS services that allow for fast model training and deployment. All of these solutions have pros and cons that differ in terms of algorithm performance as well as required skill sets and tasks to manage them, but they all require engineering resources to bring to bear on business challenges. None of these are going to fully match all your business needs and compromises need to be considered when working with them; they'll need to be customized to meet your specific requirements.

MLaaS is only feasible if you already have access to an in-house data science team. In my experience, this is challenging because most startups can't afford to build an in-house data science team, as these highly compensated and skilled employees are very expensive to hire and retain, especially with big technology companies like Facebook and Google competing aggressively for this type of talent.

Build or Buy...or Both?

There is an alternative to the build or buy dilemma: do both if you have some complicated niche use cases.

---

1 "Comparing Machine Learning as a Service," AltexSoft (blog), September 27, 2019. *https://oreil.ly/SgjlO*.

That's right—do both. If you need a solution fast and there exists an external solution that would suffice, even if it does not meet 100% of your needs, consider whether it makes sense to pay the premium until your dedicated solution is built for your specific complicated niche use cases. This option depends on favorable factors such as adequate budget, time horizon, and more. For example, you must consider whether the software is a subscription-based model and the terms surrounding contract duration and cancellation. You should also consider discussing your problem with the external vendor to determine if there are already plans on their product road map to meet 100% of your needs. In that case, you can reevaluate the decision to build.

The goal in startups is to minimize cost now and cost later. Therefore, the deciding factor is delivering something of value that your growth team can leverage to start generating revenue from it. Buy if it enables you to start generating revenue sooner. Build it if it enables you to start generating revenue sooner if you have the resources to do it successfully. Once you've built it and validated that it delivers the expected benefits, you can optimize by replacing whatever parts you need with bought or built components until there's no more benefit to optimizing further.

Investing in building an infrastructure for your company can be the right decision for the long term if you have complicated niche use cases as you scale and the economics of your AI solution become more favorable. When you buy software from a third party, it's possible the pricing model does not scale quite as linearly. On the other hand, sometimes buying from a third party turns out to be the right decision in the long term. When you consider buying it's important to fully understand whether it is capable of solving your unique problems.

Weighing It All Out

When it comes down to it, the risks, costs, and distraction factor of building intelligent, AI-powered marketing automation into your product road map will not likely outweigh the benefits of working with a SaaS partner. In addition, a partner providing an off-the-shelf solution likely has the benefit of working with and incorporating feedback and ideas from other customers that you may not have considered or explored. While there are clearly some cases where your product or business model may demand a proprietary solution, chances are you're able to get farther faster by carefully choosing a capable partner to power your intelligent marketing automation efforts.

Regardless of your decision, you'll still need a solid understanding of the business inputs necessary for properly instrumenting your intelligent machine. Let's dig deeper in the next chapter.

PART III

WHAT METRICS MATTER TO YOU?

Part III moves you into the world of choosing and measuring the right metrics for success. The key metrics for startup growth (Chapter 7) provide an overview that will help you focus on the right key metrics that align on driving long-term growth. In Chapter 8, we'll explore one of the biggest levers you have when it comes to empowering your AI machine: your creative assets and a clear understanding of how they're impacting performance. In Chapter 9, we'll explore the area of cross-channel attribution to help provide measurement for your AI machine to determine which channels and creatives have the greatest impact on the complex customer journey to achieve your desired business KPI goals. This will prepare you for Part IV's dive into picking the right approach to user acquisition.

CHAPTER 7

Key Metrics for Startup Growth

Artificial intelligence and machine learning aside, it's important to know what growth metrics are critical to your startup to give clear success goals for your "intelligent machine" to target.

In startups, the growth team is responsible for acquisition, retention, and monetization of new customers as they evolve down the marketing funnel. Therefore, it's important to have specific input metrics to enable you to measure success and benchmark the trend of whether you're getting better or worse over time in meeting and exceeding those KPIs.

The complex interplay between KPI metrics grows as your marketing investment increases, making AI a perfect way to automate your campaigns as your growth accelerates. In this chapter, we'll look at five key metrics that are most relevant for optimizing paid user acquisition budgets with an intelligent machine to help optimize the different key levers like bids, budgets, channels, creative and A/B testing across the entire marketing funnel to better meet and exceed those goals. These KPIs are among those that occur with enough data points, at a high enough frequency, and they're consistent across a range of customer acquisition and growth goals.

The added benefit of using these key metrics is that they are simple to understand for everyone in the company as well as the investors in the business who can benchmark these against other similar startups.

Customer Acquisition Cost

The CAC measures the cost of acquiring a new customer. This is one of the most important metrics, and for your business to be profitable, it is very important to make sure that the CAC is significantly lower than the LTV of a customer. Knowing your CAC is also important because it helps you figure out the right user acquisition strategies to leverage once you know the LTV to find out how much you should spend to acquire new customers cost-effectively to manage the cash burn rate in your startup.

The easiest way to calculate CAC is to pick a specific time period cohort and then divide your cost of user acquisition spend by the number of customers you gained, as shown in Figure 7-1. For example, if you spent $1,000 to get 20 customers, your CAC is $50.

$$\text{Customer acquisition cost} = \frac{\text{Costs devoted to acquiring new customers}}{\text{Number of new customers}}$$

Figure 7-1. *Formula to calculate the CAC*

The focus is always to find opportunities to continue to lower your CAC because that means you're able to acquire new customers more cost-effectively. The CAC for startups should be trending down over time as the brand awareness goes up and they identify the right user acquisition strategies to focus on. It is going to differ by your business model and industry. For example, a consumer subscription business with a more predictable revenue stream is going to have a higher CAC than a business that just sells a low-cost product.

All growth teams need to set clear CAC target goals with that data going back into the AI intelligent machines to help train the machines to optimize toward meeting your CAC goals by getting smarter around targeting new segments of prospects that match up to your best-paying customer profiles.

Retention Rate

The retention rate evaluates the percentage of customers that stay with you over a given time period. This is a key growth success metric because retaining your customers is key to building a successful long-term business, especially for subscription and advertising business models like Netflix or Facebook that depend on users engaging with your product. This is also a good indicator of customer loyalty and organic growth because customers who stick around are more likely to see value in your product and tell their friends about it.[1]

The formula can be a little complicated, but one way is to subtract the number of new customers from your total customers at the end of a given period, then divide that number by the number of customers you started the period with, as shown in Figure 7-2.

You can easily calculate the retention for any daily/weekly/monthly cohort by looking at how many people that signed up on a specific date (or range of dates) are still using your service N days later. For example, if you started the month with 100 customers, gained 20 new ones, and lost 40, the calculation is 80 (total customers at the end of the month) divided by 100 equals 80%. That means your retention rate is 80%—you kept 80% of your customers.

$$\frac{\text{Users at beginning of period - Users at end of period}}{\text{Users at beginning of period}} = \text{Retention rate}$$

Figure 7-2. Formula to calculate the retention rate

The goal is to keep your retention rate as high as possible, or your churn rate as low as possible, by leveraging AI/ML to provide great user experiences by utilizing data to enhance personalization and recommendations to reinforce the value proposition to customers so that they continue using your product. A low retention rate can be disastrous for your product if not effectively dealt with. That is where it makes sense to do your retention analysis by breaking your users down into specific cohorts (i.e., a group of users with a common defining characteristic). For example, you might group users of a mobile app by their registration date to track exactly when they give up on your app—so that you can start to identify what is making them leave. The easiest way to measure retention quickly is using acquisition cohorts.

With acquisition cohorts, you can look at the retention of a specific cohort based on when they started using your app. You can then find out exactly how many people churned per day (or per week or month). For example, the cohort chart in Figure 7-3 shows that 13,464 new users signed up on December 1 (Day 0). One day later (Day 1) 57% of those users were still using the app (7,675 users). Two days later (Day 2) 39.5% of the users who signed up on December 1 were still using the app—(5,318 users). And by Day 3, retention was at 33.6% of the December 1 cohort (4,524 users).

---

[1] "How to Calculate and Improve Customer Retention Rate," Customer Retention Rate, Salesforce. *https://oreil.ly/q_oKX*.

SEGMENT	USERS	DAY 0	DAY 1	DAY 2	DAY 3	DAY 4	DAY 5	DAY 6	DAY 7	DAY 8	DAY 9	DAY 10
All users	317,332	100.0%	49.2%	34.1%	26.1%	21.1%	18.4%	17.1%	15.9%	14.0%	12.1%	10.6%
Dec 04	11,979	100.0%										
Dec 03	11,475	100.0%	*57.0%									
Dec 02	12,464	100.0%	53.9%	*41.8%								
Dec 01	13,464	100.0%	57.0%	39.5%	*33.6%							
Nov 30	9,466	100.0%	62.1%	42.6%	32.1%	*28.4%						
Nov 29	6,467	100.0%	42.9%	42.5%	32.5%	25.7%	*22.8%					
Nov 28	7,468	100.0%	27.5%	28.8%	30.5%	24.3%	19.2%	*18.2%				
Nov 27	12,464	100.0%	32.5%	19.9%	23.0%	25.2%	20.1%	16.9%	*16.1%			
Nov 26	11,480	100.0%	57.0%	25.2%	16.3%	19.5%	22.8%	19.5%	16.2%	*15.9%		

Figure 7-3. *An example of the most popular way of displaying cohort data*

Cohort analysis is critical because DAU/MAU counts are highly distorted by growth. If your app is growing rapidly, new user signups will mask where your existing users are dropping off in your DAU/MAU numbers. If you're only looking at DAU/MAU, you'll be blind to retention issues that will kill your app if left unaddressed.

Identifying behaviors that affect retention also helps you understand the behaviors that drive engagement in your app. But once you start to run experiments to discover the actions that lead to growth, you'll need to put concrete numbers on these behaviors. By looking at the relationship between certain user actions and retention you can identify the main behaviors and actions that are correlated with long-term use. These can lead you to discover the "a-ha" moments within your product that make users stay and continue to engage with the app or product. For example, Facebook found that users who added seven friends within the first ten days were highly likely to continue to use the social networking platform long term. Users who didn't add seven friends were more likely to churn out. In this case, performing the specific event of adding seven friends in a certain time frame was highly correlated with retention.

Whatever your product's core value, your greatest growth lever is creating magical moments in which users recognize that value. Without such moments, retention will suffer and growth will be difficult to sustain. Mediocre companies focus simply on growth. A great company focuses on sustainable growth —through engagement, stickiness, and retention. Most growth teams that focus on daily and monthly active users are able to provide that retention and downstream event data back into the AI intelligent machine to train the algorithm to optimize toward better retaining existing users and targeting new users who are more likely to stick around by targeting new user segments that highly correlate with your desired retention.

Customer Lifetime Value

The customer lifetime value metric measures the revenue you receive from repeat customers. While it can be tough to predict LTV in the early stages of a business, once you have a reasonable data set you can start to make certain assumptions. All startups need to be able to figure out their LTV because it helps determine what your ideal CAC needs to be at to enable the startup to acquire new customers and reduce the burn rate. The greater the lifetime revenue of a customer, the more you can afford to spend to acquire that customer and have confidence on how long it would take to recoup back your acquisition spend. The longer a customer continues to purchase from a company or is monetized from advertising revenue, the greater their lifetime value becomes.

To calculate customer lifetime value you need to calculate average purchase and then multiply that number by the average purchase frequency rate to determine customer value, as shown in Figure 7-4. Then, once you calculate average customer lifespan, you can multiply that by customer value to determine customer lifetime value. For example, a paid subscription business that earns $10 per month on average and keeps their customers for 10 months would have a $100 LTV ($10 × 10 months).

$$\text{Average conversion value} \times \text{Average number of conversions per time period} \times \text{Average user lifetime} = \text{Lifetime value}$$

Figure 7-4. *Formula to calculate customer LTV*

LTV is important to track because it also helps you evaluate the quality of your product, brand, user experience, and customer service. It would be hard to monetize customers who are not happy with your business and that would show up in whether your LTV is trending up or down over time.

Return on Advertising Spending

All performance marketing spend is based on generating some kind of tangible monetary return for the business. This is one of the biggest investments for a startup beyond payroll, so every growth team is expected to generate a return. ROAS calculates that return and is an important KPI to determine the effectiveness on how well the growth team is spending the user acquisition budget.

The formula is quite simple, as shown in Figure 7-5. You simply divide the revenue that is produced by the campaign by the dollar amount that is spent on that particular campaign to arrive at your ROAS. So if you spent $150,000 on the campaign that resulted in $300,000 in sales, your ROAS is $2. You generated $2 for every $1 you spent. According to a study by Nielsen, the average return on ad spend is 2.87:1, meaning for every $1 spent on advertising, the average company makes $2.87. However, a good ROAS should at least be greater than 1:1 (but most likely higher than that depending on the industry).

$$ROAS = \frac{\text{Campaign revenue}}{\text{Cost of campaign}}$$

Figure 7-5. *Formula to calculate ROAS*

One of the biggest differences between ROAS and ROI is that ROAS is a ratio derived from comparing how much you spend to how much you earn, while ROI accounts for the amount you make after paying your expenses. The sole purpose of ROI is to determine whether the campaign is worth the investment or not with a focus on the profitability of acquiring new customers.

Conversion Rate

Conversion rate (CR) is the measurement of success in getting your users to perform a desired action within your campaign (e.g., making a purchase). This metric is used to track different actions for users at different stages on the customer marketing funnel. The conversion rate is a good early indicator for the performance on a campaign but not the most important metric to focus on for growth teams.

The formula to calculate CR is simply taking the number of conversions and dividing that by the total number of interactions that can be tracked to a conversion during the same time period, as shown in Figure 7-6. For example, if you had 400 conversions from 8,000 interactions, your conversion rate would be 5%, since 400 ÷ 8,000 = 5%.

$$\frac{\text{Number of users who performed an action}}{\text{Number of users who could have performed the action}} = \text{Conversion rate}$$

Figure 7-6. *Formula to calculate CR*

What is considered a good conversion rate? Conversion rates vary depending on many different factors like the campaigns, channels, offers, and/or type of business. A good conversion rate ultimately comes down to basically the one that gives you a great ROI. Higher conversion rates mean that an advertising campaign is effective at guiding visitors through the marketing funnel. Therefore, marketers should seek to optimize the factors that influence conversion rates. It's always good to track conversion rates when you're running different A/B testing experiments to find the right variables that resonate best with your users to influence the CR.

> *There are different levers to optimize to improve conversion rates.*

There are different levers to optimize to improve conversion rates including testing different offers and price points, and reducing friction to ensure that the steps to complete a desired action, or calls to action, are simple. As a growth team, you're always running A/B testing experiments to find opportunities to optimize for better conversion rates.

These five key metrics should be part of any growth team dashboard with trends to measure your progress week over week, month over month, and year over year to ensure you're moving in the right direction. They help guide you to figure out if your user acquisition strategies are working or not because the success of any AI intelligent machine is dependent on executing the right strategies to grow your startup by acquiring the right quality of customers who you can engage, retain, and monetize over the long term. All growth teams need to set clear target goals with that data going back into the AI intelligent machine to help train the algorithms to optimize toward meeting your specific KPI goals by getting smarter around targeting new user segments that match up to your best-paying customer profiles.

Beware of Vanity Metrics

As you determine how to measure what matters for your startup, you should also beware of vanity metrics, which are things you can measure that *don't* matter to the success of your business. They're easily changed or manipulated, and can mislead you into making the wrong decisions to grow your business. For example, tracking customer registrations would be considered a vanity metric because it has no correlation to getting a quality customer who is going to engage, retain, and monetize well over the long term. To not fall into the vanity metrics trap, consider centralizing user activities and milestones into a single event stream. Event streams show a comprehensive view of how people move through your product, enable you to analyze their behavior, and track how your metrics influence each other.

Once you create your event stream, count the number of active five-minute blocks your user spent with you in a day and look for clusters of action—and gaps of inaction—in their behavior (see Figure 7-7). It's a quick-and-dirty way of understanding what your customers are actually doing to answer key questions on user behavior to figure out the right metrics for your success.

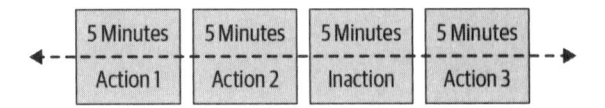

5 Minutes	5 Minutes	5 Minutes	5 Minutes
Action 1	Action 2	Inaction	Action 3

Figure 7-7. *A simple diagram to illustrate different five-minute blocks of action and inaction*

Ultimately, you want to focus on the right key metrics that align on driving long-term growth. The best way to create a unified growth culture in your startup is to always align your organization around a few key growth metrics for all teams to rally around.

> *Ultimately, you want to focus on the right key metrics that align on driving long-term growth.*

Every team's individual goals should directly ladder-up to at least one of those metrics, so that collectively everyone—the entire business—is aligned to help drive growth using your intelligent machine.

In the next chapter, we'll explore one of the biggest levers you have when it comes to empowering your AI intelligent machine: your creative assets and a clear understanding of how they're impacting performance.

CHAPTER 8

Creative Performance

The best way to acquire and retain customers is to target the right audience, with the right creative message, in the right channel and at the right time.

AI enables you to get smarter using data to optimize your creative performance to a whole new level. Marketing creative can simply be defined as the way you communicate your core message to you target audience at different stages of their customer journey through the marketing funnel. The AI "intelligent machine" needs access to a large variety of creatives to train the algorithms to figure out the right creative to show to the different user segments to elicit the desired response. The more creative variety you have, the more chances you're giving your intelligent machine to learn and optimize. This chapter will explain how creatives can be leveraged—and measured—as part of your AI machine.

The Importance of Creative Assets

The creative is the single biggest lever to impact your campaign performance. Just as comedian Ron White puts it: you can't fix stupid...well, you can't fix awful creatives with all the AI in the world. Running a variety of assets will help these platforms personalize your ads for as many ad placements as are available. Another thing to keep in mind: the better the click-through rate on creative, the less you need to pay to win competitive bids in either of the major advertising marketplaces to win the impression to get your ad in front of your target audience—a higher click-through rate is a good "signal" to ad platforms that your creative and your targeting are in a good zone, creating a positive user experience. It's important to remember that the quality and quantity of your creatives could end up making or breaking your campaign.

The better the conversion rate on your ads, the more you can afford to be aggressive with your bidding strategy. Being more aggressive on the different advertising exchanges allows you to unlock access to premium ad inventory that can give you a big competitive advantage when your campaigns are bolstered with AI managing your bidding at a detailed level based on performance.

> *The creative is the single biggest lever to impact your campaign performance.*

Having great-performing creative is one of the biggest levers in a marketer's toolbox, but most growth teams don't effectively leverage creative performance to their advantage. Great creative with performance marketing can also help build brand awareness, which can lead to more loyal customers in the long term—and help your message stand out in the busy world of highly distracted consumers. By creating innovative advertising units, marketers can increase the effectiveness of their campaigns by using programmatic media buying technology to expand the campaign reach further.

Creative Campaign Inputs

As more and more of the major paid media channels like Facebook, Google, and others leverage AI to simplify the media buying process, your AI intelligent machine will be primarily focused on controlling five key campaign input levers to optimize paid user acquisition campaigns:

- Bids
- Budgets
- Audiences
- Creative
- KPI goals

The AI intelligent machine needs to be able to figure out in real time the optimal variations and permutations of all of these inputs to help achieve the desired business output goals like ROI and CAC. Using advanced, multidimensional math, AI algorithms excel at understanding all of these inputs. But for the math to work, they need to be able to test enough different variations of creative placements, types, messages, formats, and sizes to identify the right creative to put in front of the right customer to achieve the desired business goals.

This isn't an easy one-size-fits-all approach because with AI you have the superpower of data and A/B testing to run a series of sequential creative ads at scale for different stages of the customer journey from prospecting, retargeting, reengagement, and win-backs to figure out precisely what creative will perform the best for different users at different stages of their customer journey. It's less about spray and pray and more about an ongoing Lean Startup experimentation—constantly running creative A/B tests across different customer audiences, channels, countries, etc. through the entire customer journey. This can literally lead to millions of different combinations and permutations depending on the size of your paid user acquisition budget.

The massive scale with which you can experiment, learn, and optimize creative throughout the user journey simply isn't practical (worth the time and effort) without the use of things like machine learning. A/B testing uses some of the same mathematical techniques that machine learning uses, but the key benefit with machine learning is that we can combine multiple approaches to gain insights. Machine learning and AI bring multiple dimensions to the math, which gets quite complex and unwieldy as the number of simultaneous experiments you're running grows.

AI is an ideal way to better manage the whole process of running these different creative A/B tests across all the key channels like Facebook, Google, Snapchat, Liftoff, and others because they can learn, adapt, and iterate at a much faster pace than can be achieved manually. AI gives you the power to quickly identify which creatives work and don't work and adjust budgets and targeting to increase your rate of learning and scale up growth.

Creative Scheduling

It's important to keep creative fresh and on a regular schedule. The idea is to create an ongoing "rinse and repeat" process to keep optimizing your best-performing ads for even better performance. The AI intelligent machine would allow you to better target people with the right ads and messages based on where they are in the life cycle, encouraging them to take actions that naturally lead to higher lifetime value.

The key part of the creative process is to ensure there is a virtuous cycle, with the creative performance data being passed back from the AI machine to your creative team to take that feedback to keep developing more creative iterations on a regular schedule based on what is working to feed the AI intelligent machine engine and the cycle goes on. It's important to keep humans in the loop to interpret what's behind the best-performing creatives and audiences, so they can build on that learning and keep feeding new, improved creative approaches to your always-on machine.

Using Creative Teams

Once your overall system and workflow processes are built, the creative development process should become the competitive advantage (or weakest link) that impacts your overall performance.

The whole creative development process of coming up with new ads is heavily dependent on human intelligence, but should be powered by data-driven insights surfaced through the intelligent machine. A creative brainstorming and ideation process isn't something AI can replicate today. Dynamic creative is a good option for combining images and experiences together, but the AI is not skilled at choosing the right creative concepts and/or able to figure out those dynamic ads impact on the branding. When narrow AI is rules based, it will be a long time before AI can reliably recognize a subjective aesthetic or detail that puts one creative ahead of another. I don't envision this changing in the near future and startups will need to invest into their creative throughput pipeline to help set up their AI intelligent machine for success.

Most startups don't have the budget to invest into developing an in-house creative team and so the option is to work with either a team of freelancers or creative agencies to help manage this for you. I have generally started out working with several dedicated creative freelancers or small creative agencies and then look to pivot this into hiring a small dedicated creative team in-house depending on the size of the budget being spent on our paid user acquisition.

The creative development costs would eventually help dictate your decision on whether to continue to work with an outsourced provider or bring this function in-house because you eventually reach a point where the ROI indicates it is more cost-effective doing this in-house based on the size of your user acquisition budget. At IMVU, investing into growing our in-house creative team has really helped us significantly improve performance across all our paid user acquisition campaigns as we've ramped up our use of AI for campaign orchestration and management.

Ad Fatigue

The more budget you spend, the faster your creative ads are going to experience ad fatigue—especially if you have a limited number of creatives to begin with. This is defined as the weakening effect that people seeing the same creative ad over and over again will have over time as it becomes familiar and therefore more likely to be tuned out with reduced impact (this is also known as *saturation*).

The best way to figure out if you may be battling ad fatigue is to see how long it takes for your new ad's performance to reach degradation against your specific KPI goals. For example, if your KPI is ROI, then watch ad performance closely to see when it starts to perform poorly after a certain timeframe. This would indicate the ad isn't performing as well anymore, and new creative variations could give you a much needed lift in performance.

In general, you always have to ensure your creative refresh is happening faster than your ad fatigue, so that you're being proactive against running into ad fatigue as you continue to scale up your creative testing with AI. Think of the creative as fuel to the flames, but keep in mind it needs to be revised and refreshed at least several times per month on average in order to avoid fatigue or saturation depending on your budget. You can delay ad fatigue by expanding your audience or creating new ads. Creating new ads is the more effective approach. It's important to figure out how often to refresh by looking at your creative performance data.

How many creatives should you produce? It's ultimately a practical function of budget. As a rule of thumb, you can assume you need about $10 per day per creative to give each one enough budget for your intelligent machine to gather enough data to make confident decisions. So for a budget of $500 a day across all your channels, you should plan on having roughly 50 creative variations in your arsenal to create an ideal pool for testing and learning. This number can, of course, grow as you get more granular with audience targeting and life cycle marketing.

Benefits of Great Creative

There are three key ways that great creative and AI can help scale up your customer acquisition performance:

Brand awareness
> The reality is that exposing your brand consistently to the right audience, with the right message, at the right time is going to help build awareness for your product in the customer's mind; over time, it becomes familiar and more trusted among the consumers you're reaching. An engaging witty, funny, compelling, or original creative ad is more likely to stand out and influence the customer to like your brand, then take the desired next steps in their customer journey and funnel. All great creative also needs a clear and strong call to action (CTA) to encourage the customer to take your desired next steps in their customer journey. For example, a compelling creative with a special deal or offer (say, 15% off) is more likely to get someone to purchase versus the same creative with no deal. Incorporating customer reviews and influencers to drive up "social proof" and build trust can also be a solid middle of the funnel creative tactic that appeals to customers who are less likely to act on deals or offers.

Loyalty

Data-driven creative messages get more attention and better responses about the products being marketed to their customers. Even in the era of privacy, consumers are clamoring for better use of their personal data to drive relevant and better targeted personalized ads with consistent cross-channel experiences. Any startup that can deliver an experience that respects the user's time, attention, and money will end up building more trust and an engaged community of loyal fans. An example is Amazon, which has built their Prime membership based on leveraging customer data to deliver great personalized ads to encourage more sales and loyalty.

More learning

Investing resources to develop a variety of different ad creative orientations, sizes, formats (images and video), copy variations, and CTAs would help to maximize your reach and performance by letting the AI do the work to optimize toward the best-performing creatives.

The more creative A/B testing you can do with AI, the faster you will learn to find insights to capture customer attention in today's highly distracted world. This will enable you to scale up user growth with different sequential creatives and CTAs to positively influence the purchase behavior of your product and improve ROI. At IMVU, we found after extensive testing that user-generated content (UGC) creative ads showing actual customer avatars and virtual world in-app experiences performed much better than standard creatives. These UGC creatives provided actual gameplay experiences that closely match user expectations and showed the audience authentic IMVU experiences.

Creative Best Practices

In order to grow a loyal customer base, you need to serve the right messages and designs to the right audiences. Here are some creative best practices to help guide you:

Know your target

The biggest benefit of running advertising with an AI intelligent machine is the ability to target specific customers who are most likely to make a purchase. Therefore, you should leverage this data to your advantage by creating the relevant ads that are most likely to resonate with the different target audiences. One of the best ways to do this is running a series of different A/B testing on creative ads to figure out which is the most compelling to the different target audiences at different stages of their customer journey.

KISS (keep it simple, stupid)

It's always more effective to be less cluttered than to overwhelm users with too much information on ads. It's tempting to want to get the most bang from your ads and throw as much information as possible. Unfortunately, you are not going to communicate your entire value proposition story in just one ad. It's best to be concise and get to the point with your messaging. This is where sequencing your creatives to your targeted audience can make a big difference.

The key goal for ads is to capture your target audience's attention by piquing their desire to want to learn more about you, and not necessarily to close the deal right away. Use ads to tease a product, service, or promotion. Earn the attention of the audience and entice them into following through to the richer content on your website or mobile app. It's always good to create a series of sequential ads to communicate different value propositions with "snackable content" that is easy for users to digest to break through the clutter of all the other ads that are fighting for their attention.

Most common display ad sizes are small and too much information can be overwhelming, confusing, and difficult to read. It's best to keep the ad simple and easy to understand (stupid). You have to get your message across clearly and quickly, because you only have your viewer's attention for a second. You normally don't get a second chance to make a first impression. Make that small window of attention count.

Use compelling visuals, copy, and CTA

One of the most daunting parts of designing a good piece of creative is deciding on the best combination of copy, visuals, and CTAs. You want your creative to stand out from the rest of the ads competing for the customer's attention. It's always good to A/B test different creative formats, messages, CTAs, images, or videos to figure out the best-performing ads for the different target audiences at different stages of their customer journey. Our job as growth marketers is to include a CTA that makes it clear what you want a customer to do, then make it simple for them to do exactly that. Continue to take the winners of your tests, create slight variations, then rinse and repeat the tests again. Testing should always be ongoing, and never one and done.

The color scheme of your creative should reflect your brand guidelines and the landing page that users click through to. There should be a seamless, integrated experience from the ad to the landing page, so it carries the same look and feel of the advertising. The color emotion guide in Figure 8-1 illustrates the psychology of color in advertising.

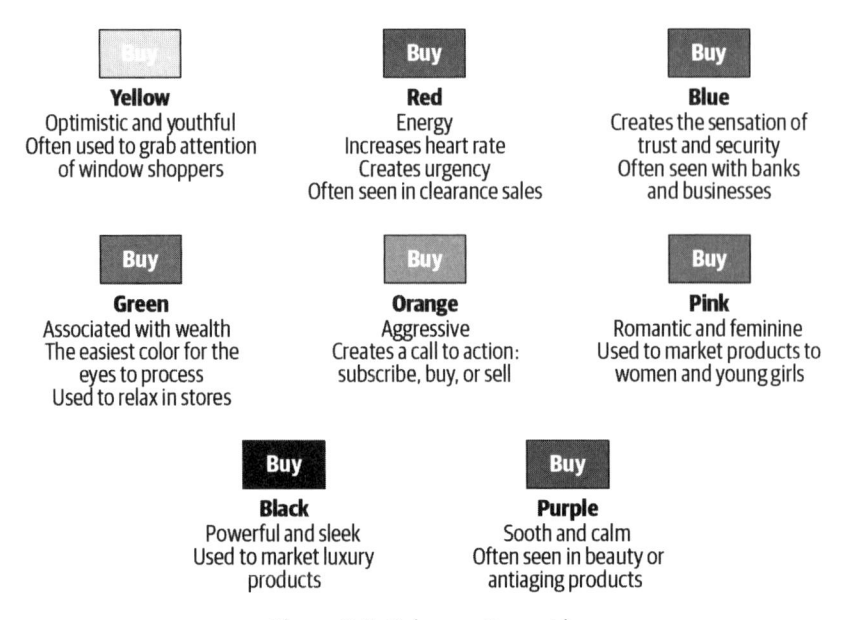

Yellow
Optimistic and youthful
Often used to grab attention
of window shoppers

Red
Energy
Increases heart rate
Creates urgency
Often seen in clearance sales

Blue
Creates the sensation of
trust and security
Often seen with banks
and businesses

Green
Associated with wealth
The easiest color for the
eyes to process
Used to relax in stores

Orange
Aggressive
Creates a call to action:
subscribe, buy, or sell

Pink
Romantic and feminine
Used to market products to
women and young girls

Black
Powerful and sleek
Used to market luxury
products

Purple
Sooth and calm
Often seen in beauty or
antiaging products

Figure 8-1. *Color emotion guide*

Use simple images that are easy for the eye to register. You should never use images to simply fill up space, and you must make sure that the image visually communicates what is written in the copy. Design your creative with clearly defined borders, which draws visitors' eyes to the ad.

Limit your typography to two fonts per ad. Make sure to only bold the important information. Try to limit the ad to no more than one-third of the real estate devoted to text. Too much copy can be overwhelming and most users won't even read it. That's why the most compelling billboards limit themselves to eight easily readable words.

Mobile Ads Best Practices

With 3.8 billion smartphones in the hands of consumers worldwide, mobile devices are fast becoming the primary way your customers are finding and consuming information. In addition, by 2021, 78% of all mobile data will be video.[1] Advertisers need to be prepared for this shift from a static mobile experience to one that takes a video-first approach. Luckily, best practices for mobile advertising and video creatives are relatively simple and there are

---

1 "Cisco Visual Networking Index," Cisco, last updated February 27, 2019. *https://oreil.ly/aA6_a*.

literally hundreds of tools available to help you build great video-powered mobile creatives. Keep these criteria in mind as you develop mobile creatives:

Core Requirements	Suggested Enhancements	Optimization Keys
Logo	Animate your text to capture attention	You have three seconds to capture the audience's attention
A single clear message you want to communicate	Use simple animations (or slideshows) to pack more information in visually	Keep your video under 15 seconds
Strong CTA		Assume that the user's device will have the sound turned off
		Shoot video vertically or square to maximize screen real estate for mobile devices

Future Creative Development and Iteration

As we noted earlier, today's neural networks and NLP advances make it possible to "train" intelligent machines to write advertising or marketing copy in your brand's voice, or recommend things like hashtags for social media posts.

Using off-the-shelf libraries and training them on a significant sample of your brand's marketing copy (the more structured, the better), you can achieve interesting results today. These exercises can be useful for idea generation, creating variations in ad copy, emails, or other types of marketing materials.

Some companies that operate in highly structured reporting environments—think sports, financial reporting, etc.—have replaced reporters with trained, special purpose machines designed to crank out quality copy that is virtually indistinguishable from an editorial product.

For now, the large amount of training data required to make automated copy generation really work for a brand and carry its "voice" in copy makes the technique a bit out of reach for most startups. But this will evolve considerably over the next few years and it's a place to watch. In the meantime, experiment with online text generators (they get better and more powerful every day) to get some ideas and inspiration. However, it's currently hard to envision a world where AI would be able to completely automate the entire creative development process without human intelligence driving the creative machine. This is one area where human creativity is far superior to AI; even though it may replace many of the mundane creative tasks, it will not usurp the entire process anytime soon.

In the next chapter, we'll explore the area of cross-channel attribution to help provide measurement for your AI machine to determine which channels and creatives have the greatest impact on the complex customer journey to achieve your desired business KPI goals.

CHAPTER 9

Cross-Channel Attribution

In today's data-driven marketing world, cross-channel attribution is a hot topic. It's defined as the science of using advanced analytics to allocate proportional credit to more than one digital and non-digital channel or touchpoint. This is very important to help growth teams gain insight into what's working and not working, otherwise they're just guessing. Having touchpoints attributed inaccurately is never helpful and leads to poor execution on a user acquisition strategy. All growth teams are responsible for knowing which campaigns are most effective to help them acquire new customers. As more and more startups spend heavily on advertising to attract new customers across a myriad of channels and platforms, the cost of acquiring new customer growth has continued to increase year over year. On top of that, the typical customer journey can take 5, 15, or more than 50 interactions with an ad or brand for someone to finally convert into a new customer.

The complex marketing landscape means that user acquisition efforts are spread out across a rapidly changing and far-reaching channel and media mix. In order to accurately measure both online and offline media, and its impact within the marketing mix and overall ROI, you need the ability to collect a variety of data to track prospects across the entire customer journey, then merge that data to map out what had the most impact to influence them into becoming a new consumer. Clearly, marketing attribution is key for any data-driven growth team to make smart decisions on where to focus resources to acquire new customers as well as plan and project future growth. This chapter will show you the different types of attribution models available to help you to figure out the right one for your business because getting the right attribution is important to making the right decisions in how you allocate your customer acquisition budget.

> *The complex marketing landscape means that user acquisition efforts are spread out across a rapidly changing and far-reaching channel and media mix.*

What Is Marketing Attribution?

Marketing attribution is the practice of evaluating the different interactions or touchpoints a consumer encounters on their path to become a customer, whether that is defined as signing up for a free trial or making a purchase. The goal of attribution is to determine which channels and creatives had the greatest impact on the decision to convert, or take the desired next step in your marketing funnel. There are several popular attribution models used by growth teams today, such as first touch, last touch, multi-touch attribution, lift studies, time decay, and more. The insights provided by these models into how, where, and when a consumer interacts with a product and brand allows growth teams to alter and customize campaigns to meet the specific desires of individual consumers, thus improving marketing ROI.

Advanced marketing attribution programs require you to aggregate and normalize consumer data across channels to ensure each interaction is properly weighted. For example, if a consumer is exposed to a video ad and an email campaign, but only converts after seeing a special promotion in the email, marketers can note that this piece of collateral played a bigger role in driving the sale than the display ad. They can then devote more resources to creating targeted email campaigns. What you need is a tool that allows you to trace every user back to the first source of contact, the last source, and all the sequential sources in between those contacts. To achieve the level of data granularity required for effective attribution, you need advanced analytics platforms that can accurately and efficiently extract big data into person-level insights that can be used for in-campaign optimizations.

Marketing Attribution Models

There are many common attribution models available that can help assign value to marketing campaigns using real-time data through statistical analysis at the user level. This is in contrast to models such as marketing mix modeling that use aggregate historical data such as syndicated point-of-sale data and companies' internal data to quantify the sales impact of various marketing activities. This person-centric approach is why attribution models are more typically applied to digital campaigns than those conducted offline, such as print advertising. It's important for all startup employees and investors to have better insights into how their growth team is spending their money to get confidence on executing the right user acquisition strategies. Most growth teams use first-touch, last-touch, or multi-touch attribution.

First- and Last-Touch Attribution Models

First- and last-touch attribution models are currently the most common methods used today because they are easier for most people to understand and implement, but they fail to provide a clear view of the holistic customer journey. These models attribute a conversion to a single touchpoint, often the first or last one engaged with by the consumer. An example of a last-touch attribution is the popular last click model, which attributes a conversion to the last piece of marketing advertising a consumer clicked on before converting. However, this simplistic approach neglects to look at the wider customer journey and touchpoints engaged with by having a strong bias for either the first or last touchpoint (e.g., Google search ad), which get all the credit for bringing in the new customer. This leaves the door open for either false negatives or false positives by underestimating the impact of all the different prior assisting touchpoints working together to influence customers further down the marketing funnel, before they get closed by a typical closing channel like paid search.

An example would be a new ecommerce customer who may first see several banner and video ads across their mobile device before finally clicking a paid search ad on Google to make a purchase. With last-touch attribution, all the credit would go to the Google search ad and the role played by the other ads is disregarded. A good sports analogy is giving all the credit for scoring a goal to the goal scorer with no credit to the rest of the team who played a part in the buildup to the goal. We all know that winning in sports or business is a team sport, so using last-touch attribution doesn't make sense for businesses who focus their efforts across multiple channels, platforms, and media mixes to acquire new customers.

Multi-Touch Attribution Models

Almost 90% of US companies are expected to be using multichannel attribution models by 2020 according to eMarketer. Multi-touch attribution models assign credit to more than one channel or touchpoint by looking at all of the different touchpoints engaged with by the new consumer leading up to a desired outcome like a purchase. In our ecommerce example, the credit would be shared by all the different touchpoints that helped influence the final purchase (banner, video ads, and Google search ads). Hence, using our soccer team analogy, this would mean giving credit to the entire group of players who were involved in the play leading up to the goal and not just the player who scored the goal. This holistic view of the entire customer journey would result in building more accurate models. Which multi-touch model you use determines how much value is assigned to the different channels or touchpoints. These models are largely differentiated by how they divide credit between the different touchpoints on the path to the final outcome (i.e., a purchase):

Linear

Linear attribution records each touchpoint by the customer leading to the final outcome. It weighs each of these interactions equally, giving each touchpoint the same amount of credit toward driving the conversion. For example, in Figure 9-1, if there are five different touchpoints in the user journey then each one would get 20% of the credit.

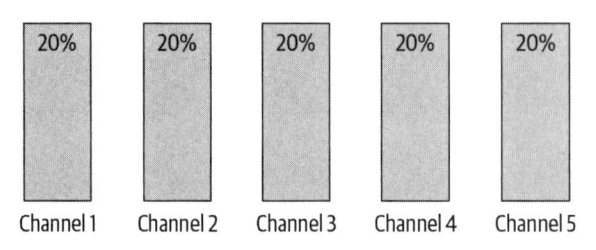

Interactions in chronological order

Figure 9-1. *Example of linear attribution*

U-shaped

Unlike linear attribution, the U-shaped attribution model scores touchpoints separately, based on the premise that some are more impactful than others on the path to the final outcome. Specifically, both the first touch and last touch are usually credited with more weighting compared to the rest. For example, in Figure 9-2, the first and last touchpoints would get credited with 40% and the other 20% is divided among the three remaining touchpoints between the first and last touch.

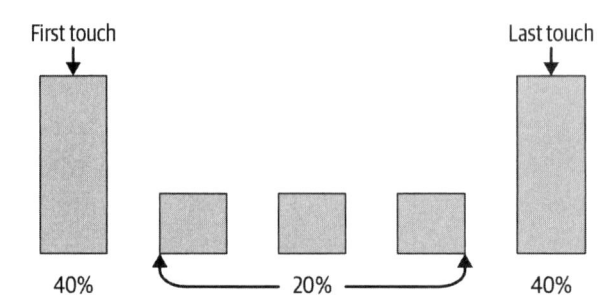

Figure 9-2. *Example of U-shaped attribution*

Time decay

The time decay model also weighs each touchpoint differently on the path to the final outcome. This model gives more credit to touchpoints that happen closer to the final outcome compared to those early on, assuming those had a greater impact on the final outcome. This model could be effective to figure out the best way to leverage different touchpoints based on your user acquisition goals to help drive top-of-the-funnel awareness or bottom-of-the-funnel conversions. For example, in Figure 9-3, each channel is credited with a different value as it gets closer to the final outcome.

```
                                           30%
                                    25%
                             20%
                      15%
               10%
            Channel 1  Channel 2  Channel 3  Channel 4  Channel 5
                    Interactions in chronological order
```

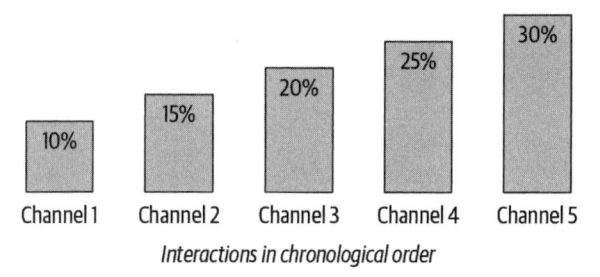

Figure 9-3. *Example of time decay attribution*

W-shaped

This model uses the same idea as the U-shaped model; however, it includes one more core touchpoint—the opportunity stage. Thus, for the W-shaped model the touchpoints credited with first-middle-last touchpoints get more credit than the ones in between them. For example, in Figure 9-4, the first-middle-last touchpoints receive 30% of the credit and the two remaining touchpoints receive 5% credit.

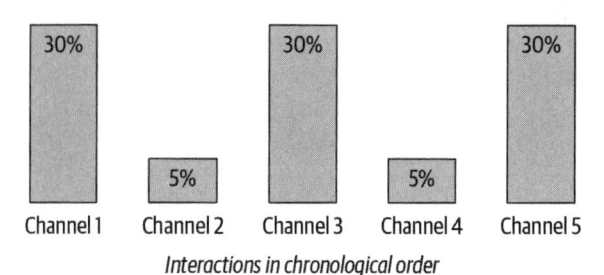

```
         30%              30%              30%
                   5%              5%
      Channel 1  Channel 2  Channel 3  Channel 4  Channel 5
              Interactions in chronological order
```

Figure 9-4. *Example of W-shaped attribution*

Choosing the Right Attribution Model for Your Startup

There are pros and cons to every marketing attribution model. There is no such thing as the perfect attribution model and the key is to figure out tools you have available to help you build the right model for your business. That's because each model works well in its own right and is dependent on the amount of resources you have to invest into leveraging the right attribution tools to help play with different attribution models to determine which works best for your startup. There are many factors that need to be considered from how long your typical purchase cycle is to the channel mix between online and offline media as well as digital and retail channels. For example, multi-touch attribution is often credited with working better for digital channels, while marketing mix modeling provides stronger insights into offline campaigns.

Ultimately deciding on the level of sophistication of your multi-channel attribution model comes down to what type of attribution tools you can afford to leverage to help you manage it because you need to be able to track and measure all the different touchpoints across the entire customer journey to help you connect all the dots.

Marketing Attribution Tools

To get the most reliable insights, marketers will need to use a combination of models and correlate the data from each to determine the correct optimizations to make for online and offline campaigns.

Doing this will require a powerful analytics platform capable of providing in-campaign insights into online and offline marketing optimizations; such a platform will be a distinct advantage.

There are several categories that marketers should evaluate when selecting a marketing attribution tool or software:

- Speed
- Accuracy
- Connection of branding and performance
- Cross-channel insights

Here are a few questions to ask when selecting an attribution model:

- Are you able to track cross-platform user journeys between different channels and platforms, as well as online and offline media?
- Can you get visibility into branding impact?
- Do you get visibility into the impact of creative during the consumer journey?
- Can you get person-level insights for non-digital, offline efforts?
- Are you only measuring lift, and not inevitable events?
- Do you use experimental design to avoid correlation bias?
- Can you get insights to optimize during the campaign, or only at the end?
- Do you get insight into external factors that impact campaigns?

- Does the solution provide quality analysis in addition to accurate data?

Here are some of the popular attribution tools available today:

- Adjust
- AppsFlyer
- Branch
- Kochava
- Singular

Benefits of Marketing Attribution

There is no argument that growth teams need to have better insight into how effectively their budgets are being spent. The challenge is how to shift from a simplistic model to a more advanced multi-touch model with added investments that need to be made into finding the right tools for piecing all this data and measurement together.

Advanced attribution models can be time and resource intensive to get right, especially complex models that evaluate a variety of data sets for online and offline campaigns. The most effective attribution models are the ones that can provide you the best direction on how to allocate your time, money, and resources to acquire new customers cost-effectively. The smarter you get about leveraging data to better understand your holistic customer journey, the more effective you will be in scaling up your customer growth with a positive ROI.

However, when done effectively, attribution brings many benefits, including:

Optimized marketing spend
    Attribution models give marketers insights into how marketing dollars are best spent by showing the value of different touchpoints over the course of the customer journey and their impact on the LTV of those customers. This allows growth teams to adjust and optimize their budget accordingly based on different success goals and metrics.

Increased ROI
    Effective attribution enables marketers to reach the right consumer, at the right time, with the right message—leading to increased conversions and higher marketing ROI.

Improved personalization
    Marketers can use attribution data to understand the messaging and channels preferred by individual customers for more effective targeting throughout the customer journey.

Improved product development
　　Person-level attribution allows marketers to better understand the needs of their consumers. These insights can then be referenced when making updates to the product to target the functionality consumers want.

Optimized creative
　　Attribution models that can evaluate the creative elements of a campaign allow marketers to hone messaging and visual elements in addition to better understanding how and when to communicate with users.

People-Based Attribution Is the Future

Measuring your spending across virtually every area of growth and determining its contribution to revenue is imperative. This includes having the attribution data to drill down, analyze, and rebalance any program, campaign, touchpoint, and/or channel to optimize revenue performance, including end-to-end visibility of how new customers are interacting with your brand through their entire customer journey. This is where leveraging advanced multi-touch attribution cross-platform technology like AppsFlyer creates a huge advantage and will end up becoming table stakes for businesses to use toward the vision of truly holistic, people-based attribution with a single, deduplicated persona for each of your human customers, available to reference across every channel and platform for accurate measurement and credit toward your final outcome. Harnessing consumer engagement data through the multi-touchpoint consumer journey and applying advanced machine-learning algorithms will help to not just understand consumer intent but also shape and engage intent at scale to anticipate new opportunities for engaging customers—and winning.

The Why of People-Based Attribution

As we have seen in previous chapters, data is the fuel that any intelligent machine runs on—specifically data that encompasses the entire customer journey. From a growth marketer's perspective, this journey begins long before a user downloads an app or makes a purchase. Instead, it starts with the very first touchpoint between a business and a future customer.

The vision of a unified and holistic view of the interactions between a business and their customers is, of course, nothing new. But while marketers in the past had to accept the limitations of how their craft was being measured and evaluated—a challenge distilled into the bon mot "Half the money I spend on advertising is wasted; the trouble is I don't know which half"[1]—the rise of

---

[1] David Ogilvy attributes this to Lord Leverhulme and John Wanamaker in his book *Confessions of an Advertising Man* (Southbank Publishing). *https://oreil.ly/QqFUA*.

digital media has brought about both a new standard and new expectations around the measurability of marketing efforts.

Performance marketers were able to achieve impressive gains in marketing efficiency and measurability; however, these achievements are often not translated into significant progress outside the realm of digital. Additionally, the fragmented mobile ecosystem introduced new measurement challenges that made it even harder to understand a customer journey from beginning to end. Most importantly, the explosion of new channels available to individuals—from smartphones to smart wearables, smart speakers, and smart TVs—means user journeys are becoming increasingly complex.

According to Forrester Research 65% of online purchases now involve multiple devices,[2] while a recent study by eMarketer found that less than 10% of companies succeed in attributing user actions holistically across devices, channels, and platforms.[3]

This creates an interesting dilemma for marketers: on the one hand, individual consumers are interacting with brands in an ever-increasing stream of channels and touchpoints, all of which form a connected experience for them. For example, their experience with a major shopping brand includes seeing a billboard on their commute, browsing a catalog online, visiting the store to purchase a new item, and using a coupon from their mobile app.

Businesses, on the other hand, are having a hard time understanding the *context* of these connected actions. Instead of seeing a shopper in a holistic way, they are working with multiple "split personalities" of the same individual. What's more, marketing teams and advertising budgets are often organized in a way that accentuates—rather than alleviates—a brand's omnichannel challenge. The results of this siloed approach are campaign inefficiencies, duplicated marketing efforts, and wasted ad spend.

People-based attribution seeks to close this gap by connecting the different touchpoints—or marketing interactions—between a business and their audience. It is driven by the understanding that people, not devices, are the common denominator between individual data points across marketing channels. As a result, the focus of people-based attribution is to match disjointed marketing interactions with a set of unique user profiles.

---

[2] Kate Leggett et al., "Engagement Costs Continue To Rise Even With Digital," Forrester, September 7, 2017. *https://oreil.ly/QpDkp*.

[3] Lauren Fisher, "Advancing Marketing Attribution," eMarketer, February 19, 2019. *https://oreil.ly/21IaC*.

The Current State of People-Based Attribution

While straightforward on a conceptual level, achieving true people-based attribution is not a trivial feat. To create an accurate, unified user profile, any attribution provider must overcome a set of serious challenges:

Lack of measurability of specific channels
　The technologies and methodologies used to measure various channels vary greatly between and even within media—and interactions with some channels (e.g., out-of-home and newspaper ads) are almost impossible to measure with any degree of accuracy.

Missing connection between channels
　Even if a channel is measurable, linking data from this channel back to a unified user profile is challenging. A single individual browsing both the desktop website and the mobile app of a brand will usually be registered as two separate users, unless the brand has technology in place that creates a match between both profiles. On the other end of the spectrum, having multiple users use the same device (e.g., a shared family desktop computer) may create false positives that group different individuals into the same user profile.

Joining and normalizing data
　Once the cross-channel data has been collected, it needs to be joined and normalized in a meaningful way. Different ad networks operating in the same channel may use varying definitions of what constitutes an interaction,[4] and this challenge is further amplified when different channels are joined—for example, if a marketing interaction on mobile is compared to a web interaction or one on over-the-top (OTT)[5] TV. This requires a deep contextual, channel-specific understanding of what a marketing touchpoint means.

Data and privacy concerns
　Finally, just because people-based attribution is technically possible, doesn't mean that the end users will agree to being measured in a holistic way. Marketers must ensure that their attribution provider is capable of keeping customer data secure by adhering to strict security standards and protocols. They also need to ensure that their solution is compliant with

---

4 For an example of how attribution providers can help standardize definitions of ad interactions between different media sources, see "AppsFlyer Clicks and Views Standardization" (*https://oreil.ly/D-jsl*) for mobile marketers.

5 OTT is the term used for the delivery of film and TV content via the internet, without requiring users to subscribe to a traditional cable or satellite pay-TV service like Comcast.

privacy-centric regulations, such as the General Data Protection Regulation (GDPR) and California Consumer Privacy Act (CCPA), and is capable of implementing opt-out requests from users across touchpoints.

Despite these significant challenges, people-based attribution solutions have become increasingly robust and comprehensive during the course of the past few years. One reason for this is the increasing digitalization of channels, which continues to open up and deepen measurement capabilities available to marketers. At the same time, attribution providers—especially ones with expertise in unifying the highly fragmented mobile ecosystem—have emerged as key innovators in the space.

Attribution Basics: Recognizing the User Behind Individual Touchpoints

Attribution providers generally rely on two fundamental methodologies to attribute a signal from a marketing interaction to a specific user or individual: *deterministic* and *probabilistic* matching.

Deterministic matching

Matching technologies based on deterministic methods utilize identifiers that are unique to a device or interaction. As such, they provide a very high level of confidence that a positive match between a marketing interaction and a user is indeed correct. Examples of deterministic identifiers are the mobile device IDs provided by operating system owners (i.e., Apple's IDFA, as well as Google's GAID and Play Referrer), cookie IDs supported by desktop and mobile web (but usually not mobile apps), and unique customer IDs assigned by a business (e.g., during signup for a loyalty program).

Probabilistic matching

Not every marketing interaction will provide a deterministic identifier: for example, 10%–15% of mobile users[6] use a "limit ad tracking" feature that replaces their unique Device ID with a blank Device ID, a string of generic zeros. Furthermore, some non-digital channels, like traditional (linear) TV, will not offer a deterministic identifier at all. This is where probabilistic matching comes in as a fallback method to the deterministic model. As the name suggests, these techniques leverage parameters and machine learning to build statistical models for device matching.

On mobile, *fingerprinting* is the main probabilistic identification method that uses a blend of publicly available parameters (i.e., device name, device type,

---

6 "Limit Ad Tracking," AppsFlyer. *https://oreil.ly/7hNBQ*.

OS version, platform, IP address, carrier, etc.) to form a digital fingerprint ID statistically matching specific device attributes. The accuracy of probabilistic matching is dependent on the scale of data and the sophistication of the model. That's why state-of-the-art probabilistic matching methodologies, like Apps-Flyer's *adaptive fingerprinting*, are informed by criteria like IP uniqueness to determine the likelihood of a positive match at a very high confidence level.

Holistic matching

At its core, the choice between deterministic and probabilistic matching is a trade-off between reach and accuracy. As a result, the most advanced attribution platforms employ a blend of both methodologies, where probabilistic matching is used as a fallback when deterministic identifiers are not available. Table 9-1 illustrates the basic principles and traits of each of these solutions.

Table 9-1. Overview of matching methodologies

	Probabilistic matching	Deterministic matching	Holistic matching
What it is	Using statistical methods to determine the likelihood of a match based on non-unique identifiers	Using a single unique identifier to determine a match between interactions	Combined approach where multiple deterministic identifiers are augmented by probabilistic ones
The benefits	Broad reach across devices and channels	Excellent accuracy with high level of matching confidence	Excellent accuracy across a breadth of devices and channels
The challenges	Risk of mismatches, especially when based on a small data set	Limited reach and applicability	Requires scale and advanced matching algorithms

Two Approaches to People-Based Attribution

The different approaches to people-based attribution today generally fall into one of two categories: *shared databases* on the one hand and *private databases* on the other.

Shared graphs

Matching based on a shared database, merging all customer data together to build an identity graph (also known as "device graph" or "persona graph") is a form of "crowdsourced" data collection that is often used as a workaround to counter limitations in scale either of individual advertisers, or the attribution platform as a whole. The basic idea is that a positive match made by one company is then made accessible to all other companies utilizing the same attribution platform.

For example, if Business A has established that a specific user with the cookie ID 1111 from desktop web uses the mobile Device ID 2222, this relationship may then be available for an unrelated Business B to optimize their marketing efforts. The advantage of this approach is that shared databases can give customers of the same attribution platform the necessary scale to attribute correctly. As such, shared databases can be the right solution for small- and medium-sized companies with a limited mix of channels or infrequent customer touchpoints.

But marketers should also consider that the shared matching data is owned by the attribution provider—not by them. This means that their data is actively used to sell a *product* provided by the attribution platform, which may benefit their competitors just as much as it benefits them. In this example, if Business A—who made the initial match—decides to switch attribution providers, they may lose access to the shared matching data, while Business B still benefits.

Last but not least, this approach may also raise questions about privacy compliance. If Business B receives a request from the user to erase their attribution data, will Business A lose access as well?

Private graphs

The alternative to the shared graphs approach is graphs that are individually built for a single company at a time, and are private to that brand or business. Using the aforementioned example, this would mean that the match established by Business A will only be accessible to them, and not a—potentially competing–Business B.

The benefits of this approach are obvious to privacy-sensitive businesses that cannot or do not want to share their customers' data with other companies, but do not want to compromise on personalization either. It also alleviates concerns about the ownership of the companies' first-party data, which often amounts to a significant competitive advantage for intelligence-driven businesses. This focus on first-party data makes private graphs especially relevant for major brands, companies with large user bases, and/or ones with frequent customer touchpoints across channels—in other words, those who have the most to gain from people-based attribution (and incur larger risks and more scrutiny when it comes to privacy).

Common and Advanced Use Cases for People-Based Attribution

As brands adopt people-based attribution as a key driver of growth and engagement, they will increasingly develop complex use cases for this new technology. When evaluating people-based attribution for your business, consider the following use cases.

Optimize media mix and budget allocation

As you can see in Figure 9-5 and Figure 9-6, having a complete view of your users' journeys provides you with insights not only into how individual channels perform in comparison to others. It also allows you to better understand how these channels work in tandem to create a multi-touch experience that increases engagement with your audience. For example, you may be surprised to find that a specific video ad on desktop that fails to generate significant traffic to the website it is promoting actually plays a vital role in increasing the likelihood of a mobile conversion later in the customer's life cycle.

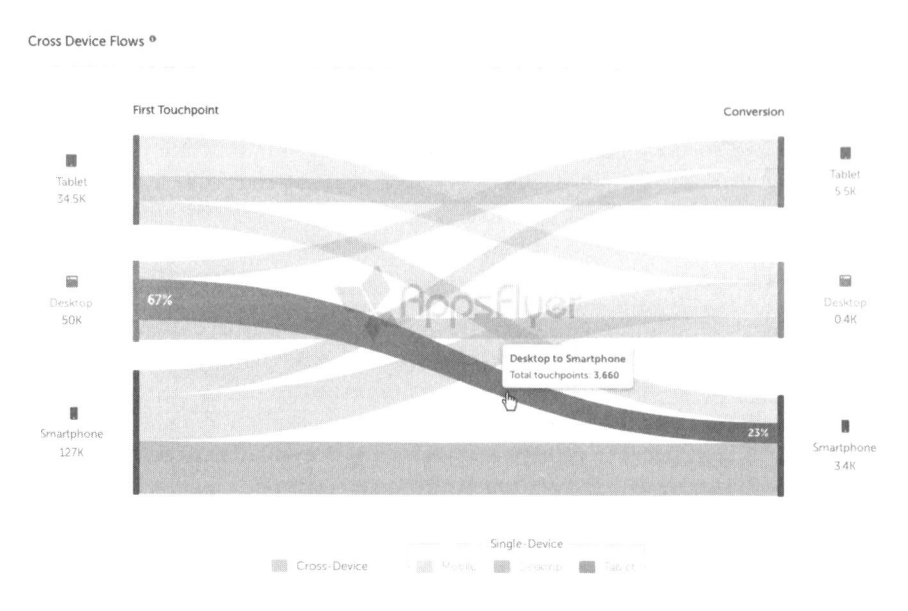

Figure 9-5. *A Sankey diagram shows the most common user journeys across devices—in this example, 15% of journeys that ended in a conversion on a mobile device started with a website visit on desktop (courtesy of AppsFlyer)*

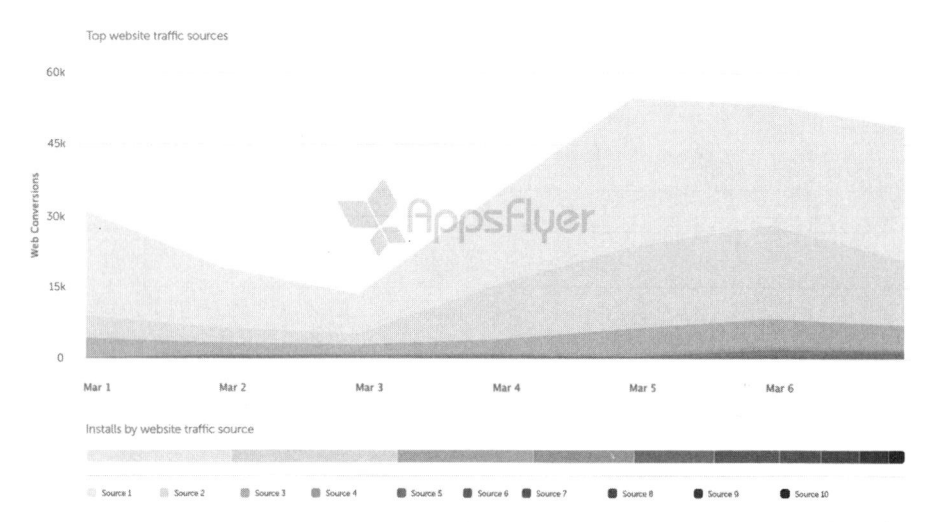

Figure 9-6. *This web-to-app conversion chart provides a comprehensive view of customer journeys by analyzing the impact of web campaigns on your native app (courtesy of AppsFlyer)*

Boost ad efficiency

People-based attribution can also help reduce ad fatigue by restricting how often a certain ad may be shown across devices and channels. When a consumer has been overexposed to the same ad repeatedly over a short period of time, the ad loses its effectiveness. This is why you may choose to implement frequency capping—for example, by setting a limit that the same user can see the same ad only three times within a 24-hour time period. Such frequency capping is most effective when implemented across devices, and can save you significant amounts of ad dollars.

Smarter retargeting

People-based insights allows you to pique users' attention on the many devices they use. For retargeting and reengaging users across screens, consider the following methods (see Figure 9-7):

Retarget web visitors who have bounced
98% of web visitors do not convert on their first visit. Connect with web visitors that have bounced with creatives and a CTA adapted to the device they're using to make sure you catch them when they are ready to engage with your brand.

Retarget based on the product last viewed on web
Build an audience of users that have viewed a specific product on your website and drive them (with or without deferred deep linking) to the

relevant product within your app with tailored messaging and contextual delivery.

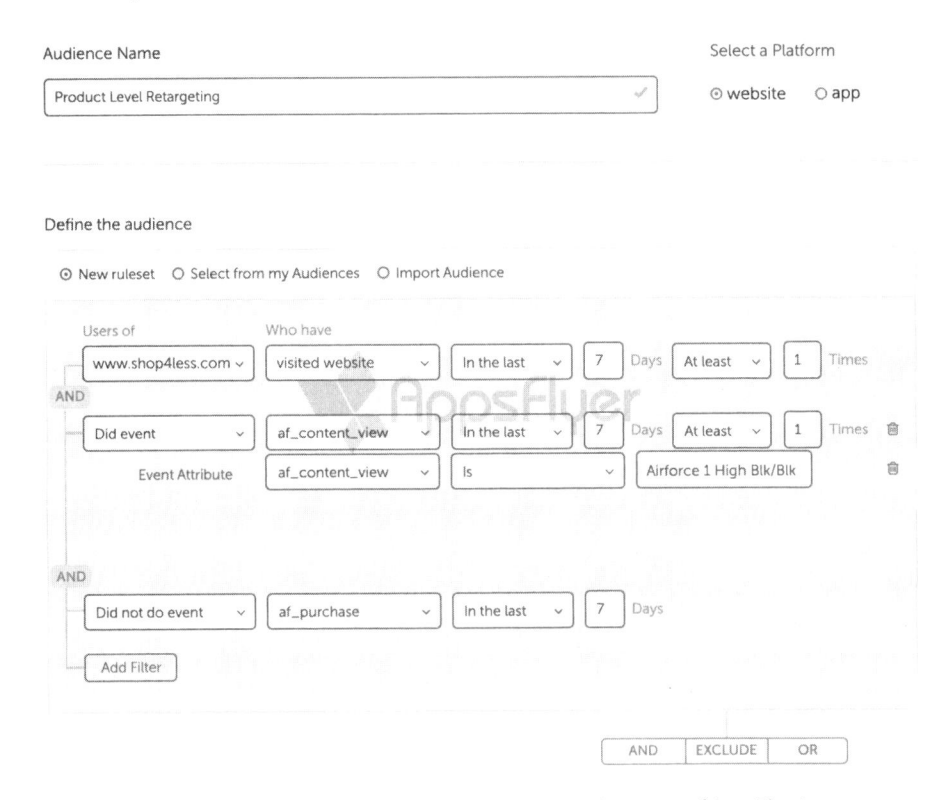

Figure 9-7. *Product-level retargeting segment (courtesy of AppsFlyer)*

Retarget based on search history

Use search history to create smart segments and retarget users based on their buying intentions. Drive them to your website or app based on the optimized user journey for your audience.

Identify and prevent advanced forms of fraud

In a world where AI-powered, fraudulent traffic from bots and complex automated scripts is becoming nearly indistinguishable from human behavior, having a large cross-channel data set of user interactions increases the likelihood to spot behavioral anomalies that differ from the norm, or the majority of users within certain segments.

For example, to a financial institution that understands that 80% of their app users also frequently interact with their website on desktop, a media source that delivers large amounts of users that only interact with the app presents itself as an outlier that should be investigated.

Improve the customer journey and user experience

As you can see in Figure 9-8, the ability to consider the full customer journey across channels and devices unlocks advanced opportunities for user flow optimization, as well as multi-touch targeting and personalization.

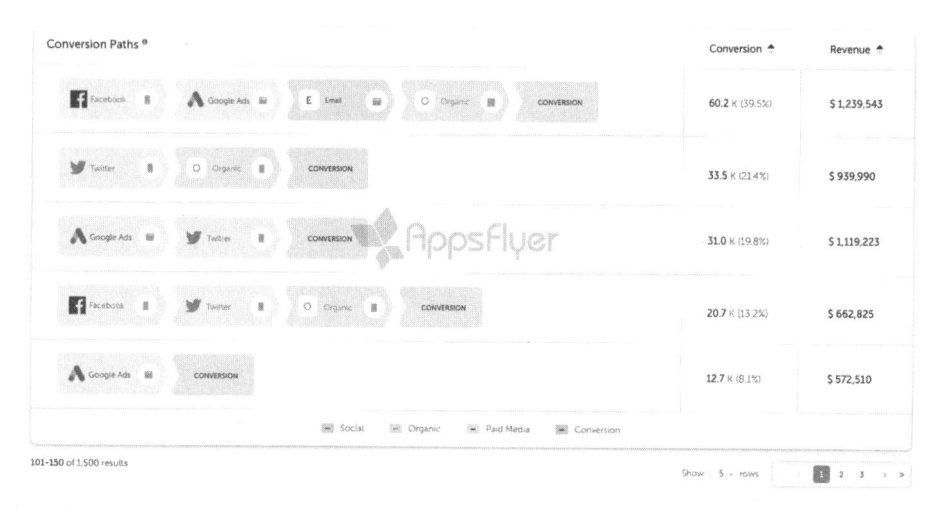

Figure 9-8. *Conversion path dashboards make cross-channel user flow data actionable (courtesy of AppsFlyer)*

For example, a prospective customer of an automotive manufacturer may see an ad for the full range of cars offered in a video ad on desktop and decide to browse the advertiser's website, looking specifically at two models they are potentially interested in. Based on this information, the user may then be targeted with a dynamic product ad on mobile that invites them to download the advertiser's app to explore customization options for these two car models. The user spends a lot of time customizing only one model in the app—and during the next sale, they receive an email inviting them to a test drive in their dream car.

In this user flow, previous interactions drive the messaging and content of subsequent marketing touchpoints independent of the channel used. And people-based attribution provides insights for an intelligent machine that delivers specific creatives or content based on the customer life cycle.

Now that we've got attribution covered, let's look at the options available for user acquisition strategies and work on picking the best approach for your situation.

PART IV

SELECTING THE RIGHT APPROACH TO USER ACQUISITION

Part IV moves you into the world of choosing the right approach to user acquisition. In Chapter 10, there is an overview of the top five proven key user acquisition strategies for you to consider to scale growth and how to pick the right one for your business. In Chapter 11, you will get a detailed overview into the "growth stack"—a set of tools that all work together to help you get the specific results you're looking for, given your situation.

CHAPTER 10

Different User Acquisition Strategies

Ways to Think About User Acquisition Strategy

The cost of acquiring new customers continues to increase significantly year over year as more brands are spending heavily on advertising to find new customers. Every time you pick up your smartphone, turn on a device screen, or open an app, you are being bombarded with advertisers trying to get your attention to help sell you something. Your attention is literally worth billions of dollars because that's how much money companies are spending on their user acquisition efforts to try to target you across different devices including mobile, desktop, TV, radio, and digital voice assistants to convert you into a new customer.

The fact is that human attention is a finite resource. There are only 24 hours in a day (no matter who you are), and every day there are more products seeking their attention. With endless demand and limited supply, human attention is probably the most valuable resource in the world. This only gets more challenging as the channels we use to live, work, learn, and play—Google, Facebook, Instagram, YouTube, Amazon, Netflix, Pandora, Fortnite, and more —continuously vie for our attention to keep us addicted to their apps and tied to their ecosystems.

The process by which you bring new users or customers to your business is customer acquisition. The goal, for any business, is to create sustainable and systematic customer acquisition strategies that keep up with industry trends. One of the top challenges for a startup is how to acquire and retain new customers cost-effectively. In the beginning, the vast majority of startups struggle to find users or customers. This is because very few people are familiar with your product or service and brand. Regardless of the size of your company or startup, this is a very important aspect of running a business besides helping you turn a profit. It also acts as evidence of traction for your startup to customers, partners, investors, influencers, and prospects. All future startup growth depends on two things—customer acquisition strategy and execution.

The key to any successful user growth strategy is finding the right balance between focusing on your acquisition and retention efforts. As a startup, you can't afford to make too many mistakes in your user acquisition strategy, so you have to be flexible on figuring out the most relevant strategies. Your customer retention and monetization are key at the end of the day because it's the foundation of growth; without keeping your existing users and making money off them, you're always filling a leaky bucket. You might be growing based on new users for a while, but eventually you'll exhaust all possible acquisitions. Your user numbers will plateau then decline while your cost to acquire users will continue to increase.

That is the route to killing off your startup because you won't be able to cost-effectively acquire new customers to offset your costs, leading to increased cash burn rate. When you're growing a startup, you need to stay on top of tracking your CAC and LTV key metrics (which were covered back in Chapter 7) by doing an ongoing cohort analysis to help you measure success on your growth strategy.[1]

> *The key to any successful user growth strategy is finding the right balance between focusing on your acquisition and retention efforts.*

There are only two phases in any startup: pre-product/market fit and post-product/market fit. If you're pre-product/market fit then determining product/market fit is the first crucial step before investing a lot of money into a user acquisition strategy.[2] The best way to get to product/market fit is to follow Eric Ries's Lean Startup methodology for developing businesses and products, which aims to shorten product development cycles and rapidly discover if a proposed business model is viable; this is achieved by adopting a combination

---

[1] Cohort analysis is a subset of behavioral analytics that takes the data from a given data set and rather than looking at all users as one unit, it breaks them into related groups for analysis. These related groups, or cohorts, usually share common characteristics or experiences within a defined timespan.

[2] Product/market fit means being in a good market with a product that can satisfy that market. Many people interpret product/market fit as creating a so-called *minimum viable product* that addresses and solves a problem or need that exists.

of business-hypothesis-driven experimentation, iterative product releases, and validated learning.

Resources shouldn't be dedicated to growth if your product isn't on a clear path to sustainable user engagement and value creation. Everything you have and everything you do should be about finding that product/market fit first, making sure there's a real tangible need for your solution, and reaching out and really talking to your initial customers to iterate fast. A good way to do this is to first leverage low-cost user acquisition options to target friends and family, blog mentions, PR, and posting on forums and other communities to cheaply acquire users to help you figure out the product/market fit. Let's get one thing clear: there is a slim chance to successfully scale up a poor product with no product/market fit. In our current landscape of user reviews and social communication channels, it's very easy for both good and bad user feedback to go viral and positively or negatively impact your ability to scale up growth.

It takes time and effort for a product to reach the desirable product/market fit. When the customers truly start appreciating the product with positive user reviews and recommending it to peers, then it has reached product/market fit. Scaling user growth is tough, but once you have achieved that product/market fit, you can move onto the exciting part of figuring out the right user acquisition strategies for your startup. This chapter will provide you with considerations to bear in mind as you make this decision.

Stages of a User Funnel

The user acquisition strategy is all about how businesses get new users or customers, keep them happy by providing value, and then figure out how to monetize them to drive revenue to make a profit. This requires figuring out the best approach for customer acquisition, engagement, retention, and monetization. The B2C funnel in Figure 10-1 is a handy visualization of how customers come to know and buy from your brand. When your business circulates around delighting and retaining customers, your marketing strategy starts to resemble a virtuous cycle, not a funnel, with the focus on being customer-centric to always over deliver on the value you provide to customers.

All these areas in a funnel are important to any successful user acquisition strategy because being able to systematically attract, convert, and retain new customers keeps companies healthy to scale growth—and investors happy by validating that the startup has the potential to become a successful business. This requires running as many A/B tests as possible in each of these stages of the customer funnel so you can test, learn, and iterate as quickly as possible, finding small wins that end up compounding into massive growth in the long term. Obviously, the A/B testing and hypotheses development process has to be scientific based on some best practices, but as a startup, you need to increase the velocity of your experiments daily, weekly, and monthly.

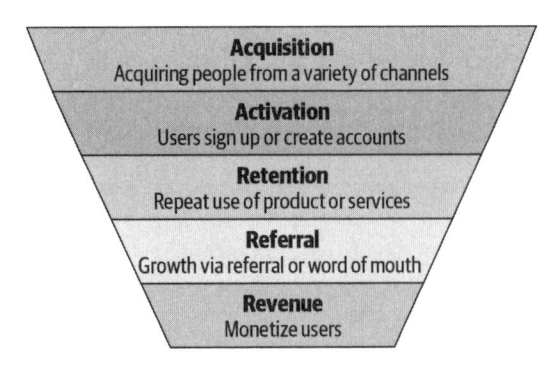

Figure 10-1. *Different stages of the business to consumer marketing funnel*

Growth is a systems-based approach to building and scaling end-to-end user value efficiently and effectively. Companies that succeed work holistically to improve their user experience across engagement, retention, onboarding, and user acquisition. By building and optimizing end-to-end experiences for the most underserved segments, companies can focus on scaling more of the newly identified segments to grow their product usage further. Identify the biggest drop-off points and key levers in your user journey and deploy the necessary tools and frameworks to rapidly test and close the gap. Holistic thinking of LTV, CAC, and user experience will differentiate the winners from the losers.

Figure 10-2 illustrates a simple "three-step" strategic user acquisition plan, with a focus on getting users to Know You, Trust You, and Love You.

Figure 10-2. *Simple framework of a "three-step" strategic user acquisition plan*

Even though this is a very simplified framework, it lays out the essential stages for an effective UA plan. And now that you're aware of these basics, we can move on to discussing more detailed strategies.

Five Key User Acquisition Strategies

The most successful startups that get to millions of users and paying customers always focus on one or two key growth strategies, which they optimize to perfection before moving on to other strategies. Here are the top five user strategies to consider to help you scale up your startup growth:

Paid acquisition

A common mistake with venture-funded startups is to start burning tons of cash to buy customers without having a business model in place to monetize those users. You really need to have a plan for a business model that has a path to solve for profitability to build a successful long-term business. If you can monetize your customers to pay you more money than the cost to acquire them, then you can experiment with many different paid channels to figure out which ones have your best potential user audiences (e.g., Google, Facebook, affiliates, paid search, TV, podcasts, etc.).

A good place to start is by sharing data on who your best LTV customers are with these paid channels to help them build lookalike audiences to help you find more users like them within those channels. The rule of thumb is that you will lose money up front testing different channels but your goal is to optimize your ideal CAC to maintain a 3:1 LTV: CAC ratio to keep the margins reasonable after other costs. This strategy can have a big impact on growth because you have much more control over the levers to scale up quickly depending on results and make a faster impact on business growth.

Virality

If your users love your product, then you can get major "word of mouth" virality driven by a high Net Promoter Score (NPS)[3] and positive user reviews. The key is to make sure you build a great product or user experience that people love and make it easy for them to share it with their network. The goal is to convert them into a community of evangelists who end up becoming your biggest advocates for marketing your product. In general, a higher NPS score correlates with generating more word of mouth marketing. Most of the successful startups have leveraged viral

---

[3] Net Promoter or NPS is a management tool that can be used to gauge the loyalty of a firm's customer relationships. It serves as an alternative to traditional customer satisfaction research and is claimed to be correlated with revenue growth.

loops to generate even more virality by testing different options to make it easy to share with your networks with the right incentives to encourage more of that behavior (e.g., Dropbox giving free storage space to both referrers and referees).

People often measure the viral coefficient to see how effectively existing users attract new users, and the best practice is to get your viral coefficient to exceed 1.0.[4] A viral coefficient of 2 means that every customer you acquire will bring in two more customers. A viral coefficient above 1 is advantageous to your customer acquisition costs because as more users come through word of mouth and other unpaid channels, the CAC declines. Other options include working with paid influencers who resonate well with your target audience and leveraging them to promote your product by seeding them to talk about their positive experiences on the product with their fans and followers (e.g., Instagram influencers for beauty and fashion products).

Content

If your product creates a ton of unique content, in the form of Q&A, articles, customer reviews, blogs, videos, podcasts, etc., you might end up with millions of unique pages that can in turn attract hundreds of millions of new users who are searching for content via search engines and other channels like social media, podcasts, app store pages, and smart audio devices. The content is an effective long-term user acquisition strategy because it takes time for the content to start getting better visibility and building a community of followers, but it is definitely well worth the investment. If you get content marketing working, then you are able to retarget people, build better lookalike audiences on different channels, and build backlinks to your content, which brings up your domain authority for SEO.

As you write and publish more content across more platforms the momentum would start to grow to influence new users, but everything starts with figuring out developing the right content first. Ideally, you should choose multiple platforms for publishing your content, even if you publish the same or slightly different variations of that content to match the desired formats on each platform. Look at a lot of media companies—they're building agency services divisions now. It's easier to build an audience first, and then from there, you can start to branch out into other areas. A great

---

4 In order to calculate the viral coefficient of your product or service, you need two numbers: the number of invitations sent per user (referrals, shares, or whatever best represents an invitation to use your product/service), and the average conversion rate of those invitations. Then multiply those two metrics to get the viral coefficient (often referred to as the *k* value).

example is Glossier (*https://oreil.ly/OSwgY*), which started as a beauty blog in 2010 and has since morphed into one of the rare makeup companies that do almost all of their business online; it is now valued at over one billion dollars.

Strategic partnerships
Capitalizing on the success of another platform or business is a great way to grow your own. Try to find a way to work with other relevant platforms, businesses, products, or services whose audiences align well with your target customers. The key is to find partners who reach similar users but are not directly competitive with your product. The partnership has to be a win-win for both sides and has an exchange of value (doesn't have to be monetary but something you both find valuable to your business). The value exchanged should be balanced, fair, and benefit you both. An example of this is Roku's early growth strategy, which included strategic partnerships with different content providers on the Roku platform to reach new users in exchange for providing co-marketing opportunities to acquire new users for both partners. This partner marketing strategy worked out well to attract key partners like Netflix, Hulu, and Amazon as well as broadcasters like Fox, CBS, and Bloomberg to promote Roku to their massive customer bases, to help create awareness for Roku to highly relevant audiences looking for ways to stream their content on the TV.

Product innovations
Most innovations improve and complement the core business of a company, taking advantage of and enhancing its most valuable assets with the potential to drive results for all companies (especially technology companies). What matters is the pace of innovation. That is the fundamental determinants of competitiveness. This makes sense as small improvements in a big business can have a meaningful impact by continuing to increase your addressable market of users (e.g., international expansion into new countries), payment options (e.g., PayPal, mobile wallets, Apple Pay, Google Pay, Amazon checkout, etc.), cross-platform experiences (e.g., IMVU desktop and mobile apps, etc.), and product or brand extensions (e.g., Apple Mac, iPhones, iPads, iTunes, Music, etc.). However, diversification outside of the core is a much more risky strategy with longer odds of success, which is why this isn't recommended for early-stage startups until they have fully developed their core user audience.

Marketing is becoming more expensive, customers are becoming less trusting of brands, and customer acquisition is going to be even more challenging for startups who have smaller budgets and low brand awareness working against them. This isn't the time to give up; it simply means startups have to get smarter with leveraging the right strategy for their business at different stages of growth. In today's distracted world, you'll only win by acquiring customers in ways that clearly differentiate you from the crowd and build an enthusiastic customer base that sticks around.

The key to success starts with building a great product or experience, which helps you attract a community of loyalists who collaborate with you on a journey to build a great brand together, as well as leveraging strategic partners and/or product innovations that can help accelerate your reach to attract more relevant customers. Once you have proven the business model, hit the accelerator pedal and invest as much as you can afford based on the economics of growth. You'll want to grow the business as fast as possible before a competitor realizes what you have done, and tries to copy you to steal your market share!

> *The most successful startups that get to millions of users and paying customers always focus on one or two key growth strategies, which they optimize to perfection before moving on to other strategies.*

Now that you have a better understanding of broad strategies for acquiring customers, it's time to dive into the "growth stack"—a set of tools that all work together to help you get the specific results you're looking for, given your situation.

CHAPTER 11

The Growth Stack

The growth stack is a framework that helps growth teams develop and evolve a user growth strategy for acquiring new customers. The stack can be applied at any stage during a product's life cycle and to many different business models, although some layers and elements of the stack will be more relevant at different stages of the startup. The framework organizes the levers for growth by the key funnel stages (acquisition, engagement, retention, and monetization), helping growth practitioners consider everything they could do to drive growth of their mobile product at each stage, which in turn helps define focus areas and build a coherent strategy. The framework can use in-house or external platforms to support the growth team.

The Mobile Growth Stack (*http://www.mobilegrowthstack.com*), shown in Figure 11-1, was developed by Andy Carvell and Moritz Daan, based on their experience working with a range of businesses worldwide as mobile growth consultants at Phiture, which is a Berlin-based mobile growth consultancy.

Deciding what not to work on at each stage of growing a startup is as critical as choosing what to do; the stack is a framework to aid this strategic planning. The framework encourages consideration of all the included elements when devising a growth strategy, but it does not follow that all elements are necessary or equally valid for every business at every stage; quite the opposite. At its core, growth is driven through measurement and iterative experimentation, with an obsessive focus on impact. There are pros and cons to different options, but the focus of this chapter is to outline all the different options as well as demonstrate that the landscape is so much more complex now and harder to manage without leveraging AI.

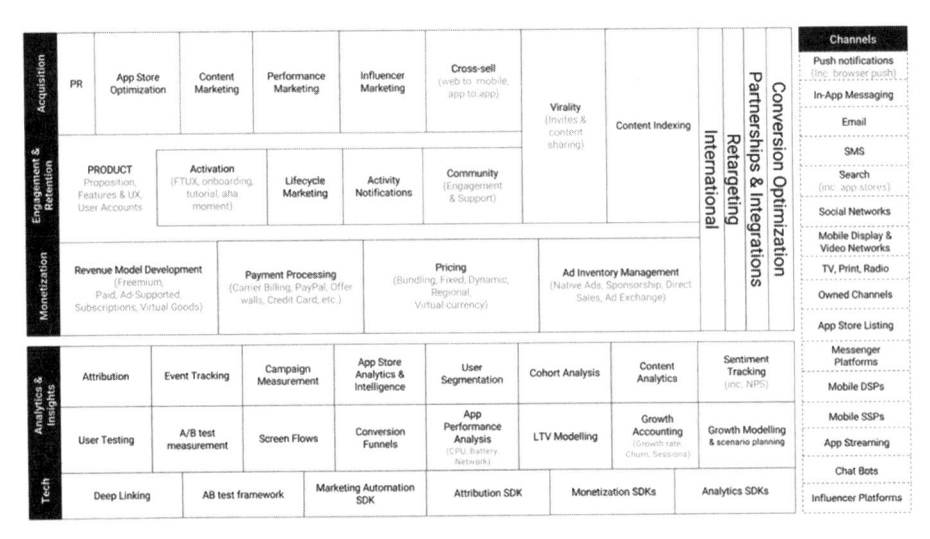

Figure 11-1. *The Mobile Growth Stack (https://oreil.ly/l8qBl)*

How Does It Work?

The stack has three horizontal layers, representing key performance objectives—Acquisition, Engagement and Retention, and Monetization—supported by a fourth layer, Analytics and Insights, as well as a vertical layer, which together represent the different channels to reach your customers. Startups at different stages of customer growth will likely prioritize different layers in order to reach their short- to medium-term business goals, but a successful strategy will need to generate impact in all three core layers at some point and will be highly unlikely to achieve this without investment in Analytics and Insights.

Each individual element cell in the stack represents an activity that could or could not form part of the growth strategy. Not all elements will be equally applicable to all startups. A smart growth strategy does not attempt to cover every element of the stack, but selects an appropriate mix of activities that plays to core strengths, provides the best opportunity for near-term growth gains, and invests in developing additional capabilities and channels for the next—hopefully bigger—phase of growth.

> *Deciding what not to work on at each stage of growing a startup is as critical as choosing what to do.*

In my experience, it's always better for startups to leverage as many third-party tools and platforms to support their growth efforts as possible, so that their in-house resources are completely focused on providing the best possible app/product user experience while not getting sidetracked into building and maintaining different growth stack platforms that aren't their core competency. The technology and best practices are constantly changing, which makes it very challenging for any resource constraint startup to build an in-house platform to outperform third-party tools and platforms. I have seen this happen time and again when startups build in-house platforms for their growth team and then that technology becomes dated quickly because they haven't continued to focus on innovating the platform to keep up with the new best practice capabilities. It's hard to compete with the latest and greatest third-party tools that always have more dedicated resources to focus on solving those problems better than your team.

The right balance is to ideally find a few external platforms that have the ability to cover the majority of the growth stack ecosystem across Acquisition, Engagement/Retention, Analytics and Insights, and Monetization.

> **NOTE**
>
> I would caution against trying to integrate a different external platform for each element of the growth stack. That would drive up costs and set the bar much higher to become ROI positive on the investment supporting your growth stack.

Analytics and Insights

Analytics and Insights, shown in Figure 11-2, is the most comprehensive part of the stack, underlying the importance of quantitative and qualitative data, metrics, modeling, and reporting in guiding growth activities, measuring impact, and identifying opportunities.

Attribution	Event tracking	Campaign measurement	LTV modeling	User segmentation	Cohort analysis
Content analytics	Sentiment tracking (including NPS)	User testing	A/B test measurement	Screen flows	Conversion funnels
App performance analysis (CPU, battery, network)	App Store analytics and intelligence		Growth accounting (Growth rate, churn, sessions)	Growth modeling and scenario planning	

Figure 11-2. *The Analytics and Insights layer of the growth stack*

Many tools and services exist to aid specific data collection or processing activities in this layer, though it's possible with enough investment to craft custom solutions or quick hacks or database queries to gain short-term insight.

Attribution

Attribution of clicks, views, and installs to specific marketing campaigns, content shares on social networks, invites, or other acquisition sources involves different tracking technology for mobile compared to the web world. Browser cookies can be used on mobile/responsive web sites, but for native apps, users are tracked using device-specific IDs such as IDFA or Android ID, or via imperfect fingerprinting technology that combines a number of data inputs to match a user (or, more correctly, a device) to a click an install. Attribution becomes even more challenging when accounting for multiple touchpoints and cross-platform traffic (e.g., desktop web to mobile device install).

Deep links

Native mobile apps are evolving; no longer are they launched solely from the phone home screen, but instead increasingly launched from deep links that take users directly to specific content within the app (assuming they have it installed). Many mobile apps implement deep-link schemas that provide additional entry points into the app. Deep links can be included in push notifications, emails, messages, other apps, links from websites, and pretty much anywhere else that a regular web URL could be launched. Not only that, content within the app can be indexed by Google and surfaced in search results (app indexing is also supported for iOS 9 and above when Universal Links are enabled). Deep links are also used in retargeting campaigns, where existing (but possibly lapsed) users are served advertisements in other apps aimed at reengaging them and bringing them back into a specific part in your app.

If your app supports deep-linked content, it's important to gather information on how these links are performing. Understanding which deep-link uniform resource identifiers (URIs) are being opened and, ideally, where the user came from (e.g., browser link, push notification, retargeting campaign, etc.) will provide valuable insight into which content is most popular and deeper understanding of how various channels and campaigns perform for reengaging existing users. Such data can inform the editorial policy for new content and aid optimization of communication activities.

Event Tracking

Measuring user engagement at a granular level is a critical prerequisite to making data-driven optimizations and evaluating adoption and performance of features.

Any action the user takes within an app/product (opens, account registration, navigation between screens, button presses, content shares, purchases, etc.), as well as things that happen within the product programmatically (e.g., an enemy spaceship is destroyed, level is complete, account successfully created, etc.) is a candidate for tracking as an "event" as part of the analytics implementation. The analytics SDK will typically transmit these events along with any additional metadata relating to this occurrence of the event (typically referred to as "Event Properties") to a server when network conditions allow.

Aggregating and storing event data server side for analysis in a web-based dashboard is by now common practice and many analytics tools exist to simplify this task. Such quantitative event data shows how users are interacting with the app/product and which features are most/least used; in addition, it can help identify bugs (e.g., if event counts suddenly nosedive, the feature associated with the event may be broken) and allow the visualization of engagement funnels for key user paths. Moreover, server-generated marketing campaigns or activity notifications can be triggered by events and possibly personalized with event property data.

Campaign Measurement

Marketing campaigns, whether they are for user acquisition, engagement/retention, or monetization, require proper measurement in order for impact/ROI to be measured. Without a quantitative understanding of campaign and creative/copy performance, advertising budgets cannot be properly allocated or scaled and campaigns cannot be optimized.

In the case of customer acquisition or retargeting campaigns, this topic is closely linked to install/deep-link attribution and event tracking; customer acquisition teams need visibility of how many installs each network and campaign variant delivers, how much they are spending to acquire these new users, and the "quality" of these users (typically measured in terms of engagement/retention or monetization events that are generated by cohorts of users attributed to the campaign) in order to optimize ad spend for performance.

Life-cycle marketing such as email, push, and in-app campaigns also require detailed measurement in order to run experiments to improve open and click rates and downstream performance goals such as increasing in-app-purchases, driving more key actions within the app, improvements in retention, etc.

App Store Analytics and Intelligence

Any mobile app publisher will be distributing their app through at least one (and likely several) app stores; aside from iTunes App Store and Google Play, many other distribution channels exist, including Windows Store, Amazon App Store, Samsung Apps, and MyApp (Tencent).

Basic app store analytics provide measurement and reporting of app installs and in-app purchases by country, device, OS version, and so on as well as those of your competitors if using a service that make this data available.

With thousands of new apps and games submitted to the app stores every single day, staying visible in the stores is a constant battle for app publishers. Observing and reacting to competitive trends, keyword search volumes, and other market intelligence can give publishers an edge over the competition. Reviewing predicted download data for top apps in a category can inform strategic planning and provide an indication of how many daily downloads a publisher needs to achieve in order to reach a specific ranking in the store (though the common download estimates—generated using predictive methods—should be treated with caution, since accuracy varies considerably between categories and analytics tools). Nevertheless, analysis of app store data, with a view to deriving actionable insight, can be helpful at all stages of the product life cycle.

App store searches also form an important part of app discovery and careful identification and testing of keywords can lead to increased organic downloads from the store. Many app store optimization (ASO) tools exist that estimate keyword search volume and the difficulty of ranking highly in searches for specific keywords.

User Segmentation

Not all users are created equal; some groups of individuals will be more engaged, more likely to spend money within the app, or otherwise display some common trait(s) that enable them to be grouped together into meaningful segments for the purposes of analysis, marketing, dynamic pricing, and so forth. Most analytics tools allow creation and tracking of dynamically updated user segments based on user metadata (aka attributes) or behavior within the app. By tailoring in-app and external messaging campaigns to specific user segments, marketers can increase the relevance of their campaigns and drive more impact.

Cohort Analysis

In order to understand how user growth and retention is evolving over time, it's important to examine users in cohorts (groups of users with some common trait, typically install/sign-up date) rather than relying on top-line metrics such as total registered users, MAUs, and DAUs, which tend to mask underlying retention problems.

A typical cohort retention table such as that shown in Figure 11-3 divides users into cohorts from the period (typically day/week/month) that they were first seen in the app and shows how many users (or what percentage of the cohort) returned to the app in the following periods.

Cohort (users)	Month 0	Month 1	Month 2	Month 3	Month 4	Month 5	Month 6	Month 7
2011-04 (1021)	24%	23%	21%	20%	18%	18%	17%	17%
2011-05 (1016)	26%	24%	22%	20%	18%	17%	16%	13%
2011-06 (973)	29%	25%	23%	21%	18%	18%	17%	17%
2011-07 (1386)	32%	26%	23%	21%	17%	15%	16%	
2011-08 (1652)	33%	33%	28%	24%	22%	18%		
2011-09 (1523)	34%	28%	24%	23%	19%			
2011-10 (1405)	35%	31%	27%	23%				
2011-11 (1312)	40%	35%	32%					
2011-12 (1137)	41%	38%						

Figure 11-3. *An example cohort table (also known as a cohort triangle)*

Content Analytics

If an app or game contains dynamic content (e.g., news articles, recipes, photos, music tracks, etc.) then tracking engagement (views, likes, bookmarking, purchases, etc.) on and sharing of content provides insight into which content and categories deliver the best ROI. In addition to tracking content engagement, it's also desirable to measure how many referred users a specific item of content generates as a result of being shared and which channels deliver the best virality.

Sentiment Tracking

Customer satisfaction is important; unhappy or disgruntled users are at high risk of churn and may also voice negative feedback on app stores or online forums, deterring potential users. Conversely, happy or delighted users can be powerful advocates for a mobile product and should be identified as such in user segmentation.

There are many ways to measure customer satisfaction; online, in-app or email surveys can be used to gather detailed feedback, but more commonly users are simply asked via a pop-up to give the app a rating from 0 to 5 stars, or else to provide their NPS rating with the simple, standardized question "How likely would you be to recommend [product] to a friend or colleague?" (with a rating 0–10 possible).

Users who give the app a high rating can be confidently targeted with requests to rate the app in the store, invite friends, share content, or tweet about the app. Users with negative sentiment can be identified and—hopefully—placated by customer service efforts and encouraged to provide feedback directly to the publisher rather than in public.

Sentiment tracking techniques can be used to quantitatively gauge user reaction to new features or content, possibly before rolling out to 100% of the user base.

User Testing

Nothing brings a growth team a reality check faster than inviting people to try out a new product or feature. While the feedback from user testing sessions is qualitative in nature, it can be incredibly revealing and often just a few user tests are required to identify common themes and usability issues within the product, which can inform product optimizations, design, and even complete product pivots.

In an early stage startup, frequent user testing is especially valuable; bringing in real people to interact with prototypes and early product versions challenges assumptions about product/market fit and wrenches teams out of the myopia and groupthink that can manifest itself in enthusiastic founding teams.

A/B Testing Measurement

A/B testing is an essential weapon in the growth marketer's arsenal. Planning, executing, and interpreting the results of A/B tests, tied to hypotheses that refine a bigger-picture understanding of the product's qualitative growth model, is the bread and butter of growth. In order to A/B test new product features, UX tweaks, marketing campaigns, and user communications, tools or frameworks must be in place to assign users to statistically significant test and control groups, measure the impact on the relevant metrics and conversion goals, and report results.

Screen Flows

Similar to event tracking, screen-flow tracking provides insight into how users navigate through the app/product, which screens they land on, and the paths that they take to get there. Analysis of screen flows can identify underutilized screens or features that might benefit from more prominence in the UI (or otherwise be cut out completely), or show that users are spending a lot of time in unexpected parts of the app/product.

Conversion Funnels

Tracking and visualization of each event in key engagement flows such as account creation, purchases, and searching helps identify underperforming flows and guide optimization efforts by showing the drop-off in users as they move through each stage.

New funnels can be created on an ad-hoc basis in most analytics suites, so new funnels can easily be created to monitor performance of new features or purchase options. Detailed event tracking is a prerequisite for funnel visualization.

Billing and Revenue Reporting

Some apps/products or platforms operate marketplaces where suppliers and consumers can trade virtual or real-world goods or services. In other cases, content within the app may be licensed on a pay-per-play or pay-per-view basis from a supplier.

If any of the above apply, accurate (and ideally automated) logging and reporting of payouts, license fees, royalties, or revenue garnered from advertising, in-app purchases, or subscriptions is a required component of the product's analytics and reporting framework.

Growth Modeling

Growth is a system, with numerous inputs and feedback loops. Developing a shared understanding—leading to an abstract model—within the organization galvanizes growth efforts, informing the hypothesis generation and ideation process. The growth model will likely be refined over time, as this shared understanding develops through experiential learning and deeper understanding of user behavior, market dynamics, and operational data.

In addition to developing a high-level qualitative model such as the one above, a spreadsheet or similar quantitative model that connects acquisition (broken down by the various acquisition channels and viral loops) and retention/churn will prove highly valuable, both for understanding the present and creating projections for different scenarios. With such a model, scenario planning becomes possible and the team can adjust their mix of acquisition and retention efforts according to what will deliver the most impact on active user growth.

LTV Modeling

Understanding the LTV of users is incredibly important once the app/product is monetizing. LTV is a present value calculation of the future expected revenue generated by a user over their lifetime. Since this is a forward-facing projection, LTV modeling is not an exact science; actual revenue generated by users may exceed or underperform the LTV calculation and as such it pays to be conservative when using LTV for advertising-buying decisions. LTV can be influenced by many factors including acquisition source, user demographics, range of monetization possibilities within the product, and so on. If user retention (lifetime) can be increased, it follows that LTV will be higher too.

Growth Accounting

While a quantitative growth model is used to generate forward-looking projections, the process of *growth accounting* involves keeping track of current and historical user growth. Active user growth can be considered a simple function (Figure 11-4).

Active users = New users + Retained users − Churned users
(for a given period; e.g., last 30 days)

Figure 11-4. *Formula to calculate active users*[1]

Another way to think about it is that customer growth comes from three separate "buckets" of users: new users, repeat users, and returning users. Repeat users are those who were active in the previous period and were seen again this period. Returning users were reactivated after lapsing in the previous period. As you can see in Figure 11-5, tracking active users in these three buckets provides deeper understanding of the active user number and what is driving the growth (or lack of it) in a given period.

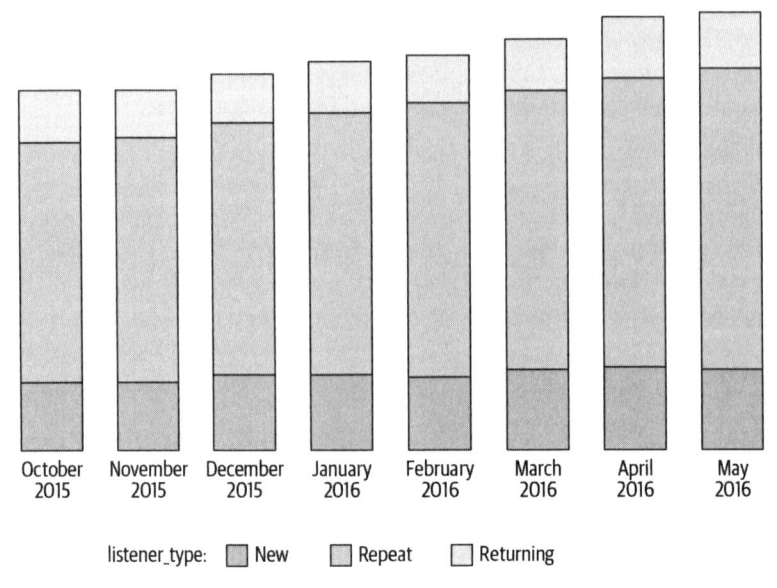

Figure 11-5. *An example chart of tracking active users in three buckets (new, repeat, returning)*

---

1 "Lapsed" users is perhaps more correct than churned users, since they may not have fully churned in the sense that they will never return, but simply were not active in the period.

App Performance Analysis (CPU, Battery, Network, Crashes)

One important way that mobile products differ from desktop apps and websites is the range of circumstances in which they may be accessed. In a desktop environment, web apps can safely assume an unmetered internet connection (likely with decent bandwidth and latency) is available at all times.

Good mobile products are designed to work in situations where bandwidth is limited, latency is high, or where there is no network connection available. Mobile devices run on batteries and users are increasingly savvy to the point where battery hogging apps may be deleted for this reason. Similarly, many users do not have unlimited data plans and expect apps and mobile sites to be data-conscious. Finally, apps that crash are swiftly uninstalled, often with a poor review left in the app store.

While performance analysis is likely to be considered primarily by the engineering team, it's worth keeping in mind that a product that performs poorly in any of the above scenarios is likely to suffer from high churn and/or reduced engagement. Paying attention to performance metrics, shown in Figure 11-6, will alert the team to any potential inhibitors to growth.

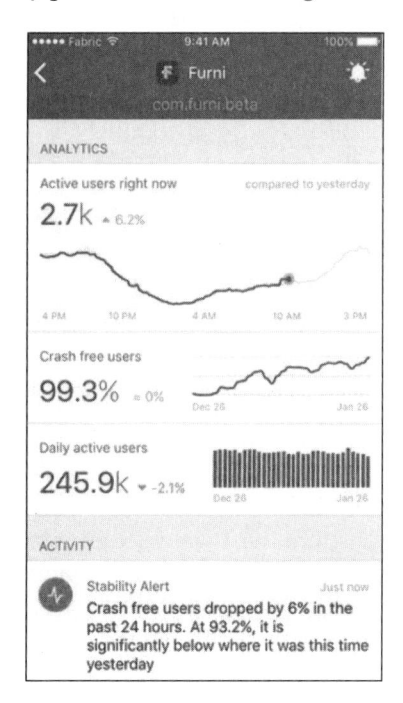

Figure 11-6. *The Fabric monitor app, which incorporates crash reporting*

Acquisition

The Acquisition layer of the stack, shown in Figure 11-7, encompasses the activities that could be undertaken to acquire new users for a mobile app, whether through paid, earned, or owned channels.

Earned media (or free media) refers to publicity gained through promotional efforts other than paid media advertising, which refers to publicity gained through advertising, or owned media, which refers to branding.

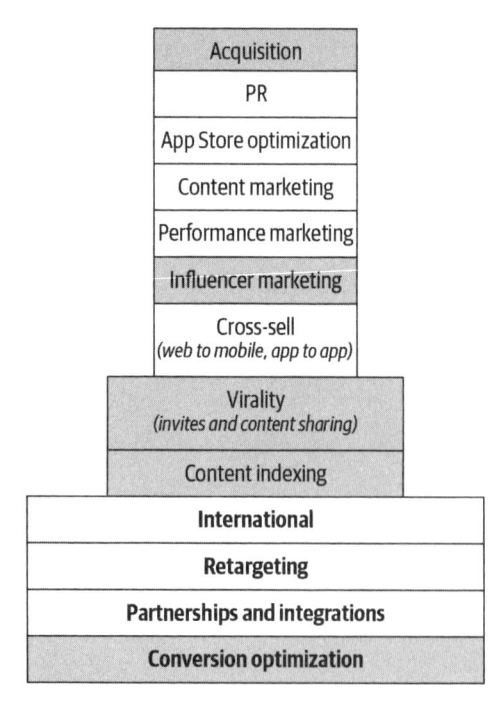

Acquisition
PR
App Store optimization
Content marketing
Performance marketing
Influencer marketing
Cross-sell (web to mobile, app to app)
Virality (invites and content sharing)
Content indexing
International
Retargeting
Partnerships and integrations
Conversion optimization

Figure 11-7. *The Acquisition layer of the growth stack*

PR

PR activity involves generation and pitching of press-worthy stories with the hope of enticing journalists to cover them instead of the glut of competing stories on any given day. Ultimately, well-executed content marketing is likely to deliver more dependable returns over time, but creative PR can provide a significant—if linear and tough to attribute—boost to organic growth. Since PR is usually not a core competency for startup founders and data-driven growth marketers, PR agencies who know the local/industry media landscape are often engaged, sometimes on a performance basis (e.g., paid per press mention).

App Store Optimization

ASO consists of three core activities:

App store conversion rate optimization
   Since the app stores are the distribution gateways for almost every consumer mobile app, systematic testing of the assets (screenshots, title, keywords, description, app icon) used to promote the app or game in the app store to optimize the conversion rate from "store page visit" to "app install" is an activity that magnifies the impact of all other acquisition activities. Performance marketing spend will stretch further if app store page conversion is increased; the cost per install (CPI) will fall, since more users who click on ads will end up installing the app.

App store search optimization
   Optimizing for the best-performing keywords that will attract high search volume and convert well with the app's target audience is a process of refinement and experimentation, which requires periodic review in order to stay ahead of competitors. For some apps, app store search represents a large proportion (up to 80%) of the organic traffic to their app store listing, whereas in other cases, search plays a smaller role in app discovery. In any case, user acquisition can be increased by at least some degree by ranking highly in search results for relevant keywords.

App store featuring
   All of the major app stores have some concept of featuring, whereby editorial teams give prominent temporary placement of banner-style advertising for selected apps, based on various editorial criteria. Getting featured by Apple, Google, Amazon, and other platform owners can deliver a significant (and free) boost to user acquisition over the period of featuring. Publishers of apps that are featured typically invest time cultivating direct contacts with the relevant app store managers and provide them with regular and timely information regarding upcoming significant app releases, though this is not always the case.

There are numerous things that can increase the chances of an app being featured: ensuring the app user interface exemplifies the platform design guidelines, supporting newly released platform features or hardware, creating custom content for special calendar events that can be tied to app store promotions, highly positive user ratings and reviews, and ensuring the app is free from bugs and crashes are some of these. Ultimately, editorial teams want to surface the best-quality apps in their stores and rarely—if ever—provide guarantees of featuring.

Content Marketing

Content marketing requires a significant investment of time and resources before it is likely to pay off, but a strong content marketing program can provide a significant, sustainable, and growing (albeit linearly) source of new users.

Content marketing can take many forms, but involves generation of blog posts, news, infographics, artwork, tips and tricks, top-10 lists, and other kinds of online content that appeals to the target audience for the core mobile product (the app, game, or constellation of apps that is being promoted) and should include prominent links to the app stores where the app can be downloaded.

Here's an example: if the product in question is a budgeting app, creative and engaging content would be generated for people wanting to save money or manage their finances; this could include tips and tricks for saving money, an infographic about the budgeting process, and so forth.

Content marketing posts are typically published on owned media such as the company blog, but can also be shared over social channels or email to amplify reach. Over time, with regular content published, the posts should climb the rankings for web searches relating to the topic and drive more organic search traffic to the posts and subsequently to the app. Content marketing builds brand awareness and can measurably increase acquisition, but might take several months to start delivering users.

Performance Marketing

Performance marketing via mobile display/video advertising networks, paid search ads, and app install ads on Facebook, Instagram, Twitter, and other channels provides an opportunity to scale user acquisition far more aggressively than most other channels, albeit for a price.

Typically, performance marketing has become a viable strategy for products that monetize at least some portion of their user base though in-app advertising, in-app purchases, subscriptions, or some combination—and when the CAC of new users from a given marketing campaign yields a positive ROI, calculated by predicting the LTV of a user within a certain confidence interval.

Performance marketing campaigns usually involve bidding against other advertisers for ad placements on a CPM (cost per thousand impressions), CPC (cost per click), CPI, or CPA (cost per action, e.g., a purchase of an item or subscription) basis.

Influencer Marketing

The term "influencer marketing," in its broadest sense, covers a broad range of activities that involve working with influential individuals or groups to obtain brand or product advocacy or endorsement from them. This concept is far from new: tobacco companies have been influencing us via movie stars for generations, commercial sponsorship of sporting personalities is taken for granted, and so on.

Working with influencers has traditionally been hard to measure, time-consuming, and potentially expensive, but often nonetheless effective. The emergence of performance-centric influencer platforms, connecting advertisers with a new generation of independent influencers—including bloggers, YouTube, Instagram, and Snapchat stars—has democratized a space once dominated by big brands and celebrity agents. It's now possible to scale influencer marketing to groups of influencers that individually have a smaller reach—albeit among loyal audiences interested in potentially niche topics—than the superstars with tens of millions of followers. Embeddable tracking links and real-time reporting of impressions and clicks, at the same time, enable marketers to be more data-driven with their influencer marketing spend; they can calculate conversion rates, CPI, and other performance metrics.

Increasingly, influencer marketing is becoming a performance marketing activity that augments or replaces traditional mobile app install campaigns, evaluated against Facebook and DSPs on the same terms. In many cases, these developments have shifted influencer marketing from being a brand marketing activity to a measurable growth tactic.

Distribution Deals

Distribution partnerships that provide access to a large audience/user base of a strong network or brand can boost reach substantially overnight. Typically they are harder to achieve as a small company that's just starting out, since there has to be some kind of value exchange taking place and the more attractive collaborations for growth tend to be with larger companies with millions of users.

Just a few examples of distribution deals include partnerships with mobile telecommunications carriers (the telco promotes your app to their subscribers in exchange for a cut of the profits, or perhaps a flat fee), traffic exchange between websites, and preinstallation of (possibly customized) versions of an app by manufacturers of smartphones, smart TVs, or other connected devices.

Virality Loops

The elusive concept of "virality" is hard to generate artificially; ultimately, sustained viral growth is likely to be rooted in a strong product or engaging content. However, paying careful attention to content sharing, item gifting, or invitation flows cultivates the right conditions for virality to occur.

Each channel (e.g., email, mobile messaging networks, social networks such as Facebook, Twitter, etc.) will display different dynamics in terms of the number of users reached (e.g., one-to-one versus one-to-many, ease and likelihood of being reposted within the network by receivers, etc.), the conversion rate of these shares and the average time it takes to close the loop and acquire a new user through this channel. The two key variables that govern the performance of a viral loop are K-factor (average number of users each invite/share reaches × Conversion rate) and cycle time (average time taken to close the loop). Of the two, shortening the cycle time yields a more dramatic increase on growth trajectory, since virality compounds over time.

Cross-Sell

When an existing user base exists on another owned product or platform (e.g., desktop web app, mobile web app, another app or game in the company portfolio, etc.), opportunities exist to cross-promote between these properties to funnel users toward a newly launched app, or to migrate desktop/mobile web users to native mobile, where there are additional ways to engage, retain, and monetize them.

Driving traffic from one owned property to another is a great source of "free" users who already have familiarity with the product/brand and hence are likely to be easier to retain than totally new users coming fresh to the app. Cross-sell is particularly useful for products with short lifespans where users may become bored of the experience after some time; game publishers employ cross-sell tactics extensively in order to deliver users to newly released games in their portfolio before the older games reach the end of their shelf life.

Content Indexing

Content indexing of deep-linked atomic content, principally via Google App Indexing and the improved Apple Search that rolled out with iOS 9, provides new opportunities to drive app discovery as well as referrals of existing users directly back into the app.

Ensuring web and mobile web content is also properly indexed and is mapped to the same content inside the app is important when implementing a coherent and optimized search optimization strategy, since Google currently still requires matching web content in order to index content within apps (though this will likely change in the future, as the relevance of web declines further).

Conversion-optimized responsive landing pages and Facebook pages should also not be overlooked as additional channels for driving app downloads and should be optimized for search, although a full content marketing program will likely yield stronger results (but also require more creativity and effort) than pure advertisement landing pages.

Engagement and Retention

Product is at the core of the Engagement and Retention layer of the growth stack, shown in Figure 11-8.

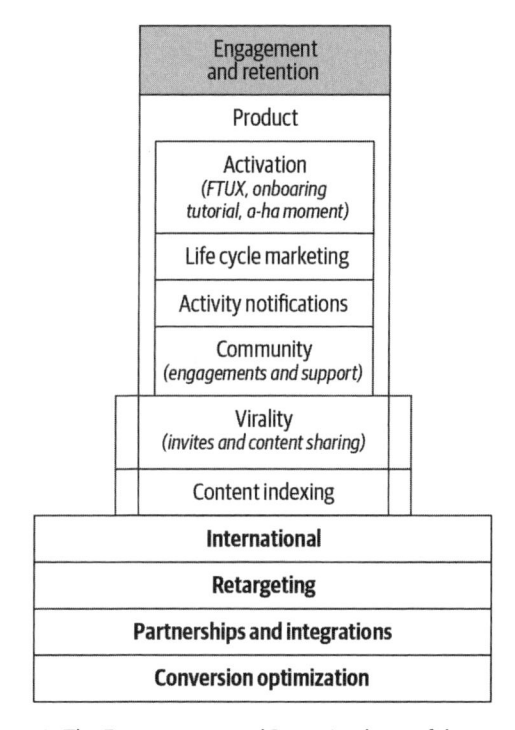

Figure 11-8. *The Engagement and Retention layer of the growth stack*

Growth as a discipline sits at the intersection of product (including design), marketing, and data science. Earlier versions of the Mobile Growth Stack may have given the impression that engagement and retention are primarily functions of growth marketing; this is manifestly not the case.

Retention stems from an engaging product experience and no amount of activity notifications, life-cycle marketing, or community engagement initiatives will keep users using a poorly designed product that they do not find engaging. Product is now explicitly placed at the core of the Engagement and Retention layer to reflect this.

Activation

The specific definition of activation is product-specific, and may evolve over time as a deeper understanding of user behavior is gathered and the drivers of longer-term engagement are established more definitively through hypothesis testing. However activation is defined in a specific product, it's a key growth objective to activate users swiftly in order that they experience the core product value quickly and begin their path to higher and prolonged engagement. This is all a fancy way of saying that users need to find the product engaging early on in order to keep using it. While this, too, is ultimately a function of core product, activation rates will typically benefit from focused effort from both product and marketing sides to assist users on their journey toward their "a-ha" moment.

First-time user experience (FTUE), also known as new user experience (NUX), is inordinately critical in the lifetime of a user; if a user doesn't "get" the proposition and reach a moment of delight—or at least appreciation—during their first few minutes using a freshly installed mobile app, the session will probably be their last.

The majority of user churn occurs in the first few days. Cohort decay graphs all take fundamentally the same shape, regardless of the app. New user onboarding efforts should aim to flatten out the curve at a higher retention rate.

User Accounts

Persisting user data by providing mechanisms for account registration and sign-in assist usability and can increase retention. US prepaid smartphone users upgrade every 7–8 months (post-paid a more moderate 18–20 months) and break them far more often than that. Thus, the challenge for retention is not just to increase session frequency, but also to incentivize users to *reinstall the* app onto new devices, or to initiate sessions on borrowed or desktop computers (assuming a web experience exists) when their main device is not available.

Creating an account arguably increases the user's investment in a product or platform. User accounts provide a way to collect more information about users such as email addresses, phone numbers, or other user attributes that can be used for life-cycle marketing purposes. They also give users a place to call home and a sense of identity within the product: offering personalization options (e.g., customizable avatar/username/profile picture, themes, etc.) further increases the user's emotional investment and reduces their likelihood to churn, at least when properly integrated into the overall experience. Finally, the account registration process can be designed to provide opportunities for users to invite colleagues or friends (e.g., via contact list import) or connect with other users on the platform, increasing network effects.

Account creation should be as frictionless as possible. Facebook, Twitter, Google, and LinkedIn, among others, offer simple account creation and sign-in without requiring users to create new passwords, which increases the chances that users will complete the process.

Deep linking

The term *deep link* refers to a URI that a smartphone OS handles by opening a specific native mobile app at a specific piece of content, a screen/feature in the app, or in some cases some specific executable code. Implementations differ between mobile platforms, but in all cases, it's possible to map web URLs to content within the mobile app.

Deep links are a valuable way to drive *reengagement* of existing users; by clicking on a deep link, the user is returned back into the native app and is not required to navigate through other screens or menus in order to engage with the content or feature that was linked, much in the same way that desktop web users can be linked directly to any content within a domain rather than just the homepage.

Various solutions exist to solve the problem of not knowing whether someone clicking on a deep link has the corresponding mobile app installed. Android apps register an intent to handle regular web URIs from a specific domain: if the app is installed, it will intercept relevant web links and map them to in-app content. iOS Universal Links (supported by iOS 9 onwards) deliver similar functionality, though earlier iOS versions do not support such mapping, necessitating a messier solution. Alternatives include the use of deep-linking features from the attribution partner, or dedicated third-party deep-linking services that handle deep links more elegantly and provide additional functionality such as redirecting users without the app installed to the appropriate app store to download it (thus driving acquisition and retention with one "smart" link).

Life-Cycle Marketing

Life-cycle marketing involves communications through relevant channels such as email, push, in-app, etc. to optimize the flow of users through the life cycle toward loyalty, high engagement, and monetization.

The growth marketer needs to invest time in mapping out and defining the key engagement milestones in the user life cycle according to the specific nuances of their target audience and their current understanding of their qualitative growth model (with the expectation that this understanding—and hence the model—will evolve over time as lessons are learned and hypotheses are tested).

A cohesive, considered, and continuously refined life-cycle marketing program facilitates and enhances the user journey (typically starting with strong onboarding and activation) and reduces user abandonment, attrition, and churn through timely, targeted interactions. Life-cycle campaigns typically aim to inform, educate, inspire, or motivate users toward higher levels of engagement, reactivate inactive users before they churn completely, or encourage loyal users to spend more, invite friends, or complete other valuable actions.

Life-cycle campaigns are targeted at segments of users at a similar stage in the life cycle or who have some common attributes. They are often triggered on some user behavior (e.g., a welcome email once the user creates an account, or a reactivation push notification when the user has been inactive for a period of time), or sent out on a scheduled basis (e.g., weekly digest or newsletter).

There is a high risk of annoying users with communications that are considered spam or unnecessary, so a smart life-cycle program is adaptive to user preferences and response (open rates, clicks, and subsequent in-app engagement). Really smart CRM implementations employ machine learning to develop a better understanding of which channels are most effective for different user segments in the life-cycle campaign. The channel mix can then be adjusted to better drive impact, possibly even down to individual user level, on a programmatic basis. Even without such an automated system in place, manual experimentation and adjustment can deliver significant gains.

Activity Notifications

Activity notifications differ from life-cycle campaigns in that they are usually driven by events that occur *outside* of the user's personal experience with the app: either things happening in the real world, or in the broader network that the app connects with. Generated programmatically, usually in real time and often personalized specifically for each user, activity notifications should inform users of things that are relevant and interesting to the user, based on the preferences they have expressed, either implicitly through their past behavior or explicitly by opting to be notified about certain events, content, or topics.

Good candidates for activity notifications include:

- Social signals such as friends joining or things friends/contacts are doing on the platform (e.g., "John just posted a new photo," "Alice achieved a new high score of 505,433")
- Social interactions with the user or their content (e.g., "John commented on your post," "Alice's army just attacked your village!")

- Things that happen in the real world of relevance to the user (e.g., "Leave now to arrive at Town Hall for your 5 p.m. appointment," "Heavy traffic on the M69 motorway")
- Content relevant to the user's tastes or preferences (e.g., "New track uploaded to the 'techno' group")
- Time-delayed events (e.g., "The video you uploaded has been approved and is ready to view")

Note that notifications are not just push notifications; while push is a great channel for delivering real-time notifications to users when they are not in the app, they are not the only effective channel and it's also not possible to reach all users since many users do not enable push notifications. Other channels suitable for delivering real-time activity notifications include email, SMS, display ads, desktop browser notifications, and in-app pop-ups. The effectiveness of notifications to drive subsequent engagement and retention can be amplified by implementing a bespoke in-app notifications feed or inbox features within the app itself, which stores all notifications in a more permanent form for later browsing and does not rely on the OS notifications tray, in which an app's notifications compete with those of other apps installed on the device.

The answer, as always, is to let the data lead the discussion: a notification system should be designed in such a way as to enable analysis not just of leading conversion metrics such as click-through rates (CTRs) and short-term engagement, but also measurements of longer term engagement, retention, and negative signals such as push opt-outs, email unsubscribes, and app de-installations (all of which are measurable, but are often not monitored) versus a control group that doesn't receive notifications.

Community (Engagement and Support)

Developing and nurturing a community of power users of the product generates a sense among even casual users of being part of something bigger, whether or not they are active participants in the community.

Building social features within the product or an online forum where enthusiastic users can meet, discuss the product, report problems, generate new product ideas, and so on requires significant sustained investment, but is not the only way to support and engage with users; often self-organized communities spring up quite organically around apps and games without any input or control from the publisher. Such users often voluntarily act as unpaid ambassadors and promoters both offline and online in other networks and forums. Engaging with these users wherever they are, and making them feel appreciated and valued, is likely to accelerate and magnify the community effect.

Supporting users who have problems or encounter bugs can turn a disgruntled user into a loyal one, reducing their likelihood of churn and potentially turning them into a promoter (this is verifiable through sentiment tracking before and after community support interactions). Support also requires investment, although generation of self-serve resources such as FAQs, chatbots, and how-to guides can reduce the resources required in answering emails, phone calls, or online inquiries.

Monetization

Figuring how you to make money in your business model is at the core of the Monetization layer of the growth stack, shown in Figure 11-9.

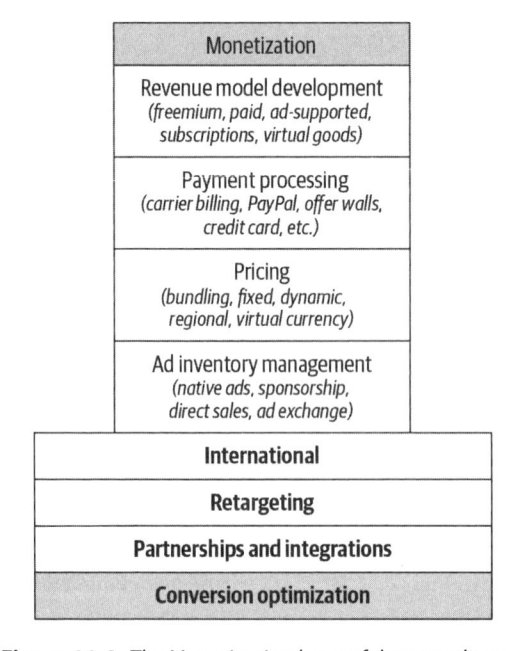

Figure 11-9. *The Monetization layer of the growth stack*

Revenue Model Development

Due to the all-time-low barrier to developing and publishing apps/products, it's perfectly possible to build an app/product and achieve impressive user growth without ever trying to generate revenue from it. However, for all but the most simple standalone apps, a publisher will face escalating costs (in the form of engineering, maintenance, support, servers, third-party tools licensing, etc.) as app usage increases. VC-funded startups often focus on growing active users and engagement before attempting to monetize and often have a significant runway to nail product/market fit, but at some point the product must demonstrate tangible value if the investment is to be recouped. Bootstrapped startups or lone developers do not have the luxury of months or even years and typically monetize their apps and games from launch day.

Typical monetization strategies include:

- Paid apps/products—user pays up front to download in the app store, or a one-off fee to buy or create an account on the service (e.g., Apple iPhone).
- Freemium with in-app purchase—basic product is available and usable for free, but upgrades or special items can be purchased as in-app purchases, sometimes intermediate with virtual currency (e.g., IMVU).
- Subscription apps—typically monthly or yearly fee for access to some or all of the features (e.g., Netflix); often used in conjunction with the freemium model, but possibly require subscription from the outset.
- Ad-funded—the app serves adverts, usually in the form of banners, full-screen interstitials or videos, which generate revenue from click-throughs to advertiser sites (e.g., Facebook).
- Affiliate—the app features products or services from third-party vendors and takes a cut from purchases, which may happen within the app or via the vendor website/app (e.g., Amazon Associates).
- Offer Walls—often used in conjunction with other payment methods in freemium apps and games: the user completes "offers" from brands or advertisers and is rewarded within the host app, usually with virtual goods/currency or other in-app/in-game upgrades (e.g., Ironsource).

A publisher may experiment with different revenue models over time, combine multiple models (e.g., ad-funded free tier, premium tier as pay as you go with in-app purchases, or subscribe to get full unlimited access), or use different models for different platforms.

Payment Processing

If the app offers subscriptions, in-app purchases (virtual goods/services, content, or in-app functionality/upgrades) or facilitates any kind of ecommerce transactions, there must be a way to accept payment from users. In-app purchases (IAPs) are by far the simplest option, since payments are handled by Apple, Google, Microsoft, etc. as part of their app store ecosystems, taking a 30% cut in the process.

For ecommerce apps selling real-world goods or services (anything outside of the app itself), the onus is on the publisher to process user payments from credit/debit cards, PayPal, bitcoin, Boleto, or whatever payment methods are most popular with their users. Payment processing is a complex business, but many third-party services exist that can be integrated to facilitate payment processing and billing.

Pricing

When selling IAPs or in-app subscriptions, it's important to understand the policies of the store. Apple uses price tiers, which to some extent normalize prices across currencies but require careful consideration to optimize profits across regions. Google Play implements price tiers for paid apps, but permits granular control of IAP prices in each currency.

Virtual currency

Employing a virtual currency brings both complexity and fine control over the app economy and may make dynamic pricing or price experimentation easier to achieve. While virtual currency is usually considered the preserve of games, there are other notable examples, including Skype Credit, which is sold in bundles to provide talk time to landline and mobile telephones.

Apps and games usually sell virtual currency bundles as in-app purchases, and/or give them away to incentivize high-value actions such as account creation and viewing adverts or simply launching the app on consecutive days. Use of virtual currency or other virtual rewards to incentivize engagement in non-game applications is an example of gamification.

Bundling

While currency is usually sold in bundles (e.g., boxes of gems in Clash of Clans), virtual goods, content, and functionality within the app may be retailed for amounts far less than the smallest bundle size in so-called micro-transactions. Micro-transactions and virtual currency bundling not only enable fine-grained control over pricing and more control over in-game item inventory, but also make it harder for users to calculate how much they are spending in real money, which can distort their estimation of value within the virtual economy.

Bundling is also a classic retail strategy for goods sold for real currency: McDonald's "menu" deals combine burgers, fries, and a soft drink at a cheaper price point than buying them separately, although research suggests that consumers (at least in some industries/product categories) value the option to buy bundled items separately when evaluating buying options. Bundling is supported for regular IAPs, so a virtual currency is not a prerequisite for testing such pricing tactics.

Discount coupons and sales

Much like bundling, other traditional retail tactics work just as well in the app economy. Offering discounts through virtual "coupons" or app store issued promo codes can be helpful to promote increasing demand for items, to reward loyal users, or to incentivize purchase completion in abandoned cart scenarios.

Since IAP prices can be adjusted at any time, it's possible to put items on sale for a limited time and promote them using regular in-app and external channels, or by highlighting them in the UI.

Ad Inventory Management

With products that serve adverts, whether display (banners/interstitials), audio, video, or some other format, consideration should be given to the placement, type, and number of advertisements that will be shown, as well as how these adverts will be delivered.

User experience, and hence user behavior, may be altered by the decisions made regarding advertisement:

- Serving too many adverts or interrupting the user experience with intrusive ad formats such as videos (even if skippable) may reduce user engagement and retention with the core product and cause negative user sentiment (though may also generate more advertising revenue).
- In some cases, users may be less inclined to make purchases if they encounter adverts before becoming a paying customer. Conversely, some products offer an "ad free" experience to users who upgrade to a premium subscription or pay a one-off fee via IAP.
- "Click-outs" (clicking on advertising and being redirected to a website/app) halt the user's current session in the product; in the worst case, they may never return.
- Loading times for advertisements that are not precached natively could cause performance issues and consume mobile data. If partnering with an ad exchange, it may be hard for the publisher to directly control these factors since ads may be downloaded from the exchange via a black-box SDK with little configurability.
- Advertisements from unscrupulous (or downright fraudulent) advertisers may be served in the product, which could result in irate users and increased churn. Ad quality is hard to police, since adverts are often served programmatically via bidding platforms, making checking every advert impossible. The only way to be 100% sure that all adverts will be suitable is to directly sell advertising units in the product to brands, which is

unfeasible for most publishers. Working with trusted networks can help, although many networks trade traffic and ad inventory between themselves, which increases the chances of a weak link that lets in poor quality adverts.

When considering these factors, trade-offs will be made between short-term ad revenue and longer term retention and engagement.

Activities That Cut Across the Stack

Certain activities do not fall within just a single area of the growth stack. The following activities should all be considered at different stages of your business growth, but generally the sequencing on when to consider them is usually determined by the budget and resources available to execute on it.

Internationalization

"International" growth is a broad topic that transcends any particular layer in the framework. Growth tactics in international markets are likely to be quite specific to your product/service and the competitive landscape in which it operates. However, done right—which likely will mean more than simply translating the product and localizing the app store listing, though this would be a good place to start—internationalization will act as a catalyst for your acquisition, engagement, and monetization efforts and hence complement activities across the stack.

A strong international strategy will likely take into consideration supporting locally relevant payment methods, integration with the most popular social networks in target regions, country-level or regional partnerships, and so on, and hence works in combination with many of the individual cells in the stack.

Retargeting

Effective retargeting of users or potential users with targeted messaging can be used to drive acquisition (by retargeting visitors to a web app or landing pages with adverts for the mobile product), increase engagement, or boost monetization; it cuts across all three layers. Ideally, a growth marketer would be able to pinpoint users who had dropped out of—or got stuck in—any stage of the user life cycle and deliver a message that will hopefully nudge them toward a goal.

Partnerships and Integrations

Business development, technical integrations, and partnership activities can drive impact for acquisition, engagement and retention, or monetization, depending on the nature of the deal.

Partnerships can take many forms and are limited only by the creativity, persuasiveness, and perceived value by the parties involved. Some common types of partnerships that could be employed to drive growth include:

- Traffic exchange between websites or native apps
- Preinstallation of mobile apps by device manufacturers or mobile carriers
- Co-marketing activities
- Sponsorship of events, individuals, or organizations
- Licensing of intellectual property (e.g., a movie, book, song, or image rights)
- Affiliate deals
- Loyalty schemes

In many cases, such partnerships will include a commercial component such as revenue share, licensing fee, or guaranteed minimums, though the specifics are very much subject to negotiation and will depend largely on leverage.

Conversion Optimization

Conversion (rate) optimization (aka CRO) is an activity that forms the basis of the majority of data-driven growth efforts. In the stack, the term "conversion optimization" is used broadly to refer to efforts to increase the rates of conversion between one state to another, as opposed to specifically referring to purchase or subscription events.

In the acquisition layer, conversion optimization forms an important part of app store optimization (optimizing conversion from app store listing impression to install), performance marketing (ad impression to click, or click to install), and cross-selling efforts between products and platforms.

In engagement and retention, conversion optimization efforts center on moving people between non-engaged or low engaged to higher states of engagement via numerous means. Conversion optimization is a core activity in life-cycle marketing, where email, push, and in-app campaigns are relentlessly optimized for higher open and click rates, as well as improvements in downstream engagement metrics. Product and marketing efforts around activation often aim to convert users from having not performed an activity in the app (e.g., used a feature) to having done so (or done so more often than before), often within a specific conversion measurement window such as the first few days of their lifetime.

In the monetization layer, optimizing for conversion to a purchase, subscription, incentivized video view, or ad-unit click are key to increasing profitability and CRO is hence at the core of monetization initiatives.

Upsell describes the activity of driving even more upgrades, subscriptions, or purchases (and hence not applicable for all revenue models). In a nutshell, efforts should be made to convert freemium users from free tier to subscription or purchase and to increase the average revenue per paying user (ARPPU) by driving additional ongoing purchases with tactics like special offers, bundles, and discounts to help with increasing frequency, value, or ideally both.

Channels

Although certainly not exhaustive, this list includes the channels that the majority of growth practitioners are using today. As with all elements of the stack, some channels will prove more or less effective in reaching a particular target audience for a particular business.

It's often worth experimenting with the channel mix itself; a reactivation campaign might yield poor results when delivered over email, yet drive high impact when the message is refactored for push, or vice versa. More likely still, greater impact could be gained when lapsed users are reached via a multi-channel campaign, possibly even including retargeting users in other apps.

Channels and tools are secondary to the core activity; they can—and should—be swapped out or augmented over time.

Push

Native push notifications and browser notifications provide a way to reach the user when they are not using the product and hence are highly effective channels—when used wisely—for reengagement of existing users. Push is an opt-in channel, so not all users can be reached, but the impact on the opted-in is often worth it. In order to increase the reach of push as a channel over time, many growth marketers invest significant effort in experiments designed to increase push opt-in rates.

In-App Messaging

In-app messages appear within the main product user experience and can be delivered either on web or native mobile. Any in-app dialog, pop-up, or information screen can be considered an in-app message, though in recent years mobile marketing automation (MMA) frameworks have abstracted this technology from the main app to allow marketers to design, test, and measure targeted campaigns without requiring engineering resources or new native app builds to be submitted.

In-app messages are a very powerful channel, since they grab the user's attention during their regular app or game usage and click-rates of 20%–50% are not uncommon. However, due to the intrusive nature of such campaigns, they should be used carefully and sparingly to avoid ruining the core experience and increasing user churn.

Email

While arguably not as effective as it once was, email remains a valuable channel for marketers across both web and mobile. Mobile users can be reached with emails in real time and often receive push notifications from their mail app when new messages arrive. When considering email as a channel for activity notifications or life-cycle campaigns targeting mobile users, extra attention needs to be focused on how the email will display on small-screen devices and how any links are implemented (best practice dictates that users should be directed to a website if the native app is not installed and deep-linked into the app if it is).

To use email as a channel, it's a prerequisite to request the user's email address and many countries also have strict laws governing opt-in, permissions, and what constitutes lawful email communication.

SMS

Every mobile device, including non-smart feature phones, supports SMS. As such, SMS as a channel has a huge potential reach. As well as being used as a channel for notifications, SMS can be used to drive acquisition by sending a link to a mobile website or app store page to users who provide their phone number (usually on a product's landing page). This method is particularly useful for less smartphone-literate users who are unaccustomed to finding apps in the app store, but know their phone number, and for effectively acquiring users from desktop to mobile.

As with email, SMS is quite highly regulated in many countries and requires the collection of user phone numbers.

Search

Search as a channel covers organic and promoted app discovery via search engines and app store searches. This could be via targeting specific keywords, or through indexing in-app content that appears in the search results. The channel description in the stack has been updated to reflect paid search opportunities on both the Android and iOS platforms and in particular Apple's Search Ads.

Search engine marketing is a powerful user acquisition channel for browser-based users on both web and mobile, with Google AdWords dominating the market. Advertisers bid on keywords or phrases in order to rank highly in the results and drive traffic to their app or site.

In addition to paid search, SEO (and by association content marketing), ASO keyword optimization, and mobile content indexing can be significant sources of "free" traffic to the app stores, or—in the case of content indexing—deep-link referrals back into the app for existing users.

Social

Social networks—including messenger apps—provide access to potentially huge numbers of potential users. Social media marketing can be a great way to connect with potential and existing users, drive acquisition, deepen engagement, or develop communities.

Referring to all "social" as one channel is a major simplification; each social network has different characteristics in terms of the potential for connecting to or building audiences, methods of communication that are possible, support for paid or promoted posts, and myriad other factors.

Social networks represent only a small portion of ecommerce referrals, but their role in the path to purchase is growing fast. More people turn to their social network to help get feedback prior to purchasing different products and services. As a last-touch channel, social networks have doubled in visit share to US retail sites in the past two years. And the overwhelming majority of social referrals come from smartphones and on Facebook according to Q1 2019 data from Adobe Digital Insights. As social commerce takes off, social networks could become the point of purchase, rather than a driver of referrals. Social networks at the forefront of social commerce, particularly Instagram, could play a larger role in driving ecommerce purchases with more ecommerce transactions moving to smartphones.

Ad Networks

Advertising networks provide opportunities to advertise your product or service in other mobile or web apps and websites. There exists a multitude of companies in the "ad-tech" ecosystem and many options for advertisers seeking to acquire or reengage users. Targeting options, traffic volume, regional/national traffic availability, and pricing options (CPM, CPI, CPC, etc.) vary greatly between players in the ad-tech space.

When buying users for your mobile app from paid channels, the goal is to find the right mix of providers that deliver the volume and quality of users (usually defined by their propensity to monetize or at least engage with the app) at a

CAC that is sustainable for the business: this requires heavy investment in analytics, CRO on campaign creatives, and attentive budget and campaign management.

TV, Print, and Radio

Television advertising has seen a remarkable resurgence over the past year, as CPIs from popular channels such as Facebook have risen sharply due to saturation and marketers hunt for more economical acquisition sources. New TV attribution partners have sprung up to help mobile advertisers match app installs with TV campaigns and—despite the inherently noisy data—many marketers are reporting strong results and favorable CPIs (i.e., actual performance, rather than a brand boost) from this traditional media channel.

Other traditional media such as print and radio may also prove to be valuable in connecting with the target audience, though most growth marketers eschew these old-school techniques due to the difficulty in measuring the effects.

Billboard display advertising and even hand-distributing flyers can be a great way to saturate the consciousness of a city and are relatively cheap compared to high-priced online and mobile advertisements. For this reason, such old-school marketing channels are often used when launching hyper-local, mass-market services such as food delivery, laundry, and taxi-hailing apps, albeit always in combination with digital campaigns.

Owned

Owned channels may include a company website (including mobile web), company blog, landing pages, and other apps from the same publisher. These channels provide a great opportunity to cross-sell and drive traffic between owned properties, acquire new users through organic search engine traffic, and inform existing users about new products, features, services, or marketing offers.

Messenger Platforms

The meteoric rise in messenger platforms such as Facebook Messenger, Whats App, Snapchat, Line, WeChat, and others has led many to speculate that messaging *is* the new platform, relegating all other networks and apps to also-rans in the race for smartphone users' attention.

Despite the competitive threat posed by messaging apps themselves to all other apps, they also provide opportunities for apps to reach new and existing users through content sharing, direct messaging (if they provide an API that allows apps to do this), and invites/referrals. Each network is different, with some permitting external links, chatbots, and API integrations and others not. In addition to product-level integration, some platforms (e.g., Snapchat) lend themselves to more traditional marketing activities where awareness and acquisition can be achieved by building an audience through content and/or performance marketing.

Each platform is different; some messaging platforms lean toward group messaging and one-to-many broadcasts while others are predominantly used for person-to-person interactions. Consideration of the dynamics of the chat platform—as well as the messaging habits of the target audience—will help the savvy growth practitioner to prioritize and tailor efforts toward the networks and integrations or marketing efforts most likely to reach and resonate with their ideal users.

Chatbots

Closely related to the topic of messaging platforms is that of chatbots. Chatbots, AI, NLP, digital assistants, and conversational interfaces are increasing in prominence and—despite the immaturity of many current experiences—will play an increasingly disruptive role in the way users interact with many platforms and products in many categories.

The fact is that nobody knows exactly what the future of "chatbots" (itself a vague definition) will bring, or how exactly bots will merge with the current distribution and value chain for mobile products. It's not too much of a stretch, however, to suggest that chatbots currently present opportunities for integration with—and promotion of—mobile products, as well as presenting another potential touchpoint with existing users.

Mobile DSPs and SSPs

The 2017 edition of the stack added mobile DSPs and supply-side platforms (SSPs) as additional channels to recognize the rise in programmatic advertising. DSPs allow advertisers to buy ad impressions across a range of third-party apps or sites, often providing access to multiple ad exchanges, sophisticated targeting criteria, and a broad range of options for ad placement. As such, DSPs are an increasingly important part of the performance marketing mix for some companies.

SSPs are the publisher-side equivalent: facilitating finer control of monetization via ad inventory inside the product by allowing programmatic buying of ad placement within the app.

App Streaming

Streaming apps and games offer users the chance to experience some or all of the product without ever downloading it as a classic native app from the store. Typically facilitated via HTML5 and with the potential to be distributed over some messaging platforms, app streaming can present a real alternative to traditional distribution and hence is an interesting emergent channel. It remains to be seen to what extent streaming apps will replace traditional app store distribution versus augmenting it, growing overall reach and becoming another touchpoint (like HTML5 web apps) with the user along their journey toward native app adoption.

Applying the Stack in an AI World

The good and bad news is that there are many options for growth teams to leverage the different elements of the growth stack to enable them to get smarter to acquire, engage, retain, and monetize new and existing customers. The challenge for any startup is to make the right decisions on what elements of the growth stack to use at different stages of the startup growth and find the right balance between using in-house and external platforms to support them. The Native Advertising Institute 2018 chart now has grown to over 400 vendors (see Figure 11-10), making it even more complex with a myriad of advertising vendors for user acquisition teams to potentially test, which requires a lot of internal resources to manage and execute.

It's time for startups to fully embrace the power of AI and ML to streamline marketing processes across the entire customer marketing funnel to help growth teams work smarter by leveraging an "intelligent machine" that can help them automate as much as possible across the growth stack in the following areas to accelerate their testing and learning to scale fast once the product/market fit is achieved:

- Segmentation
- Personalization
- Media buying
- Campaign optimization
- Predicting customer behavior
- Data analysis and reporting
- Customer support
- Better cross-platform attribution
- Combating fraud
- Creative development and iteration

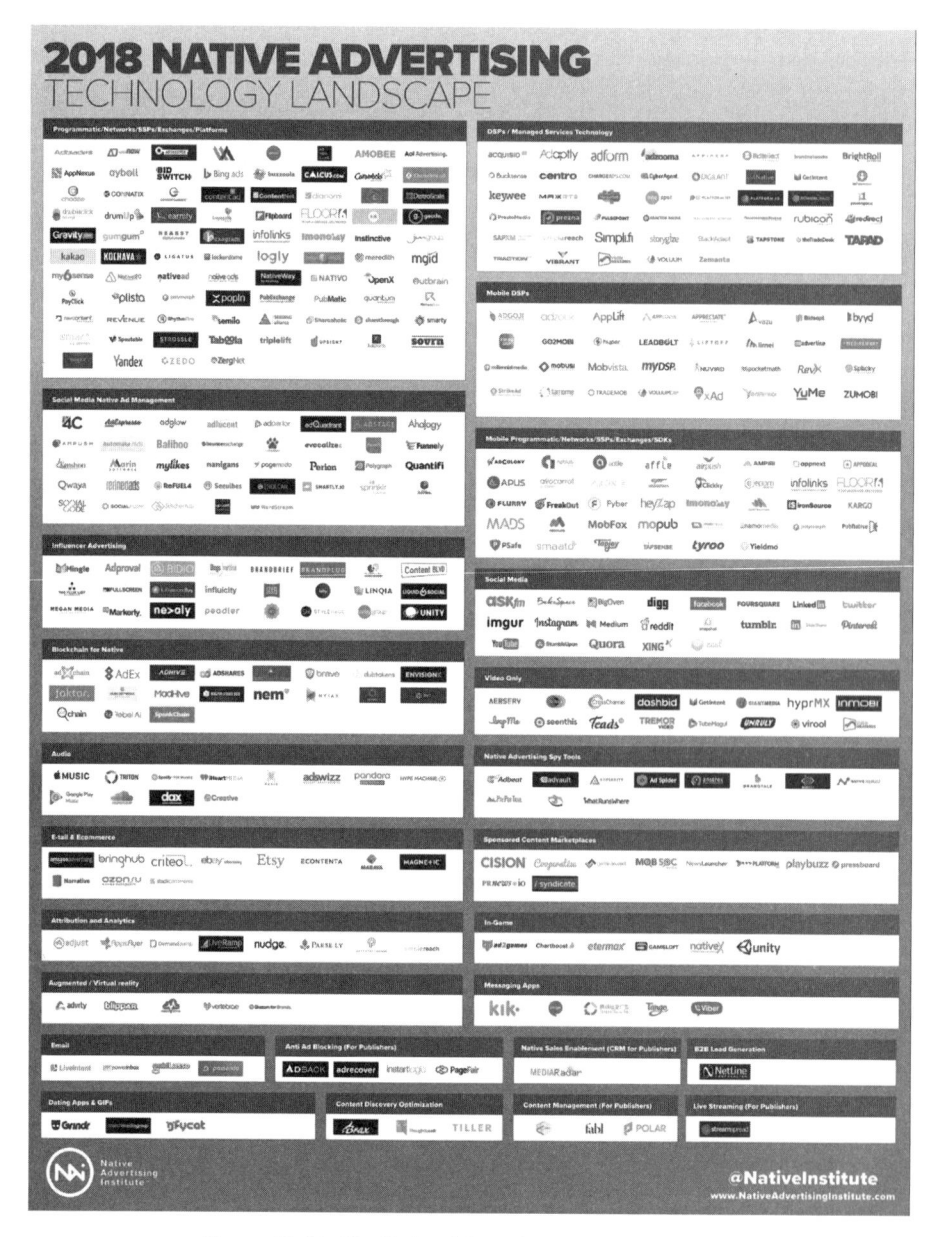

Figure 11-10. *The Native Advertising Institute 2018 chart*

We've found plenty of examples of ways that AI is transforming growth marketing to allow us to achieve things that would never have been possible without it. With AI, you can work smarter and gain a holistic, real-time view of your customers and their relevant interactions throughout the entire journey. AI lets you act quickly on your data and makes it easier to focus on the higher value work by getting fast actionable insights.

> *The challenge for any startup is to make the right decisions on what elements of the growth stack to use at different stages of the startup growth and find the right balance between using in-house and external platforms to support them.*

Sooner rather than later, your user acquisition efforts will need to rely on artificial intelligence, machine learning, and automation to adapt, customize, and personalize cross-channel user journeys and deliver optimal results. At IMVU, we're doing it today in ways that would be impossible to orchestrate using last-generation business intelligence software or reporting dashboards. Managing complex, cross-channel campaigns with multiple targeting, creatives, and sequencing requires an intelligent operational layer *above* the out-of-the-box solutions provided by individual platforms to deliver great results.

It's easy to see that this can get incredibly complex, so next, let's explore ways to manage that complexity to reduce risk, cost, and expense along the way.

PART V

MANAGING INCREASED COMPLEXITY AND RISK

Part V moves you into the world of managing increased complexity and risk with the data needed for AI. We will explore ways to manage that complexity in Chapter 12, how to reduce risk in Chapter 13, and how a future growth team might coexist with humans and machines working together in Chapter 14.

CHAPTER 12

How to Manage Complexity

There will always be complexity with any AI project because of the codependency on different technologies and coordination required of cross-functional teams necessary to be successful. In Part II, we covered in detail the concept of Customer Acquisition 3.0, which showcases the core dependencies required to get the consistent flow of good, clean first-party customer data to Athena Prime—our "intelligent machine" from Nectar9—which enables the AI to perform to its fullest potential.

Our challenge at IMVU was very similar to most startup growth teams. Imagine the complexity that goes into managing all the different user acquisition experiments and campaigns. First, you need to think through your overall strategy. You need to take into consideration setting up and managing all the different experiments across different platforms and campaigns with the right budgets, bids, goals, audiences, landing pages, and creative assets that need to be monitored and adjusted depending on the results.

There is a practical limit to how many of these experiments humans can run and make sense of. In addition, human-driven experimentation is typically a sequential endeavor—you design your experiments, you run them for a period of days, weeks, or months, you consider the data, make adjustments, then start the process over again. Not only does this lead to longer feedback cycles, but the more experiments you conduct simultaneously leads to exponential complexity that's prone to error and even human bias.

The key takeaway is that there's already a lot of complexity built into the processes with growth teams. They are under intense pressure to acquire new customers by running as many different experiments as is humanly possible based on the bandwidth of the team.

The most tangible benefit of AI when it comes to marketing automation is to help growth teams to run tens of thousands (not hundreds) of different experiments a month in parallel. A properly instrumented intelligent machine can orchestrate and automate the delivery of sequenced campaigns on multiple channels in a synchronized way and take action without supervision or human intervention to get optimal results dramatically faster than in times past.

To say executing this type of sophisticated campaign with a complex array of audiences, channels, creatives, and dynamic sequencing using manual processes is "challenging" is a euphemistic understatement. But by applying artificial intelligence and data science strategies, we make it possible to identify the right sequencing for different cohorts of people at different stages of their life cycle. Patterns emerge, and humans can then build on those insights to further fuel improvements. Rinse and repeat.

> *The most tangible benefit of AI when it comes to marketing automation is to help growth teams to run tens of thousands (not hundreds) of different experiments a month in parallel.*

Scaling growth doesn't come easy. To turbocharge your performance, I would argue that working with, or building, an intelligent AI machine to help you automate the key levers like blending segmentation models with cross-channel creative placements, achieving data-driven results far beyond manual capabilities, ends up reducing the complexity of managing all this work manually because machines are always better adapted at this type of detail-oriented work and are far less prone to make errors compared to even the most well-intentioned and talented of teammates.

In this chapter, we'll look at some recommended best practices to manage the complexity of implementing an AI solution at your startup.

Identifying Use Cases

Get to know and understand AI use cases and successes from other growth teams who have successfully implemented AI into their technology solution. You should look to find and understand all the different use cases where AI has been successfully adopted and whether the team decided to build a solution or license software as a service. As we explored previously, the investment to fully build an AI solution in-house is beyond the reach of most startups, so the better place to start is to see what third-party solutions are being leveraged by other growth teams to fast track their way into adopting AI for growth on their team. Be sure to ask for tests or pilot programs to ensure any third-party software you're considering will perform as promised.

By identifying use cases and successes, you can identify exactly which problems you're trying to solve and find recommendations to catalog potential MarTech vendors who have a proven track record of solving those exact problems.

"MarTech" is defined as the blending of marketing and technology. It allows growth teams to look at a process and automate areas where it makes sense to become more efficient, streamline data, and ultimately allow companies to adopt things faster and scale marketing efforts.

Typically, most use cases center around the following three themes:

Cost reduction
> The general financial savings to the company in money that results from the improvement in running a lean team to scale up growth using AI solutions to do most of the heavy lifting tasks that would replace hiring user acquisition managers. People are a startup's most expensive resources.

Better ROI
> The improvement in campaign performance on key growth metrics like CAC and ROI, which occur due to better optimized results from the increased velocity of A/B testing that increase breakthroughs in learning to find small wins that compound over time at a much faster rate than doing this manually.

Risk reduction
> Implementing AI tech solutions reduce the risk of the business being heavily dependent on humans managing all the key campaign levers and the risks that come from employees who would churn on the team, especially at the user acquisition manager level.

Tying back all the different use cases to any of these three themes would positively impact getting the cross-functional support needed to support the project as well as getting executive sponsors to champion this effort from the top of the org structure—something critical for long-term success.

Expected Value

AI holds powerful potential, but it suffers from a lot of hype in the media and around boardrooms. The best way to build trust with other stakeholders is to navigate a narrow path between what is hype and what is reality. Bear in mind that those who watch from the sidelines will risk being left behind as the rate of change is accelerating rapidly every day. The challenge is to walk a fine line between being transparent and conservative on the expected value. As a champion, I recommend you lean toward a bias to "under promise and over deliver." It's good to get all the different key stakeholders to work together with the growth team from the start to fully vet all the AI solutions being considered to make sure they work to reduce uncertainty and resistance to change in an effort to maximize potential positive outcomes.

When it comes to implementing AI, there is no substitute for sound business principles. You should apply the same rigor in the adoption of AI as you would in the adoption of any other new technology. You have to focus on problems to be solved, where considerable value can be extracted to impact key growth metrics, and where the value statement is evident and can be clearly articulated.

It's good to start by first solving small problems, get some early wins, and then continue to solve more complex problems over time. The idea is to continue to engage internal teams to keep them excited about small victories along the way to maintain their support for your AI efforts.

> *It's good to start by first solving small problems, get some early wins, and then continue to solve more complex problems over time.*

At IMVU, we took our own advice in this regard. We started small with a proof of concept to validate our approach. We started exclusively with only one major partner (Facebook) using our AI intelligent machine behind the scenes to optimize the ad campaigns for one country (the United States), channel (iOS), and campaign (prospecting). We ran multiple experiments to see how well the software's AI-powered algorithms could drive more ROI compared to the baseline metrics from the same campaign managed without AI. With this, we were able to get a good clean read on the data. As performance improved with more training data, we slowly continued to scale up growth by moving beyond Facebook. We added more channel partners and more complex cross-platform campaigns to focus on the entire customer journey with an emphasis on downstream success metrics like acquiring new customers and better ROI and LTV.

The Operational State

A key must-have when implementing an AI system is a clear vision of an organization's operational state and business goals; very often, there is a desire to see what the AI tool can do versus thinking about the operational state and business outcomes. This requires thinking about a number of things up front. How often do you anticipate interacting with the system? Daily, weekly, monthly? What will be the ongoing inputs to the system? What will be the ongoing outputs to the system? What is the expected audience of users? What is the plan to expand usage over time?

If one begins the project with the intent to have it be operational versus some proof of concept, one will make better, more informed decisions and increase the chances of success. The second thing to understand is how the organization intends to validate the findings of the system. Getting transparency into what the machine is recommending helps to build trust, which is required to be successful in any long-term AI system.

Focus on Outcomes

When implementing AI technology, the focus should be on *outcomes*. Set goals and make sure you have ways to benchmark the success of the AI solution—and know how long it will take to see meaningful outcomes. Because AI systems can take smaller subsets of data (structured) and/or larger more holistic data sets (structured and unstructured), there tends to be a question of what results one's data can produce.

Before you work with any AI vendors, always ask them to help define specific measurables that can be seen within a specific timeframe with the data you've got readily available on hand. It's good to hold all the vendors accountable for delivering tangible results within a certain timeframe. There is a trade-off between costs to gain accuracy and benefits gained from improving accuracy.

Will the vendor conduct a preimplementation evaluation to help determine ROI or outcome areas and their related measurement and target? Will they provide best practices or recommendations for processes/resources to support the new workflow and technology? It's always good to conduct a proof of concept to test run the AI solution before you're fully committed to it in general, considering how nascent the market is. As a client, you'd typically like more hand-holding from AI vendors during the implementation period.

Customer Data

Companies generally classify their data in one of two ways: it's either high-fidelity data that's closely governed and religiously maintained (e.g., customer and transaction data), or its raw unstructured data that's archived or disposed (e.g., user interaction data). With the rise of cloud technologies, the cost of storing and processing data has fallen dramatically, which now makes it cost-effective for companies to keep all their data. What would have once consumed an entire IT budget is now a tiny drop in the bucket, and now we have the rise of "data lakes" in the cloud to store all this information in hopes that someday we'll know what to do with it.

Data is what powers algorithms. Therefore, it's a competitive advantage to have all your data passed into an AI solution to help the machines learn faster and surface insights that would be nearly impossible for a human brain to fathom without the assistance of AI.

In one sense, the more data you have, the better your AI gets. Now that collecting and storing large data sets is widely accessible, there's no reason for any startup with their sights set on AI to dispose of data. Gather as much data as you can about your customers to help optimize metrics to address business outcomes.

Keep in mind that if you put garbage in, then you will get garbage out. The easiest approach is to get all your structured and unstructured data pipelines set up correctly up front using an API or software development kit (SDK) from all of your key data sources from cloud storage into (or accessible on demand by) your AI intelligent machine. An API is a programming interface that allows software programs to communicate and interact with each other, whereas an SDK is a set of tools that can be used to develop software applications targeting a specific platform. So, an API can be seen as a simple SDK without all the debugging support and other tools.

Choose the Right Metrics

As decisions are increasingly based on data, it becomes all the more important to identify what you are optimizing for and define the key performance metrics you are tracking against.

Generally speaking, choosing metrics that are a proxy for customer growth is a tried-and-true approach.

For example, IMVU focuses on two key post-install optimization goals like "App Events Optimization" (purchases or registrations) and "Value Optimization" (revenue or ROAS) for Google and Facebook. You want to identify the type of customer you're targeting with your campaign and assign a value to each conversion (new user registrations or in-app actions such as purchases). Ultimately, the more data events you pass back based on your user success metrics, the better these platforms can help you target the right users.

As IMVU has the dual goals of increasing unique and first-time purchasers, along with maximizing the return on ad spend, we knew this could be done by prospecting for new customers while simultaneously encouraging our current customers to reengage with the platform. We use different optimization goals for delivery based on the user's stage of the funnel. For example, lower in the funnel, we optimize for purchase conversions, but higher in the funnel, we may optimize for clicks or even daily unique reach.

While AI is all but useless without good data, it's worth repeating that AI-powered marketing automation efforts actually start with a clearly defined business problem focused on cost reduction, better ROI, risk reduction, or any combination thereof. We will now explore how to reduce risk in the next chapter.

CHAPTER 13

How to Reduce Risk

A startup is a human institution designed to deliver a new product or service under conditions of extreme uncertainty.
Eric Ries

Being part of any startup business is inherently risky. The odds for success of any given venture-backed company are slim.

Unfortunately, there isn't a linear path to success. The whole startup journey is an adventure full of many twists and turns, with no guarantees of fame and fortune. Every day you're risking your own future on the power of your personal work ethic, market conditions, and other factors—some within your control, many outside of it—and hoping that your growth team will succeed in acquiring new customers and scaling up growth based on your success metrics.

I'm confident that fully embracing AI will lead to more rewarding outcomes than trying to drive growth without it. Embracing AI could help increase your probability for success because it accelerates your velocity of testing, learning, and making data-driven optimizations throughout the entire complex customer journey to better acquire, engage, retain, and monetize customers.

With great risk often comes great reward. There are failures, setbacks, and even complete reboots along the way, but if you don't risk something, you'll never gain anything. Great innovation comes from asking what could be and trying to mitigate the potential risks along the way.

In this chapter, we'll discuss the key risks to beware of with AI and steps to take to help mitigate them.

Data Dependency

The biggest risk is that *AI is highly dependent on good-quality data*. A big challenge for any startup is to combat data fragmentation by creating a data-driven culture within your organization. It's critical that you feed the right data for the problem you want to solve. Good data is the bedrock of AI modeling. If a project doesn't have the right data, the results will be less than optimal. However, not having perfect data at the outset shouldn't prevent growth teams from getting started. It's best to have a plan in place to ensure all the data is being passed back into your AI machine in a timely fashion, so it's able to use the most recent data set to analyze and provide the best insights and solutions.

All the major AI advances have been fueled by advances in data sets. Collecting, classifying, and labeling data sets used to train algorithms is difficult, tedious grunt work—especially when you're working with data sets comprehensive enough to reflect the real world. You need to have consistent checks and balances in place to frequently audit the campaign results to ensure the continued integrity of the data being passed is correct and not broken.

> *The biggest risk is that AI is highly dependent on good-quality data.*

For example, every time your engineering team makes a product update, you want to double-check to make sure that nothing gets broken with the data that is being passed back into your AI intelligent machine. In my experience, there is always a risk whenever product updates are made, and having a robust QA process is needed to help mitigate this risk—or else you will end up sending incorrect data that will end up messing up your algorithms. If your data is coming in from multiple sources, it's important to check the data from one source against another before applying any machine learning. An example would be trying to eliminate malicious fraudulent data from bots and other scammers that would compromise the quality of training data that determines the performance of your AI intelligent machine.

AI is going to become a key part of your growth strategy sooner or later, and getting on top of your data management processes now is going to help set you up for success. Data quality, ownership, and governance can all be enhanced by having a dedicated executive assigned to manage this function.

Transparency

Because AI systems can crunch through vast amounts of personal data from different sources, transparency and trust are becoming increasingly important. Some approaches to AI systems operate like a black box and don't provide any transparency into what is going on behind the decision-making process. That's going to raise concerns internally and externally, especially where no humans are in the loop when machines are making decisions on the key optimization levers like bids, budgets, creative, segments, and so on.

Most growth teams who leverage AI systems to help them manage significant user acquisition budgets have to be held accountable to not just hit performance goals but also provide some level of transparency to the rest of the organization to continue to build the trust that they are using the technology in responsible ways.

Many AI intelligent machines are built with so-called neural networks serving as the engine; these are complex interconnected node systems that are less capable of indicating their "motivation" for decisions. You generally only see the input and the output. These systems are incredibly complex and nuanced. They are often tasked with orchestrating multiple campaigns across and among key marketing platforms and across channels—dynamically allocating budgets, pruning creatives, surfacing insights, and taking actions autonomously 24/7/365—in ways that can make decisions hard to follow for even the smartest of humans. Depending on the depth of the algorithm's neural network, you'd get very limited explanation and transparency. While a human would be able to understand a machine optimizing 10 levers, most would struggle to explain something with 1,000 variations and permutations. An example would be an AI model that detects over 1,000 customer data signals to identity the most promising customer prospect segments to target on major advertising platforms from a list of tens of millions where humans are out of the loop, because it would be prohibitively effort-intensive to check them all.

This black box problem of artificial intelligence is not new, and its relevance has grown with modern, more powerful machine learning solutions and more sophisticated models. Meanwhile, models can outperform humans in complex tasks like the classification of images, transcription of speech, or translations from one language to another. And the more sophisticated the model, the lower its explainability level.

Here are five main approaches to consider in your startup for AI models:

Use simpler models
  This sacrifices accuracy for something that can be explained to team members, which can be an invaluable part of making progress and winning support for the application of AI to your marketing toolbox.

Combine simpler and more sophisticated models
> The more sophisticated model provides the recommendation, while the simpler model provides rationales. This often works well, but there are gaps when the models disagree.

Use intermediate model states
> For example, in computer vision, states in intermediate layers of the model are excited by certain patterns. These can be visualized as features (like heads, arms, and legs) to provide a rationale for image classification for different creative assets.

Use attention mechanisms
> Some of the most sophisticated models have a mechanism to direct "attention" toward the parts of the input that matter the most (i.e., setting higher weights). These can be visualized to highlight the parts of an image or a text that contribute the most to a particular recommendation.

Modify inputs
> If striking out a few words or blacking out a few parts of an image significantly changes overall model results, chances are these inputs play a significant role in the classification. They can be explored by running the model on different variants of the input to see the impact on the results.

Ultimately, human decision making can only be explained to some degree. It is the same for sophisticated algorithms. However, it is the software providers' responsibility to accelerate research on technical transparency to build further trust in intelligent machines.

Biased Algorithms

Even if you have the data, you can still run into problems with biases hidden within your data sets. When we feed our algorithms data sets that contain biased data, the system will logically confirm our biases. It's common to find that customer data sets that include gender, race, and age biases because they are focused on targeting user segments that closely match your best customers. The risk is that this level of bias is counterproductive if you're looking to expand and attract new audiences that are different from your current user profiles. It's important to look at whether the data and the algorithms that analyze the data are in line with the principles, goals, and values of the organization. It's currently hard for AI to make judgments on the ethics and values of their recommended outcomes.

There are currently many examples of systems that disadvantage ethnic minorities to a greater degree than is the case with the white population. After all, when a system is fed discriminatory data, it will produce this type of data. Garbage in, garbage out. And because the output is from a computer, the answer will tend to be assumed to be true. We found this to be the case at IMVU, where we uncovered our AI machine had a bias when targeting new lookalike segments toward targeting females 18-24 on social media platforms. And when systems are fed new biased data (because that is what the algorithm says) it turns into a self-fulfilling prophecy, which at IMVU led to excluding other segments that were a lost opportunity for us. And remember, biases are often a blind spot.

Companies still have too little expertise at their disposal to be able to properly assess these data sets and filter out any assumptions and biased data. The most vulnerable groups are disadvantaged by these systems even more than usual. Inequality will increase. In the worst-case scenario, algorithms will choose the winners and the losers. Always continue to verify the results of the output of smart intelligent machines by trying to get insights into knowing how the algorithms and data achieved their result. For example, at IMVU we always monitor the user profile data on lookalike segments across different media platforms where we target new customers to ensure they are in line with the principles, goals, and values of our organization.

Compliance

Compliance is also an issue with data sources—just because a company has access to information doesn't mean that it can use it anyway it wants. We're starting to see more of a political backlash to how companies are capturing so much customer personal data with the sole goal to profit off it either by selling more products or advertising. All of this is leading to a new generation of technology addiction to our devices that isn't healthy. There is so much data flowing through different interconnected devices with the Internet of Things (IOT) and this will continue to increase as more of the world is connected onto the internet and broader adoption of 5G.

There is so much negative attention stirred up in the media around how all the tech companies are basically Trojan horses that get customers hooked to their apps and products with the sole purpose to extract personal data to profit off their customers. Facebook is a good example as they leverage AI to keep their customers on the platform as long as possible to monetize them with advertising, with their AI algorithm focused solely on the output of making more money and complete disregard for any harmful consequences this entails with all the political ads they run from different special interests.

There is going to be wider adoption of regulations like the GDPR on data protection and privacy for all citizens of the European Union (EU) and the European Economic Area (EEA). It also addresses the export of personal data outside the EU and EEA areas. The GDPR aims primarily to give control to individuals over their personal data including names, home addresses, photos, email addresses, bank details, posts on social networking websites, medical information, and computer IP addresses. It looks increasingly likely that the United States Congress will pass a federal privacy law similar to the GDPR by 2020 giving users more control to opt out of having their data shared with companies. All businesses need to develop and implement a comprehensive data privacy program or risk major penalties for any violations. The golden rule is to ensure businesses executives treat their customers' personal data the way they would like other businesses to treat their personal data.

Clearly, the risk of having more regulatory oversight on how companies capture and use customer first-party data will have an impact on the AI models that clearly perform better with more personal data events to learn from. I feel the biggest impact would be felt in how companies can target customers through different communication channels (emails, retargeting), personalized recommendations, and offers as well as building new customer segments from lookalike profiles. All of this is important for running user acquisition campaigns because it enables growth teams to leverage AI to be so much smarter on how to target the right customer segments, with the right creative messages, in the right channel, at the right time with precious accuracy that would be lost without these data signals. There is a reason why the days of spray and pray are gone thanks to AI being smart about leveraging first-party customer data to draw better user insights and predictions.

> *Clearly, the risk of having more regulatory oversight on how companies capture and use customer first-party data will have an impact on the AI models that clearly perform better with more personal data events to learn from.*

Increased wider adoption of GDPR-type regulation in the United States would make companies that already dominate the digital advertising market (i.e., Facebook, Google, and Amazon) even more dominant. If people are asked to consent before allowing a company to collect their personal information, they might be more likely to give that consent to well-known brands like Facebook, Google, or Amazon than to unknown startups that would need that information to build up an advertising business in order to compete with these established brands. This virtuous shift in cycle will result in shifting even more budget toward these media giants by growth teams, making their algorithms even smarter, which would impact their competitor's ability to continue to invest significant R&D budget into further improving its own AI capabilities.

At this point, the absence of a stringent federal privacy law is almost no longer an option, considering the numerous privacy fails at Facebook and other companies. The irony is that the new federal privacy law could end up giving these big companies even more of a competitive advantage, unless it includes a data portability provision, so that people would be able to take their data from a platform like Facebook, Google, or Amazon to another platform that could use that data to grow its business. The concern that a federal privacy law could favor these companies may necessitate increased antitrust enforcement. What is still unknown is how much first-party data advertisers will need to continue to share with Facebook, Google, or Amazon as these algorithms get even better at predicting user intent with all the data signals they collect about users. Maybe their AI won't need as much invasive privacy data to achieve the same level of results.

Clear Goals

You need to set clear goals for the AI intelligent machines to identify the targets of what they are supposed to achieve. The benefit to measuring the efficiency and effectiveness of any AI-powered machine is the ability to monitor performance to ensure it's leveraging the training data to optimize toward your clearly defined output target success goals for ROI or CAC. There would be a risk if the machine isn't on the same page with the goals you set for growth. An example is if you don't set a specific ROI goal for your user acquisition campaigns, then the machine would have no sense of boundaries on how much to spend to acquire new customers and could end up spending your budget inefficiently in the pursuit of acquiring new customers.

Adaptability of Machine Learning Models

In predictive analytics and machine learning, the term "concept drift" as defined in Wikipedia means that the statistical properties of the target variable, which the model is trying to predict, change over time in unforeseen ways. This causes problems because the predictions become less accurate as time passes. The term "concept" refers to the quantity to be predicted. More generally, it can also refer to other phenomena of interest besides the target concept, such as an input, but, in the context of concept drift, the term commonly refers to the target variable. Clearly, we live in a world of constant change where future trends are unpredictable. It's important to make sure AI systems are built to be agile to adapt to new needs, new sources, and new training models to find new ways to solve new problems that are currently unforeseen in the user acquisition landscape.

The inability for a machine learning model to adapt to frequent change impacts AI model usability in several ways. Without adaptability, the retraining of models must be performed by submitting new training data sets, where new features can be seen in the context of previously learned information. Training a new model is a massive exercise requiring many, many hours to complete and requires the use of large-scale computational facilities. Countering this risk requires startups to have the right infrastructure in place for data control so they can adapt to support larger and larger data sets to support frequent model builds.

But what's best left to the humans, and what's best turned over to the machines? Let's explore that in the next chapter.

CHAPTER 14

Human Versus Machine

All startups are on a mission to try to disrupt the status quo by coming up with better innovative solutions to solve an existing problem that hasn't already been addressed. Growth teams have a similar mandate to continuously run as many experiments as possible to test, learn, and iterate to keep challenging the status quo to come up with new and improved ideas to acquire new customers. And everyone on a growth team is constantly in a race to become more intelligent and discover the next best thing that will give them the competitive edge to successfully scale up growth at their startup to hit their success metrics. Every new marketing technology innovation now is or will be leveraging AI, and the choice is how quickly startups will embrace it or get left behind.

We all know that AI is here to stay and more growth teams sooner or later will be using AI-enabled intelligent machine platforms as a key centralized element of their growth team. The future of Customer Acquisition 3.0 rests on the shoulders of intelligent machines orchestrating complex campaigns across and among key marketing platforms—dynamically allocating budgets, pruning creatives, surfacing insights, and taking actions autonomously. These machines hold the potential to drive great performance with a far more efficient, hands-off management approach powered by AI. Control your levers, focus on creative and strategy, and turn the drudgery and math over to the machines to get data-driven results far beyond manual capabilities. The end goal for any growth team is to ensure they successfully scale growth better, faster, and more cost-effectively. They are not going to win in the new world of growth using old-school manual processes executed with bloated teams.

This same principal should be applied to the startup growth teams that need to continue to find new and innovative ways to help them outsmart their competition to meet and exceed their success metrics. As more growth teams open up to fully embrace AI, they need to figure out the best way to find the optimal balance between how humans and machines can coexist to form the ultimate dream team. It's always better for any team or business to be proactive in the evolution of disrupting themselves before someone else does it to them. The focus should be on automating tasks and not jobs to make the team leaner and more productive to be able to scale up performance.

> *Every new marketing technology innovation now is or will be leveraging AI, and the choice is how quickly startups will embrace it or get left behind.*

Some people think of AI as just one specific technology, but it's not. The future growth team would comprise of essentially a mix of automated intelligent machines that track, measure, and scale growth on user acquisition campaigns across the entire customer journey. These tools are excellent for analyzing large data sets, automating systems and workflows, running A/B tests, and optimizing audiences for paid ads. As a growth marketer, much of what you once did manually can now be done by an AI tool. The main goals of a growth team has always been to acquire, retain, and monetize as many customers as possible while spending the least amount of money. This isn't going to change in the future, but the way to go about executing the user acquisition strategies to achieve those goals will because AI saves time and money, by being better at executing complex campaigns, uncovering data insights, and getting performance results faster with less human manpower.

Skill Set for the Future Growth Team

There will be a risk of a lot of job losses in the future across all different areas of the workforce as AI continues to be adopted to deliver better results while also saving time and money. AI is usually perceived as a threat to employees—but many senior managers and executives are worried too. Management has to invest heavily in areas that AI doesn't excel at, such as critical thinking, empathy, customer satisfaction, and creativity. Machines are only meant to replace tedious, repetitive tasks, whereas a personalized approach shines on its own. Therefore, whether your business makes this investment or not, you should take responsibility to invest into building the right skill set to ensure you're too valuable to be replaced and safeguard your career.

The skill set of the new growth teams will be humans who possess a blend of business and technology acumen, to not only understand all the different key levers of the intelligent machine but be able to support them. They need to be able to develop customer acquisition/retention/monetization strategies, manage budgets and new product launches, design creatives (ads, images, messages, etc.), manage cross-functional relationships internally (product, engineering, data, creative, marketing, etc.) and externally (media partners, ad networks, channels, agencies, etc.), and provide oversight to mitigate the risk factors discussed in the previous chapter—these are still beyond a machine's capabilities. These tasks take insight, creativity, management, leadership, communication, empathy, critical thinking, and strategic planning skills that only humans possess, which means that humans and machines are codependent on each other to be successful in the new paradigm shift into the future with AI-driven growth. It will take humans to build all the key relationships to evangelize the whole AI revolution within your startup and to continue to help secure the resources to see it succeed for the long term.

> *The skill set of the new growth teams will be humans who possess a blend of business and technology acumen, to not only understand all the different key levers of the intelligent machine but be able to support them.*

As AI becomes more popular, we need to adjust the skill set of the growth team. AI can handle the day-to-day, repetitive tasks that used up a lot of human time, energy, and patience. Humans still need to take the lead when it comes to user growth strategy, design, and communications—we can save the boring work for our machines. Popular online fashion retailer Zalando (*https://oreil.ly/s4tkW*) plans to replace the majority of their marketing team with algorithms and artificial intelligence to scale future growth.

As a growth marketer, much of what you once did manually can now be done by AI tools. But humans still have to decide which of those tools to use in order to solve different user growth challenges. In the example of analyzing creative results, a human still needs to look at the data to glean insights to provide feedback to their creative teams to continue to come up with new iterations to improve results as well as ensure all those new creative assets stay in line with brand guidelines. The humans still need to handle this cross-functional project management and delegation of tasks to different teams.

This unique ability to build relationships internally and externally to continue to feed the intelligent machine inputs and see past the data is a crucial skill that only humans have. As growth teams continue to move toward fully embracing AI, it doesn't necessarily mean that everyone on that team would be out of a job, but more so that their roles and capabilities would change. The innovative growth marketers would work together with a few AI intelligent machines to focus on the different stages of the customer journey and funnel to take advantage of every opportunity. At IMVU, we used AI to empower our growth team because even though AI replaces many task-oriented roles on the team (such as managers and analysts), we upgraded our skills on the team to hire more senior-level growth marketers with experience in user acquisition strategies, project management, A/B testing experiments, paid and organic channel portfolio development, management of intelligent machines and the AI tools necessary to control them, and the handling of personal relationships with teams and partners.

Hybrid Growth Team

Future growth teams will be lean with less people, but the jobs will get more fun with the ability to be the drivers on the team and provide the right inputs into the intelligent machines to solve specific business goals and challenges. So, smart growth marketers who adapt to change will continue to thrive and find innovative ways to make a difference through AI-powered marketing. They'll play a different role alongside AI and be faced with new and exciting challenges as things continue to evolve.

> *The choice isn't humans versus machines, but rather how best to leverage the strengths and weaknesses of both of these groups to work well together by complementing each other's strengths and weaknesses.*

The choice isn't humans versus machines, but rather how best to leverage the strengths and weaknesses of both of these groups to work well together by complementing each other's strengths and weaknesses. The end goal for any growth team is how to acquire new customers cost-effectively to ensure your startup is successful. We already know that machines are better than humans at processing large volumes of data within a short amount of time. AI intelligent machines can learn and make smarter and faster decisions based on the successes or failures of their previous tasks, and over time will produce better results to hit your success metrics like CAC, LTV, and so on. That means AI is much better than humans for replacing menial repetitive marketing tasks that would take humans a lot of time to complete. But when it comes to strategic thinking, or any task that exceeds the platform's capacity for learning or statistical analysis, it is woefully inadequate. The most powerful uses for AI have to be guided by skilled humans with broad domain expertise to ensure all the right levers and dials are being optimized for optimal performance. This empowers more human creative minds and strategic thinkers to focus on the work they love rather than the boring data-rich tasks that drive them crazy.

Adopt a Growth Mindset

The fear of losing jobs to automation has always been widely spread in the news media with stories about robots stealing factory jobs; bots taking away customer service jobs; self-checkouts gutting the service sector; and artificial intelligence replacing most skilled laborers with smart algorithms. The truth is that growth teams will get leaner but smarter and more productive so they can manage extremely complex campaigns at scale to achieve much better performance with less active human dependency. There is a big risk if you don't continue to upgrade your skills to be relevant and valuable to businesses in the AI world; if you don't then you are more likely to be out of work.

The good news is that you already know this is coming and you can take action now to acquire the relevant skills and experience to be more strategic, creative, and well versed with technical skills to manage AI intelligent machines. There will be plenty of new opportunities to learn to add value on the growth team by being an early adopter championing an AI intelligent machine for your startup. Always adopt a growth mindset, which is to have an underlying belief that learning and intelligence can grow with time and experience. When people believe they can get smarter, they realize that their effort has an effect on their success, so they put in extra time trying new things, leading to higher achievement. I'm confident that you will increase the odds for a successful career in the AI era by approaching AI with a positive, open mindset —you'll need resourcefulness to figure it out, a willingness to experiment, and the ability to help and teach others.

Both humans and machines will work much better together than against each other; humans just need to figure out how to provide value in the future with the AI intelligent machine at their command. It's about becoming a hybrid team, with algorithms supporting human decision-making prowess. AI-based solutions compensate for human weaknesses and vice versa. The new coexisting team isn't going to be 1 human + 1 AI machine = 2 humans of output productivity; rather it will be more like 1 + 1 = 1,000 due to the power of AI and its multiplying effect on a team's productivity. Ultimately, the complexity of decision making is reduced for humans with access to the many more options and recommendations generated by AI intelligent machines.

AI is quickly becoming a mainstream solution—but there's a lot more to AI than plugging it into your existing strategy. The most powerful uses of AI for growth must be guided by humans who can leverage intelligent machines to help inform them on the best strategy and lead the day-to-day tactical execution of automating most of the time-consuming tasks, specifically those around data points. To stay relevant, growth marketers need to embrace AI and work well together. Algorithms are not sentient. They need guidance to successfully interact with humans on the team. When given a choice, always be the driver and not the passenger on the rocketship that everyone hopes their startup becomes. That way you always get to control the destiny of your career as you embark into the exciting world of growth marketing with AI. So, go all in to fully leverage AI as your competitive advantage to give you the edge to outsmart your competitors.

AI Will Create More Job Opportunities

AI is going to revolutionize society as we know it. Gartner estimates that by 2020, AI will create more jobs than it eliminates. By 2022, one in five workers engaged in mostly nonroutine tasks will rely on AI to do a job.[1] AI innovation will be creating many new job opportunities. There will be plenty of opportunities for those who dive in and embrace the AI tools provided to advance productivity and value to the team. There will be job losses not only on growth teams, but many different areas of the workforce as more AI will be adopted to automated tasks to improve the productivity of teams.

The most critical—and most difficult—task of any growth team is making the right decisions every day around how to focus their time, resources, and budget to acquire, retain, and monetize customers. Knowledge is power. There is always pressure to be more productive with limited resources. Therefore, the question is not if startup growth teams should leverage AI, but when and how best to leverage AI tools to help their team be more productive and aid them in making smarter, data-driven decisions that not only positively impact their jobs but also the survival of their startup. Humans must become comfortable with the idea of working with AI intelligent machines as colleagues, and people who can manipulate AI intelligent machines to perform well and meet and exceed business objectives will be in the advantageous position of seeing more job opportunities open up for them in the future. It will only be a matter of time before humans and machines work symbiotically to produce the best work—and that "next frontier," as well as its potential for triumphs and its challenges, is the focus of Part VI.

---

1 Gartner, "Gartner Says By 2020, Artificial Intelligence Will Create More Jobs Than It Eliminates," 2017. *https://oreil.ly/UfDNb*.

PART VI

THE NEXT FRONTIER

It will only be a matter of time before humans and machines work symbiotically to produce the best work—and that "next frontier," as well as its potential for triumphs and challenges, is the focus of Part VI. Chapter 15 provides an overview on implementing the right support system to ensure your organization is set up for success. Then in Chapter 16 you will learn how to prepare for the challenges that come with any new undertaking. We'll wrap everything up in Chapter 17, which covers the future of artificial intelligence and human intelligence working together as a team to fully leverage this emerging AI "superpower" to turbocharge your growth efforts.

CHAPTER 15

Planning for Success

If you fail to plan, you are planning to fail!
Benjamin Franklin

I hope you're excited about fully embracing an AI "intelligent machine" to help your growth team thrive by turbocharging their customer acquisition growth. To fully leverage this emerging "superpower," it's important to have the right support system in place to ensure you're set up for success.

This chapter offers crucial considerations to bear in mind as you plan to implement an AI intelligent machine in your growth team.

Success Goals and Measurements

All businesses use KPIs to evaluate their success at reaching targets. This means you'll need to feed your AI intelligent machine clearly defined KPI goals and make sure you and your machine have the ability to track KPIs in a real-time reporting tool or dashboard.

Most startups have different KPIs against which to measure growth. You should determine which ones are right for your business and industry. Once you have identified these goals, then it's easier to objectively measure and evaluate the performance of your AI intelligent machine.

Luckily, there are five key KPI metrics recommended for growth teams to consider as goals for their AI intelligent machine to optimize toward:[1]

- Customer acquisition cost
- Retention rate
- Customer lifetime value
- Return on advertising spending
- Conversion rate

The key is not to choose all of these goals, but focus on a few that clearly correlate with the long-term success of your business. For example, IMVU used CAC and ROAS goals as inputs to measure the effectiveness of AI-powered marketing efforts.

The value of certain KPIs will change depending on the stage of your startup (early, mid, or late stage) and they should evolve as your business grows. An example is that your CAC will typically be much higher when you're launching a new product, which will naturally suffer from low awareness. Your CAC will come down as you get better at acquiring new customers and creating more brand awareness over time.

Certain metrics will be more important than others. Early-stage companies typically focus on metrics related to business model validation like retention, while more mid-stage or late-stage startups focus on scaling up user growth with metrics like CAC and LTV. As you continue to make those KPI goal adjustments within your AI intelligent machine, be sure to give it sufficient time to capture enough training data to be able to optimize toward your new desired KPI goals and smooth out any anomalies that may come up (e.g., seasonal bid pressure on ad prices).

It's much easier to measure success for AI when it's completely aligned with supporting your business KPI goals. This makes it much easier to demonstrate the business value of AI back to the management team, and helps you continue to secure more internal support for scaling up your AI growth efforts, adding capabilities, and delivering greater returns going forward.

> *It's much easier to measure success for AI when it's completely aligned with supporting your business KPI goals.*

---

[1] These are covered in more detail in Chapter 7.

AI and Humans Working Together

By now it should be clear that the choice isn't between humans and machines, but how you can best leverage artificial intelligence and human intelligence to work well together by complementing their strengths and weaknesses. The end goal for any growth team is to continue acquiring new customers cost-effectively and keep achieving more growth with fewer resources. The best way for startup growth teams to stay lean is to find a way to figure out the right roles for your different human team members, so they can support the AI intelligent machine with data, creative, budgets, goals, new ideas, and experiments to ensure that your investment in AI is set up for success.

We already know that machines are better than humans at processing large volumes of data within a short amount of time. AI intelligent machines can learn to make smarter and faster decisions based on the successes or failures of their previous tasks, and over time produce better results to hit your success metrics (e.g., CAC, LTV, etc.). That means AI is much better suited to menial repetitive marketing tasks and calculations that would take humans a lot of time to complete. In addition, those tasks, when done manually, are prone to errors, which can be costly. But when it comes to strategic thinking, or any task that exceeds the platform's capacity for learning or statistical analysis, AI in its current state is woefully inadequate.

The most powerful uses for AI must be guided by skilled humans with broad domain expertise to ensure all the right levers and dials are being optimized for optimal performance. This empowers more human creative minds and strategic thinkers to focus on the work they love rather than the boring, data-rich tasks that drive them crazy. Being flexible and adaptable is critical to working well with AI, and it's important for anybody who wants to stay relevant on the growth team.

Now and into the future, growth teams will need to attract more well-rounded individuals with critical thinking, technical, creative, problem-solving, and data-driven skills. As you can see in Figure 15-1, the growth team organizational structure is broken up into lean squads that focus on the different growth areas: Acquisition, Retention, and Monetization. The early stage startups will start off with just one squad managing all three growth areas, but will continue to add individual squads to manage the different functional growth areas as the business scales up.

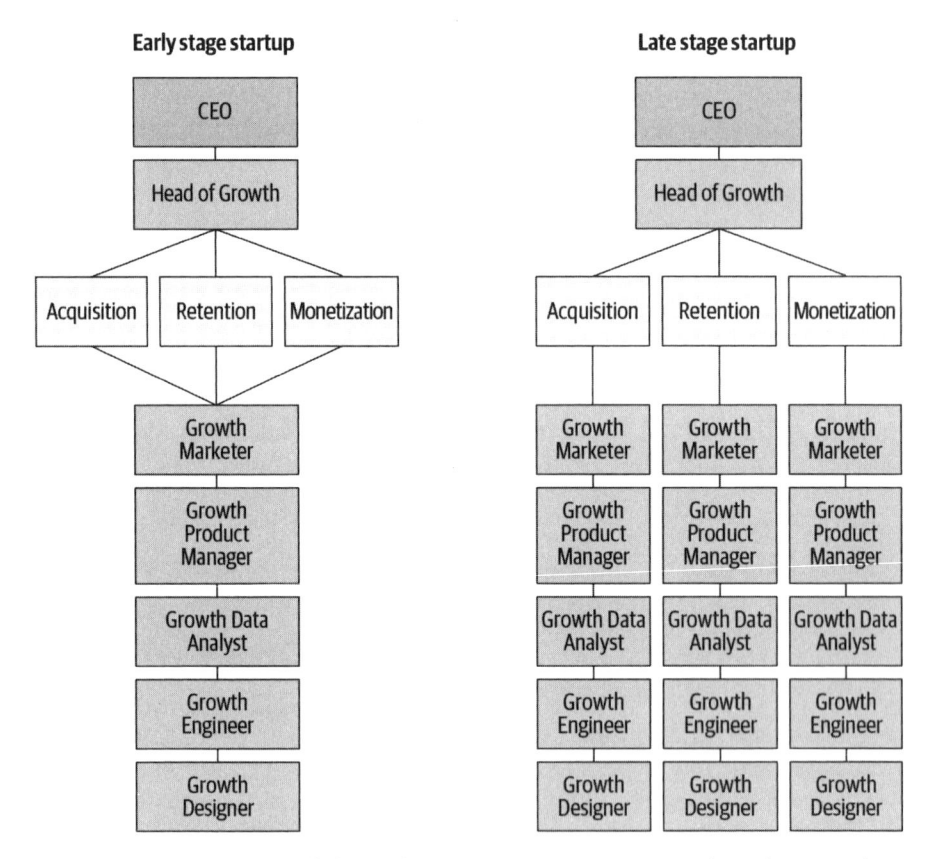

Figure 15-1. *Recommended growth team organization structure utilizing lean squads*

These "squads" need to be independent teams that operate in a highly co-dependent fashion with each other and the AI intelligent machine you've set up to enable each group to successfully hit their goals. This codependency is a critical element because it forces both AI and humans to work well collectively as a team, because none of these squads is going to be successful alone.

However, I would add a note of caution that breaking out squads has some risks of silo-thinking, and optimizing for local maxima rather than what's holistically best for growth. The Head of Growth needs to mitigate against this by providing oversight and managing trade-offs between the silos.

Here is a brief description of the different roles on the future growth team organization structure:

- The *Chief Executive Officer (CEO)* is ultimately responsible for everything related to the success or failure of the company and should provide air cover for the Head of Growth to get access to the resources needed to help their startup survive and thrive, both through financing activities and managing the overall company revenue goals.

- The *Head of Growth* is responsible for overseeing the entire customer acquisition, retention, and monetization process that impacts generating revenue in the startup. This encompasses managing the holistic growth strategy, goals, plans, and budgets—and the growth team to execute it. They would be the chief evangelist for all things related to growth and AI, as well as a member of the executive team and a direct report to the CEO. It's important for the Head of Growth to report directly into the CEO to be able to make decisions fast to enable their team to move quickly to take advantage of new growth opportunities as they continue to present themselves.
- A *Growth Marketer* is a multifaceted marketer with expertise across the entire marketing funnel and different channels within their specific growth areas (acquisition, retention, monetization). For example, in acquisition they would be experts in both paid and organic user acquisition channels like Facebook, Google, Search, SEO, ASO, DSP, and so on.
- A *Growth Product Manager* is responsible for all the experiments and the A/B testing road map across their specific growth area within the AI intelligent machine. For example, in retention they would be experts coming up with different A/B tests to run on CRM channels like email, push, and in-app across the entire customer life-cycle and on-boarding experience.
- A *Growth Data Scientist* is responsible for producing insights from experiments to inform areas of opportunity as well as overseeing that the data inputs and outputs are performing as expected within the AI intelligent machine. They would also build dashboards to track different KPI results within their specific growth areas. For example, they would present all the analysis for the different experiments on the road map.
- A *Growth Engineer* is responsible for implementing and executing all the different experiments and campaigns within the AI intelligent machine. For example, they would manage executing all the cross-channel experiments to support the growth marketer and growth product manager.
- *Growth Designer* is a versatile designer responsible for developing all the creative assets for the different experiments and A/B testing being run within the AI intelligent machine.

As the role for AI expands, the growth team organization structure would evolve as well. The future growth teams will be lean (regardless of the size of the business) because AI will empower them to achieve significantly more results with less human dependency as most of the tasks would be automated.

Growth would be less related to a specific role or a set of tactics and more about the foundational work around supporting an AI intelligent machine process with the right inputs to achieve the desired business outcomes. A lot of the heavy lifting execution work would now be done by machines with guidance from a small team of highly skilled humans with expertise in product management, engineering, design, data science, and growth marketing. Each team would be set up as an individual squad to support the different areas of growth.

> *Businesses that have successfully implemented AI have strong executive leadership support for the new technology.*

It is important to understand the idea that tactical marketing is made up of two joining minds; AI and human thinking equally support greater outcomes when effectively used together. The human brain is creative and understanding and cannot be replaced by AI. The AI will continue to supplement human decisions at a strategic level. Although AI is successful in uncovering and determining a defined set of activities, it still needs the human brain to understand patterns, extract ideas, and provide insights.

Businesses that have successfully implemented AI have strong executive leadership support for the new technology. The Head of Growth would be the C-suite sponsor who would take an active role to ensure that the company-dedicated resources are aligned to fully support the AI intelligent machine. The AI level of disruption is often directly proportional to the need for a sponsor. This is important to avoid the common conflicts within most organizations about who owns the features that KPIs most depend on between product, engineering, and growth teams. It is crucial to get all of these teams aligned so that they do not work on conflicting goals that end up negatively impacting customer growth.

Data Is at the Core of Everything

Even though AI technologies have existed for several decades, it's the explosion of data that has unlocked the power for AI to advance at incredible speeds. Intelligent machines can't work without access to your first-party customer data. It requires a lot of training data for algorithms to learn and become smarter over time. With enough decisions and data, patterns emerge that can be leveraged to make predictions for future decisions, which is what companies mostly are looking for. A 360-degree view of every customer is a concept that has eluded organizations for decades. Breaking data silos and delivering a consistent customer experience remains a priority. But very few startups have been able to put it into practice.

The challenge is that most of this rich customer data lives in silos in different databases, so integrating all the different customer data events that are captured throughout the customer journey to make that insight available for analysis is missing. The most innovative growth teams are taking steps to break down the data silos that once separated their apps from everything else. These startups are using APIs to connect their app data to their web data, and to their marketing channel data, to their business intelligence systems, in simple and secure ways that don't degrade the user experience or consume needless engineering hours.

Your data also needs to be labeled in a structured way—this could be fields in a system, a database, or a spreadsheet with rows and columns.[2]

It can happen that an organization does not have enough labeled data. In that context, you need to start gathering the factors and decisions in a structured way, so that you can use it to feed the AI platform in the near future. Another issue could be the data set. A *data set* is a collection of data.

Having the right data set is crucial. However, the size of the data set isn't the real problem, it's the scope. The challenge with AI is not so much with implementation; the big question is going to be how do you train the AI? That's why you need to spend time to make sure your data is compatible with the AI intelligent machine.

Customer Data Platform

In general, you need to modernize your data management technologies simultaneously. Data is the foundation for successful AI strategies—ensure that your data integration, database, and data warehouses are ready to power your AI initiatives. Moreover, you should invest in the infrastructure hardware required for your AI transformation. Machine learning requires a high level of computational power, as well as high bandwidth and storage.

The starting point is to have a plan to centralize your customer data on a single platform—specifically, on a customer data platform (CDP), such as Segment. As originally defined by the CDP Institute, a CDP seeks to unify customer data into a single database that is persistent and shareable with other systems. This allows organizations to create a 360-degree view of customers

---

[2] Labeled data is a group of samples that have been tagged with one or more labels. Labeling typically takes a set of unlabeled data and augments each piece of that unlabeled data with meaningful tags that are informative.

and create better customer experiences. It is part of a unified customer data management system that is comprised of three core layers: data systems, decisions systems, and delivery systems, as shown in Figure 15-2.

Data Systems	Decision Systems	Delivery Systems
Create and store customer data	Decide which treatments to give customers	Deliver customer treatments

Figure 15-2. Machine learning and the customer data platform (source: David Raab's blog (https://oreil.ly/Y83Fk))

The CDP industry more than doubled in 2018 with $740 million in revenue and the market is expected to reach a whopping $1 billion in 2019. CDPs are no substitute for a well-thought-out data strategy and architecture, but they can greatly accelerate your infrastructure road map and increase your chances of success. A full-service CDP like Segment provides numerous benefits:

Data-driven customer engagement
The right CDP helps marketers access previously inaccessible data. This helps improve their audience segmentation and personalization strategy.

Campaign measurability
With a 360-degree view of the customer journey, growth marketing teams are able to build the right metrics for acquisition, conversion, and customer churn. It helps them identify ways in which they can improve their marketing campaigns.

Improved ROI and competitiveness
Being able to determine the most preferred action, channel, and time to reach customers gives marketers that edge to remain competitive. They can budget better, and optimize on costs for improved ROI on campaigns.

In addition to integrating data that already exists in other systems, CDPs also address the "first-mile" instrumentation challenge with native SDKs that provide a standard mechanism for collecting data from the point of origin. These ensure consistency in how tracking works across all devices and screens and allow growth teams to act on data "from the edges" in real time to support moment-based use cases (like sending a message to someone who has just entered a geofence).

Figure 15-3 provides an illustration of the CDP framework.

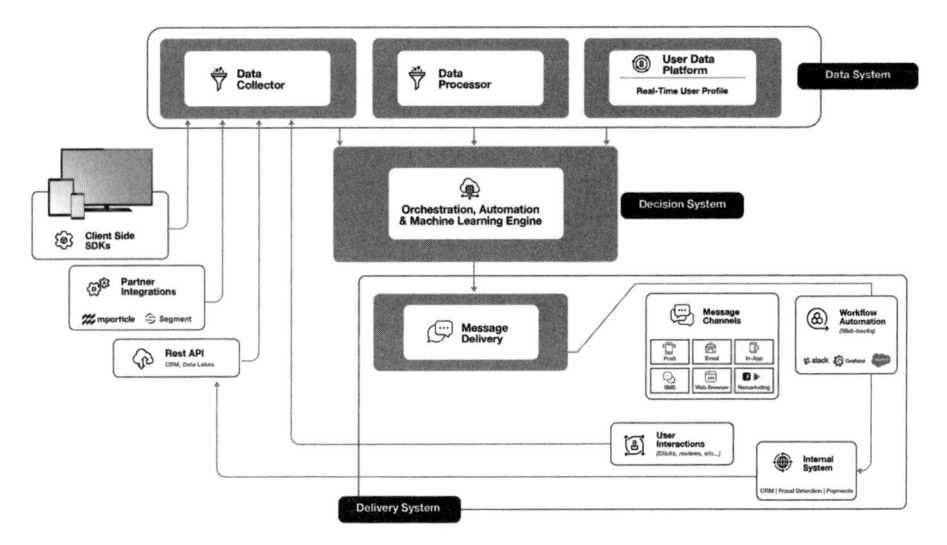

Figure 15-3. *CDP framework*

In the future, a CDP would use a delivery system on a single platform. This consolidated approach helps to reduce ambiguity and ensure data integrity. This makes it easy for any AI intelligent machine to unify data, decision, and delivery systems to make it easy for any AI intelligent machine to:

- Understand users better
- Segment them effectively
- Reach users with contextual messaging in real time

By bringing these capabilities into a single platform, growth teams are able to reduce their tech stack complexity, remove data silos, reduce moving parts, and give the team complete control over their process—from hypothesis to testing to measurement to calibration.

In the next section, we'll look at why having a CDP is integral to fully powering AI intelligent machines and creating an end-to-end customer experience.

Data System

The data system is comprised of the following two parts:

Ingest data from online and offline sources in real time
It's important to be able to ingest user data in real time from any number of online and offline applications. The data sources can be one or more of the following:

Native SDK integration on the client side
> To track user actions across devices and channels. This includes individual level data from websites, mobile browsers, and mobile apps. A user profile may include any number of custom fields and event-level behavioral fields that are specific to one's business. For example, a ride hailing service can create custom profile fields like app launched, ride booking initiated, and payment successful.

Public REST API
> OpenAPI allows customers to push user profile and event data from any source into one centralized system. This may include data from online and offline applications such as data warehouses, CRM systems, data lakes, point-of-sale, payment, fraud detection, customer support, and other systems. This user-level data can be demographic, geolocation, psychographic, and so on. Transactional data (e.g., payments or purchases) and behavioral data (e.g., recency and frequency of visits) can be easily stored as well.

Third-party applications
> These are partner integrations that include platforms for attribution, acquisition, communication, and customer experiences. A technical integration enables you to send relevant user information right into a dashboard. You will be able to see all your data in one place. These integrations enable app developers to track, segment, and engage their users.

Persistent, unified user profiles

CDPs not only store user profile data but also keep the user identity intact when they bring data from numerous channels. This creates one profile for a user across all of their devices.

You are able to specifically identify user profiles using a database ID or other unique identifier captured or generated by the customer. Using the same identifier across devices allows for user/device aggregation. For unknown visitors, you should assign a unique anonymous device ID to each device.

The user profiles should be persistent in that we store every single snapshot of user data. You can track every pattern or change in customer behavior and attributes over time, and across all channels.

Any changes in a profile are normalized and maintained regardless of whether they continue to remain present in the source systems. For example, this could be demographic attributes such as address and email or more behavioral attributes such as search history, purchase trends, or interests. This allows you to run advanced segmentation and personalization use cases that leverage all of a user's profile attributes.

Decision System: Real-Time Customer Analytics, Segmentation, and Personalization

Startups benefit from a CDP because it is an in-memory database. This database stores and accesses the most recent snapshot of user data. Any changes that happen to it in real time are rendered to customers in real time.

This custom built in-memory database also allows AI to query millions of user profiles in real time, making it an advanced analytics and segmentation tool for growth teams. It provides answers for queries that span millions of data points in near real time without any precomputation. The architecture provides the flexibility of breaking larger data sets into smaller shards spread over multiple physical servers to scale limitlessly. The platform should also have a message delivery service (MDS) that greatly complements its CDP capability. MDS is an end-to-end, omnichannel orchestration and marketing automation system that makes insight from the analytics and segmentation engine actionable.

What makes it exciting is that a lot of the segmentation and orchestration capabilities are automated. Powered by AI and machine learning, they enable marketers to define granular user segments and send omnichannel engagement campaigns in real time.

Customers are able to send campaigns across a number of channels on the web, email, mobile, and desktop as well as build rich, lookalike prospecting and retargeting customer segments that perform across all the major media channels like Facebook, Google, DSPs, and countless other channels worldwide.

Delivery System: Make User Data Shareable and Accessible to Other Systems

CDPs enable organizations to access customer insights across external systems. The OpenAPI allows growth marketers to send the insights to CRMs like Salesforce, BI tools like Microstrategy, data visualization tools like Grafana, communication channels like Slack, customer support systems, project management tools, and many others.

As a result, it enables startups to resolve differences in cross-channel efforts and bring more certainty to their analyses. The REST API provides endpoints, webhooks, server-side SDKs, and error handling that supports the most complex use cases, including:

- Enriching external systems with user data and metrics (e.g., updating a customer account in your CRM with the customer's purchase history)
- Triggering campaigns in external systems based on real-time events tracked (e.g., sending a checkout reminder to users who have abandoned an item in their cart)
- Sending user data and metrics from external systems (e.g., updating a user profile with support tickets from your issue management system)
- Creating campaigns based on external events, in real time (e.g., sending a campaign with price drop alerts when a customer views a certain product)

Data Privacy and Integrity

You need to keep a current view of the customer to maintain the accuracy of the user profile. This processes PII strictly based on instructions from the customer. Customer data is stored in an encoded format optimized for performance, rather than stored in a traditional file system or a database. Customers should own all rights to their data and can choose to download it via an API or delete it from the systems, if they need to.

CDPs Are the Lifeblood of AI

A CDP is only as valuable as the use cases it supports. Customer data has been growing at an exponential rate and is key to the success of all the AI intelligent machine use cases. Your CDP has to meet the volume, variety, velocity, and veracity needs of the future. Getting access to your customer data is non-negotiable for any successful growth team. To best unlock that knowledge, you have to consider the type of data you need, where to look for it, how to get it, and how to build the right data models to analyze your business questions. And just as importantly, you need to continually update your data to retrain and enhance the algorithms. There's certainly a lot that goes into data collection, but it's worth it. As the lifeblood of AI, getting a CDP in place is critical to help you get the business insights you need to move your business forward to fully tap into the superpower of AI. The excitement around the capabilities of data management platforms and related technologies, like CDPs, are going to lead to broader consolidation in the space, which is inevitable to deliver better ROI.

Even as you plan for success, you also need to be ready to face the challenges that come with any new undertaking. We'll take a look at some of these challenges in the next chapter.

CHAPTER 16

Ongoing Challenges

AI and machine learning are starting to hit their stride, and many of the obstacles along the way have been addressed—the availability of computing power, data management systems, and so on. However, there are still many challenges ahead. In this chapter, we'll take a look at some of the most significant challenges you're likely to encounter and how you can mitigate them.

Data Acquisition

A fundamental challenge for startups using AI is how to acquire enough first-party customer data from their users. It is hard to be explicit about how much data a company needs to truly leverage AI—that depends on what use cases they want to start with. This could be based on conversion goals or historical conversion rates; for example, this could just be for analytics or segmentation and targeting.

I like to think about AI and ML like a tool chest. With things like deep learning, the tool chest just got deeper and has more powerful tools. Depending on the problem at hand, you can use different techniques that will have their own requirements for things like training data, test data, and how accurate the model needs to be to get the best results.

Therefore, all companies from early-stage startups all the way to big multibillion dollar businesses can take advantage of leveraging AI provided they have the right data acquisition strategy in place. I think it's fair to say that startups have to be even more strategic in what data they collect and how they collect it; for example, in some cases they can bootstrap their algorithms by licensing third-party data sets to start with—and improve the performance of their models with their first-party data. To some degree, this blank slate represents a potential advantage over larger, more established organizations they may be competing with. Ultimately, the data acquisition goals come down to the problem they are trying to solve, and each of those will have its own magnitude of data needed.

We have already mentioned that good data is the key element your business needs in order to successfully implement AI. For an AI intelligent machine to perform optimally and to develop smart algorithms for say, cost-effectively acquiring new customers, a business needs to capture enough unique customer data events on a frequent and consistent basis.

However, the more data fields you add to the signup/registration/checkout procedure for customers, the more likely they are to abandon the process. Remember that all online forms are a transaction. A company needs to look at them as an exchange of information and value, in return for something of value it is giving to the user. If you don't think about online forms that way then you're going to fail to capture the data you need.

Most of the friction in data collection results from customers' lack of trust in startups that lack brand awareness or do not provide a compelling value proposition for solving their problems. When you ask for personal identifying data (name, age, gender, email addresses, credit card numbers, phone numbers, preferences, etc.) to enhance your AI efforts, it is going to impact the conversion rate of new customers. The challenge is to find the right balance between asking for too much or too little user data during the signup/registration/checkout flows and on-boarding. Customers pay close attention to the data you are asking them to provide, especially if they have no prior relationship with your company. It is critical to build trust and a strong relationship quickly when you're asking for data from new customers, and the way to do that is to consistently reiterate value.

If you want to establish long-term success in leveraging an AI intelligent machine to support growth, data capture comes even before the algorithms. The value of first-party customer data is priceless, and no publicly accessible data is ever going to provide the same competitive edge.

Access to unique data isn't a problem for major platforms like Google, Facebook, and Amazon because they are well-established brands that continue to provide clear value in return for capturing user data. However, most startups are beginning at ground zero at the task of convincing people to share their data with them. Unfortunately, AI is not useful until enough people are using your product or service for you to capture a critical mass of data events. Only with this flow of information can the AI intelligent machine help with your acquisition, retention, and monetization efforts across the entire customer journey. Getting the data flywheel process started and keeping it going is something all businesses face with AI, but this is true even more for startups. Startups should not give up on AI, however, because in the long run it offers so many opportunities to disrupt, innovate, and solve problems faster. The key is to ensure you have a good product/market fit that compels people to give up their data before you have reached the scale to provide optimal value from the data flywheel kicking in.

> *The value of first-party customer data is priceless, and no publicly accessible data is ever going to provide the same competitive edge.*

This means you need to invest effort up front to develop a strong data acquisition strategy that provides value or incentives to customers for giving up their data. An example is Amazon Prime, which offers much more than free two-day shipping to members, all because Amazon knows that Prime members have significantly higher LTV than non-Prime members. Because of the value add, Amazon captures a wealth of customer data that enables it to better target new users and make product recommendations to current customers. This allows it to boost customer purchases, build loyalty, and create strong brand advocacy among its customers, who refer their friends and family to Amazon. This is a case study in how to build a customer-centric brand driven by data, and create a successful ecommerce business.

Let's not forget that Amazon was once a little startup as well. The key to their success was investing in a data acquisition strategy from the beginning, then using that data to consistently give value back to their customers. For startups to succeed, the top priority is to create the right data acquisition strategy for building proprietary data sets within their AI intelligent machine to empower their growth team. Establishing a strong product/market fit to create a strong use case is the way to go. It's never easy, but neither is building a successful startup and changing the world.

Privacy Controls

Data is a commodity that will continue to increase in value as more data regulations like GDPR and privacy controls are adopted worldwide. I would expect more of the major media platforms like Google, Facebook, and others to use proactive "privacy" measures as a way to combat all the negative publicity Facebook received when the Cambridge Analytica data scandal hit after the

2016 US presidential election.[1] They are taking steps to give their customers more transparency and control over their personal data in order to maintain trust. As an example, Facebook recently announced a new feature called Clear History. This will let users see which external websites send information to Facebook about them, as well as clear any information about the user from Facebook's analytics tools. Users will also have an option to turn the data collection feature off on Facebook, as well as on third-party sites that use Facebook's data collection tools.

Google is also tightening its Chrome browser's privacy controls. It will be similar to Firefox and Safari, which already have some cookie blocking controls built in. The trend across the board is for companies to give users more transparency about what data they would like to share with advertisers.

Another concern for these big technology companies is that the United States government is preparing an antitrust investigation into whether the biggest tech companies like Google, Facebook, Apple, and Amazon have stifled competition. It's hard to predict how this will impact these companies regarding their customer data policies, but it will surely be a major distraction for them. It could lead to more challenges for growth if the companies end up sharing less data to identify and track users coming from their platforms, where the bulk of the paid acquisition budget is spent.

> *Cross-platform attribution about the customer journey is already challenging, but it's going to get even more so in the near future as these major technology companies are scrutinized on all fronts regarding user privacy.*

There is a big risk that Apple and Google may decide to completely stop sharing mobile device app IDs with the attribution platforms, which play a key role in tracking customers on mobile devices. This could lead to AI intelligent machines being forced to make decisions with less accuracy and transparency in the attribution data they depend on. Cross-platform attribution about the customer journey is already challenging, but it's going to get even more so in the near future as these major technology companies are scrutinized on all fronts regarding user privacy.

The privacy policies of Facebook and all the other major media partners will be an ongoing challenge, as they continue to evolve over time. They all want to

---

1 The Facebook–Cambridge Analytica data scandal was a major political scandal in early 2018. It was revealed that Cambridge Analytica had harvested the personal data of millions of Facebook profiles without consent and used it for political advertising purposes.

empower users more in order to influence the regulatory debate around data privacy. The truth is, by requiring users to make so many changes to opt out, most people will just ignore it and end up using the Facebook and Google default permission settings (which will let the companies scoop up their information). A deal with the Federal Trade Commission[2] (FTC) to finalize this is in the works right now. It's unclear at this point how many people will actually exercise their right to stop sharing their data, because personalization recommendations, content, and offers are highly valued by most customers. The reality is that these major media partners have already aggregated a lot of user data to train their AI models to become ever more sophisticated, and so they will need less data in the future to perform well.

The biggest losers are startups, who will be forced into adopting all these new stringent "privacy" measures that hinder them from capturing the customer data needed to be successful with their AI efforts in the future. It's also likely there will be a grassroots effort to take control away from the corporations through user blockchain aggregators. This is a way for users to maintain full control over their personal behavior data and with whom it is shared (VR headset, mobile devices, audio, etc.) through a unique identifier like a social security number that is created on a blockchain ledger.

Team Downsizing

There are plenty of scary headlines in the news about AI killing off jobs. A new report by McKinsey Global Institute[3] predicts that by 2030 as many as 800 million jobs could be lost worldwide to automation. The study says that advances in AI and robotics will have a drastic effect on everyday working lives, comparable to the shift away from agricultural societies during the Industrial Revolution. In the United States alone, between 39 and 73 million jobs are expected to be automated—making up around a third of the total workforce.

Businesses are going to see transformational change in all areas of their organizational structure. This will require them to both retool their business processes and reevaluate their talent strategies and workforce needs. They will have to carefully consider which workers are needed, which can be redeployed to other jobs, and where new talent is required. There is danger of a political backlash if unemployment goes up. Many companies are finding it is in their

---

2 The FTC is an independent agency of the US government that aims to protect consumers and ensure a strong competitive market by enforcing consumer protection and antitrust laws.

3 James Manyika et al., "Jobs Lost, Jobs Gained," McKinsey & Company, November 2017. *https://oreil.ly/jv8j1*.

self-interest—as well as part of their societal responsibility—to train and prepare workers for a new world of work.

There will be an impact on the growth team as more roles and tasks get automated with AI. This will be especially evident on bigger growth teams where a lot of campaign, media buying, and data scientist roles become obsolete as machines prove they can handle that work better, smarter, and more efficiently than humans. If you know AI is going to be a part of your future growth strategy, you have to make sure your team is aware of this and willing to learn how it will improve their jobs. It's important to invest time and resources into training employees who will be key to the success of the AI intelligent machine.

Future growth teams will be much leaner as the organizational structure evolves for humans and machines to coexist. Machines will become much smarter, more productive, and achieve better results leveraging artificial intelligence, with humans playing the supporting role to empower them. This process will start with the automation of small tasks, but will scale up over time.

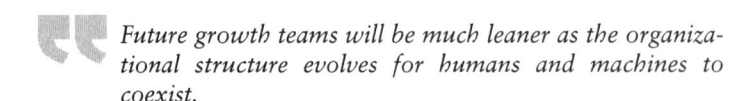

> *Future growth teams will be much leaner as the organizational structure evolves for humans and machines to coexist.*

The best safeguard for workers is to take proactive action now to build up their skill set, so they are relevant in the future of work. The growth team has many roles with rudimentary tasks that are ripe for automation. Instead of worrying about job losses, spend time acquiring new and relevant skills that will allow you to perform higher level tasks in the technical, strategic, creative, problem solving, communication, and leadership arenas. AI will create a demand for new jobs that will benefit workers if they stay open to developing the talents and capabilities that are needed.

New Channels and Opportunities

There is an old saying that is very appropriate for this dawning age of AI—"don't put all your eggs in one basket." In other words, a business should use multiple channels and diversify across different paid and organic platforms to maximize its ability to acquire customers. The key is to reduce risk by not being highly dependent on any one source of traffic. A mistake many startups make is to use paid user acquisition teams that focus on a few highly dependable channels like Google and Facebook. Both of these are good-quality traffic sources, but your startup paid customer acquisition risk is tied to them not imploding, or else you're done as well.

The challenge is to ensure that the different channels you test are easily integrated into your AI intelligent machine. The best way to do that is to make sure that they have APIs and are already set up within your attribution measurement partner, so you can easily manage new campaigns by adjusting the business inputs (bids, budgets, creative, and goals) to test, learn, and iterate at scale using AI to achieve your desired business outcomes.

Staying on Top of Fraud

In our modern world, nothing is certain except death, taxes, and fraud. As soon as advertisers caught up with incentivized traffic and bot farm schemes years ago, fraudsters quickly devised new mechanisms to swindle advertisers out of their budgets. According to the eMarketer Digital Ad Fraud 2019 report, estimates of fraud vary widely but even the most conservative estimates put the money involved well into the billions annually worldwide. Recent estimates vary from $6.5 billion to as high as $19 billion, a range that points at the difficulty of measuring fraud's true impact.

There are plenty of co-conspirators in the ecosystem who are incentivized to keep fraud alive because they are personally benefiting from it. Unfortunately, there is no consistent definition of fraud, and no alignment among the key stakeholders in the attribution platforms, ad networks, ad agencies, and media buyers. Ultimately no one is motivated to solve this problem because it would impact their future compensation and revenue.

One approach used by many high-volume advertisers is to work with a third-party fraud detection tool from their attribution provider to monitor and filter traffic for anomalies. This can be effective because of the sophistication of detection algorithms, as well as their multi-advertiser view of fraudulent traffic. However, the simplest way to minimize fraud is to avoid ambiguous, non-transparent channels, and to buy media directly from reputable sources. The ongoing challenge is that fraud impacts attribution by injecting bad data signals into the AI intelligent machine, which play havoc with the algorithms. Despite the advances in technology, ad fraud will continue to be a big problem due to the growth of digital ad spend—or, at least until there isn't enough easy money to be made by the fraudsters.

Facing Challenges

These challenges are ongoing and ever changing because AI is still in the infancy stage with a lot of untapped growth ahead. However, going all in to tackle these ongoing challenges presents many opportunities for learning and growing individually and/or collectively as a team. At the end of the day, it's always better to learn to be the disruptor than being disrupted. We'll take a look at how to win together with AI in the next chapter.

CHAPTER 17

How to Win Together with AI

The reality is that startups face many challenges in hiring the right people, acquiring and keeping customers, and optimizing for revenue growth. While every startup would like to be the next unicorn, it's only those who are prepared to overcome these key challenges that end up becoming successful. Actually, the financial pressures and constant resource constraints that beset startups are really some of their most significant advantages, because they foster a creative, agile environment where teams are encouraged to experiment, learn, and outmaneuver incumbents and the competition. Startups have a very low probability of success, so anything you can do to increase your chances of success or decrease your rate of failure is huge.

One of the make-or-break questions for any startup is to determine if your product and market fit your customer acquisition efforts. An amazing product and brand alone isn't a guarantee of success. To be successful, you have to be great at customer acquisition. The best growth teams look at the entire customer funnel as an object with many working parts. They see it as a place where they can experiment with messaging at the top of the funnel and do down-funnel hypothesizing and testing to increase customer acquisition rates, while trying to keep customer acquisition costs under control. For most companies, growth marketing is the way of the future, leveraging data and agility to scale revenue and increase customer lifetime value.

> *The Lean AI approach to modern artificial intelligence, machine learning, and automation offers companies large and small the ability to conduct far more experiments simultaneously.*

Taking the wisdom of *The Lean Startup*'s approach into the golden dawn of artificial intelligence, we can radically improve our chances of successful outcomes. The Lean AI approach to modern artificial intelligence, machine learning, and automation offers companies large and small the ability to conduct far more experiments simultaneously. Conducting experiments at scale improves the likelihood of finding successful experiments, some of which you'd never have taken the time to test in a pre-AI world. Incremental experiments that otherwise would have been sidelined for cost or complexity are now valid for observation in the world of autonomous marketing.

Jeff Bezos, the founder of Amazon, said the true secret to business success is to focus on the things that won't change, not the things that will. The key takeaway for any startup should be to continue to focus on things that will add value to their business—like a growth engine for new customer acquisition, retention, and monetization—which is essential for any long-term successful business. The difference between good and great growth teams in the future will come down to the ones who leverage Lean AI to help them with accelerating their rate of learning with better, faster, smarter execution.

The growth team plays a key role in the long-term success of the business because they are ultimately responsible for developing user acquisition strategies and managing resources to achieve business growth metrics. The question isn't if but when future growth teams will leverage an AI intelligent machine to give them a competitive edge.

The future of Customer Acquisition 3.0 rests on the shoulder of intelligent machines orchestrating complex campaigns across key marketing platforms—dynamically allocating budgets, pruning creatives, surfacing insights, and acting autonomously. These machines have the potential to give startup growth teams the edge to drive great performance with a far more efficient, hands-off management approach powered by AI. Control your levers, focus on creative and strategy, and turn the drudgery and math over to the machines to get data-driven results far beyond manual capabilities.

> *The future of Customer Acquisition 3.0 rests on the shoulder of intelligent machines orchestrating complex campaigns across key marketing platforms—dynamically allocating budgets, pruning creatives, surfacing insights, and acting autonomously.*

Whether you choose to build or buy an AI intelligent machine, your success is going to come down to getting cross-functional support for it within and outside of the growth team. The "winning together" mindset is key because AI cannot win without other teams supporting it. The best way to win together is to ensure you have the right incentives across the entire startup organization, by having the entire company financial bonus tied to hitting a customer growth or revenue goal. Everyone succeeds if the business succeeds, and that mindset will ensure that all teams are thinking about growth and prioritizing their resources to support it. At the end of the day growth isn't about one team, but about every team contributing to the greater goal, which is to acquire customers you can monetize to generate revenue and make a profit. The startups with the best ideas don't always win; it's the startup teams that are able to execute well and leverage the right resources for optimal efficiency to get the job done well.

The choice isn't humans versus machines, but how you can best leverage artificial and human intelligence by complementing each other's strengths and weaknesses. The winning together mindset has to be built into the startup culture so that AI is seen as friend and not foe. The objective is to automate tasks, not jobs, and make it easier for teams to be more productive by removing the mundane, boring, repetitive tasks from their jobs. There are many new opportunities for people to become good stewards of Lean AI within their startup and provide the data, train the models, and explain the outputs to other humans.

It has to start with the CEO fully embracing AI, hiring and training the right people to augment AI across different teams, leveraging the right data and marketing technology stack to support it, clearly identifying the problems and use cases to solve with AI, and being fully transparent in sharing all the growth team key learning and results from AI with the rest of the company. Always start by solving small problems first to get some early wins before solving bigger problems and use cases. It's always good to do an internal PR campaign to spread early AI success stories with results. This will continue to encourage people to embrace AI in the workplace. The more employees you can convert into AI subject matter experts and turn into internal evangelists to spread positive AI stories, the better.

The goal of every startup is to accelerate business growth and reduce the time to a successful exit (which should result in a big payday for the investors, executives, and employees). The CEO has to be the biggest advocate for the company to fully embrace AI not just in the growth team, but in every area of the business as a way to reduce operational costs, increase efficiency, grow revenue, and improve customer experience.

Final Thoughts

My hope is that as we come to the end of the book, you're excited by the possibilities of how Lean AI and automation can be useful in your startup. AI is poised to transform every industry—and you're either with the program or you're not. The best time for your company to identify opportunities and develop strategies to implement AI is right now. This technology is on fire across many industries, and is poised to disrupt almost every sector. Getting ahead of the game and embracing the technology as it works best in your field will set you apart as a leader. That's a position all of us want to be in, especially the growth team on the front lines fighting for every customer and justifying that every dollar you spend has a positive ROI. It's a daily challenge for any startup, and you want to ensure you have AI on your side to stack the odds in your favor.

The pre and post results of IMVU fully embracing Lean AI on the growth team has had a significant impact on team performance. We have gone from running hundreds to tens of thousands of experiments across all the different touchpoints and channels in the customer journey per month. This has accelerated our rate of learning exponentially—putting *The Lean Startup* premise of continuously running experiments on the growth team on steroids. The feedback loop to "test-learn-scale" faster powered by AI + data to test different user acquisition strategies, shorten the learning cycle, and then scale it up fast could have the same profound impact on your startup. Beyond extraordinary productivity and results, our team morale has never been better, with everyone excited to see how AI has put more fun into their roles.

There is no doubt that AI is going to disrupt many functions in your business, especially your growth team, and you need to have a plan for how to embrace it and help the team be successful. There is a lot more AI being incorporated into different marketing and advertising technology stacks, but ultimately you need to customize an AI intelligent machine with your business inputs to achieve your particular business outcomes. The smartest way to embrace AI is to find a business that has already built an AI intelligent SaaS platform that can be customized to work for your growth team. The benefit of leveraging a SaaS platform is that they already have dedicated resources allocated to support and improve the product to ensure it's going to stay relevant with all the best practices in AI.

There will be a lot more innovation coming as the AI intelligent machine continues to evolve to integrate more AI features and new channels like voice assistance (e.g., Alexa, Google Assistant, and Siri) and over-the-top media services (e.g., Netflix, Hulu, Amazon Prime, and HBO Now) to reach new customers. It's a very exciting and challenging landscape, as the battle to capture attention for your product and brand with a highly distracted consumer is only going to get harder every day. Lean startup growth teams need to leverage technology to keep up with the ever more crowded landscape of communication and advertising options for reaching new customers.

AI is usually perceived as a threat to employees—but many senior managers and executives are worried too. Management has to invest heavily in areas that AI doesn't excel at, such as critical thinking, empathy, customer satisfaction, and creativity. Machines are only meant to replace tedious, repetitive tasks, whereas a personalized approach shines on its own. Artificial intelligence, machine learning, and deep learning are just the beginning of a revolution that will transform everyday life and how we interact with technology.

The future is about AI and humans working together as a team. Therefore, whether your business makes this investment or not, you should proactively build the right skill set to ensure you're too valuable to be replaced, and thus safeguard your career. The best thing you can do is to educate yourself on what AI could mean for your particular industry and role. If you can stay ahead of the curve, you will end up handling this new AI era better than those who don't. The same old way of managing growth is going to change with or without you. The choice to survive and thrive is up to you. I hope you choose to become part of the next evolution of *growth teams* with artificial and human intelligence working together to build successful startups that will change the world for the better. I encourage you to continue to evolve your startup growth team as well, to ensure you have the momentum to propel your performance to the next level with AI + growth marketing working together. There's never going to be any shortcut to scaling user growth. If you zoom out into the future and look back, the biggest impact of AI intelligent machines will be giving startups a competitive edge to increase customer acquisition at a much faster pace to disrupt the status quo and make the world a better place through more business innovation.

> *The future is about AI and humans working together as a team.*

In growth teams you have an opportunity to either be the driver or a passenger. I challenge you to step up and be one of the drivers in your startup, and influence the role of AI instead of being a backseat passenger who has to react to change with little control. The best part about technology is that it's always evolving. Many effects of AI are unknown, but one thing is certain—that the best growth teams will fully embrace Lean AI in some way, shape, or form.

It is up to you to join the the Lean AI movement as a champion for Customer Acquisition 3.0, which—as you have learned—depends on leveraging "intelligent machines" and orchestrating complex campaigns across key marketing platforms: dynamically allocating budgets, pruning creatives, surfacing insights, and taking actions autonomously. These machines have the potential to drive great performance with a far more efficient Lean team using a hands-off management approach powered by artificial intelligence. I encourage you to be one of the early innovators, to go all in and embrace the future of customer acquisition today, and to pave your startup's path to sustainable massive user growth and a successful exit. Good luck, and may the AI superpower force be with you.

Index

A

A/B testing, 8, 86, 126
acquisition cohorts, 75
actionable insights, 27, 36
activation, 136
activity notifications, 138
ad fatigue, 84
ad inventory management, 143
adaptive fingerprinting, 101
advertising networks, 148
advocacy phase, 41
AI-based service agents, 35
AI-generated video content, 37
algorithms
    biased, 168
    building better, 17
    common principle underlying, 16
    semi-supervised, 47
    shaping behavior with, 16
    supervised, 46, 49
    supervised or unsupervised, 47, 51
    unsupervised, 50
    uses for, 16
AlphaGo, 47
Amazon Machine Learning services, 69
Amazon Prime, 12
Amazon Web Services (AWS), 32
Android ID, 122
app indexing, 122
app performance analysis, 129
app store analytics and intelligence, 123
App Store Optimization (ASO), 131
app streaming, 150
Apple Search, 134
application programming interfaces
    (APIs), 9, 33, 54, 162
AppsFlyer
    adaptive fingerprinting, 101
    conversion path dashboards, 107
    Sankey diagram, 104
    used as source of truth for mobile
        attribution, 54
artificial general intelligence (AGI), 37
artificial intelligence (AI) (see also Lean
    AI)
    bedrock of, 166
    benefits of, 20, 158
    black box problem, 167
    CDP as lifeblood of, 192
    changing definition of, 12
    customer acquisition and, 27
    defined, 12
    future of, 201
    hype and realty of, 159
    job opportunities created by, 178, 183
    key drivers of
        algorithms, 16
        availability of data, 15
        computing power, 15
    versus machine learning, 11

multiple technologies involved in, 174
predicting and shaping behavior with, 16, 36
streamlining marketing processes with, 20
trends for AI marketing, 17-20
winning together with, 201-206
artificial neural networks (ANNs), 47
Athena Prime
    Audience Selection, 56
    collaboration with Nectar9, 65
    Custom Audiences, 57
    data sources, 54
    key components abstracted by, 55
    Message Placement, 58
    optimization engine, 58
    parameters fed into, 55
Athena Sense, 56
attention economy, 6-9
attention mechanisms, 168
attribution, 122 (see also marketing attribution; people-based attribution)
attribution accuracy, 34
audience behavior
    creating lookalike audiences, 36
    predicting and shaping, 16
audience selection, 56
automated media buying, 33, 37
automation
    creation of job opportunities by, 178
    fear of job loss due to, 177, 197
autonomous marketing
    assessing maturity of, 21
    benefits of AI for, 158
    IMVU customer journey, 59
autonomous vehicles, 5, 21
awareness phase, 39
Azure Machine Learning, 69

B

B2C funnel, 113-115
Bayes's theorem, 52
best practices
    creative best practices, 86
    mobile ads best practices, 88
Bezos, Jeff, 46, 202
biased algorithms, 168

billing and revenue reporting, 127
black box problem, 167
blind spots, 169
brainstorming, 84
brand awareness, 85
browser cookies, 122
budget
    build versus buy analysis, 65
    financial savings of AI, 159
    for testing new channels, 29
    optimizing media mix and, 104
build-measure-learn feedback loop, 17
bundling, 142
business goals, 161, 171

C

California Consumer Privacy Act (CCPA), 101
call to action (CTA), 85, 87
Cambridge Analytica scandal, 195
campaign measurement, 123, 188
Carvell, Andy, 119
challenges, preparing for
    data acquisition, 193-195
    fraud prevention and detection, 199
    new channels and opportunities, 198
    privacy controls, 195-197
    team downsizing, 197
channels (see also platforms)
    experimenting with mix of, 146
    new channels and opportunities, 198
chatbots, 35, 150
Chief Executive Officer (CEO), 184
churn rate, 28
cloud computing, 32
cohort analysis, 75, 112, 124
color emotion guide, 87
community engagement and support, 139
complexity management, 157-163
    customer data, 162
    expected value, 159
    focus on outcomes, 161
    metrics selection, 162
    need for, 157
    operational state, 161
    use cases for, 158
compliance, 169

computing power, 15
concept drift, 171
consumer behavior, predicting and shaping, 16, 36
consumer marketing funnel, 113-115
content
   snackable, 87
   unique, 116
content analytics, 125
content curation, 34
content indexing, 134
content marketing, 132
contractors, 7
conversion, 38, 107
conversion funnels, 126
conversion rate (CR), 78
conversion rate optimization (CRO), 145
cost reduction, 159
creative generation, 36
creative performance
   ad fatigue, 84
   creative best practices, 86
   creative campaign inputs, 82
   creative scheduling, 83
   future development and iteration, 89
   importance of creative assets, 81
   mobile ads best practices, 88
   scaling customer acquisition, 85
   using creating teams, 84
cross-channel approach
   advantages of each platform, 28
   challenges of, 28
   consistent, 86
   marketing orchestration, 33, 37
cross-channel attribution
   defined, 91
   marketing attribution
      benefits of, 97
      defined, 92
      model selection, 95
      model types, 92
      people-based, 98-107
      tools for, 96
cross-functional approach
   benefits of, 6
   complexity created by, 157
   winning together mindset, 202
cross-selling, 34, 134

custom audiences, 57
customer acquisition
   artificial intelligence and, 27
   best approach to, 81
   build versus buy
      analysis of, 64-66
      combined approaches, 69
      Machine Learning as a Service (MLaaS), 69
      product requirements document, 63
      recommendations for, 70
      risks of building, 66-68
      risks of buying, 68
      stakeholder involvement, 64
   defined, 7, 111
   framework of an intelligent machine
      audience selection, 56
      basic elements, 45
      diagram, 56
      exploration and optimization, 58
      final steps, 62
      importance of data, 54-56
      IMVU customer journey, 58-61
      message placement, 58
      ML for marketing, 46-48
      supervised learning algorithms, 49-50
      supervised or unsupervised algorithms, 51-53
      unsupervised learning algorithms, 50
   future of, 202
   goal of, 17
   levels of, 23
   manual versus automation
      business case for automation, 43-44
      challenges of automation, 28
      customer life cycle management, 38-41
      IMVU's strategy, 41-43
      intelligent machines in digital marketing, 31-37
   new dimensions for scale and learning, 25-27
   scaling, 8, 85
   selecting the right approach to

growth stack framework, 119-153
    user acquisition strategies, 111-118
    using intelligent machines, 27-29
customer acquisition costs (CAC), 28, 29, 38, 74
customer data platforms (CDPs)
    as lifeblood of AI, 192
    benefits of, 188
    data system, 189
    decision system, 191
    delivery system, 191
    framework of, 188
    layers of, 188
    role of, 187
    single platform delivery, 189
    volume, variety, velocity, and veracity needs, 192
customer engagement, 188
customer life cycle management
    benefits of, 38
    classic customer purchase funnel, 38
    stages of
        advocacy, 41
        awareness, 39
        diagram of, 38
        engagement, 40
        evaluation, 40
        post-purchase, 41
        purchase, 40
customer lifetime value (LTV)
    calculating, 77
    increasing, 58
    LTV modeling, 127
    maximizing, 62
customer relationship management (CRM), 13, 35
customer satisfaction, 125
customer segmentation, 34, 35
customer support and service, 35
customer-centric approach, 113
Cycle Time, 134

D

Daan, Moritz, 119
daily active users (DAU), 28, 76, 124
data
    amount handled by global internet, 35
    as the core of everything
        customer data platforms, 187
        data structure and scoope, 187
        data system, 189
        decision system, 191
        delivery system, 191
    availability of, 15, 162
    biased, 168
    importance of high quality, 54-56, 162, 166
    increasing amounts of, 17, 186
    ongoing challenges of acquiring, 193-195
    persisting user data, 136
    rich user data, 26, 187
    shareable and accessible, 191
    shared versus private databases, 102
data ethics, 16, 100, 168-171
data flywheel effect, 17, 26
data fragmentation , 166
data privacy and integrity, 192, 195
data sets, 187
data silos, 186
decision trees, 51
deep learning, 20, 47
deep links, 122, 137
"deepfakes", 37
demand-side platforms (DSPs), 28, 150
deterministic matching, 101
digital fingerprint IDs, 101
digital marketing
    advances in, 31
    areas ripe for innovation
        automated media buying, 33
        content curation, 34
        creative generation, 36
        cross-channel marketing orchestration, 33
        customer support and service, 35
        insight generation, 36
        segmentation development and management, 35
        virtual marketing assistants, 34
    best applications of, 37
discount coupons and sales, 143
discriminatory data, 168
display ads
    A/B testing creative ads, 86

ad inventory management, 143
boosting ad efficiency, 105
color scheme of, 87
compelling visuals, copy, and CTAs, 87
key goal of, 87
mobile ads best practices, 88
simple and easy to understand, 87
distribution partnerships, 133
dynamic learning, 26
dynamic pricing, 142

E

email, 147
engagement phase, 40
ethics
　AI-generated video content, 37
　data ethics, 16, 100, 168-171
evaluation phase, 40
event tracking, 122
expected value, 159
experimentation
　A/B testing, 8
　benefits of, 5
　growing businesses quickly with, 14
　rapid-fire, 60
exploration and optimization, 58

F

Facebook
　accelerated adoption of AI, 27
　advances in digital marketing, 32
　Cambridge Analytica scandal, 195
　diversified mix of platforms, 28
　monetization of customers by, 169
　Universal App Campaigns, 42
Federal Trade Commission (FTC), 197
financial savings, 159
fingerprinting, 101
first-party data, 26, 57, 186, 193
first-time user experience (FTUE), 136
first-touch attribution model, 93
Fourth Industrial Revolution, 11
fraud detection systems, 34
fraud prevention, 106, 199

G

General Data Protection Regulation (GDPR), 101, 169
Glossier, 117
goals, setting clear, 171
Google
　accelerated adoption of AI, 27
　advances in digital marketing, 32
　diversified mix of platforms, 28
　Universal App Campaigns, 42
Google App Indexing, 134
Google Cloud, 32
Google Cloud AI, 69
Google Home, 12
Google's Tensor Processing Unit (TPU), 15
GPT2, 37
graphics processing units (GPUs), 15
growth accounting, 128
Growth Data Scientists, 185
Growth Designers, 185
Growth Engineers, 185
Growth Marketers, 185
growth marketing
　attention economy and, 6-9
　benefits of, 3-6
　defined, 4
　focus on sustainable growth, 76
　key to successful, 112
　primary function of, 5
　working with contractors, 7
growth metrics (see metrics)
growth mindset, 177
growth modeling, 127
Growth Product Managers, 185
growth stack framework
　Acquisition layer
　　App Store Optimization (ASO), 131
　　content marketing, 132
　　cross-selling, 134
　　diagram of, 130
　　distributions deals, 133
　　influencer marketing, 133
　　performance marketing, 132
　　PR activity, 130
　　virality loops, 134

activities cutting across the stack
  ad networks, 148
  channels, 146
  conversion optimization, 145
  email, 147
  in-app messaging, 146
  internationalization, 144
  owned channels, 149
  partnerships and integrations, 144
  push notifications, 146
  retargeting, 144
  search, 147
  SMS, 147
  social networks, 148
  TV, print, and radio, 149
Analytics and Insight layer
  A/B measurement, 126
  app store analytics and intelligence, 123
  attribution, 122
  billing and revenue reporting, 127
  campaign measurement, 123
  cohort analysis, 124
  content analytics, 125
  conversion funnels, 126
  deep links, 122
  diagram of, 121
  event tracking, 122
  growth accounting, 128
  growth modeling, 127
  LTV modeling, 127
  screen flows, 126
  sentiment tracking, 125
  user segmentation, 124
  user testing, 126
app performance analysis, 129
applying the stack in an AI world, 151
defined, 119
Engagement and Retention layer
  activation, 136
  activity notifications, 138
  community (engagement and support), 139
  deep linking, 137
  diagram of, 135
  life-cycle marketing, 137
  user accounts, 136
layers of, 120

messenger platforms
  app streaming, 150
  chatbots, 150
  mobile DSPs and SSPs, 150
  opportunities created by, 149
Mobile Growth Stack, 119
Monetization layer
  ad inventory management, 143
  diagram of, 140
  payment processing, 141
  pricing, 142
  revenue model development, 140
growth teams
  being influencers rather than followers, 205
  challenges of team downsizing, 197
  five key KPI metrics recommended for, 182
  future of, 185
  hybrid, 176
  leaner, smarter, and more productive, 177
  recommended organizational structure, 183
  role in startup success, 202
  skill sets for future, 174, 183
  team members' roles in, 184

H

Head of Growth, 185
Henderson, Bruce, 25
holistic matching, 102
human attention, 7, 111
human image synthesis, 37
human intelligence
  versus intelligent machines, 29, 173-178
  role in creative performance, 84
  simulating, 12
  working with AI
    complementing strengths and weaknesses, 183, 205
    growth team future, 185
    growth team organizational structure, 183
    growth team roles, 184
    winning together mindset, 203

human–AI interaction gadgets, 12

I
IBM Watson, 69
ideation, 84
IDFA, 122
implementation (see complexity management; support systems)
IMVU (see also Athena Prime)
   business case for automation, 43
   challenges of complexity faced by, 157
   collaboration with Nectar9, 65
   customer journey at
      applying ML and AI to, 58
      autonomous marketing, 59
      iterative testing, 59
      lapsed purchaser findings, 61
      meaningful optimizations, 60
      rapid-fire experimentation, 60
   data bias discovered at, 169
   data collected by, 13
   empowerment of growth team at, 176
   growth automation strategy, 41-43
   growth metrics chosen by, 162, 182
   impact of AI on team performance, 204
   KPIs around customer acquisition costs, 29
   leading the way on the AI frontier, 27
   proof of concept as validation, 160
in-app messaging, 146
in-app purchases (IAPs), 142
industrial revolution, fourth, 11
influencer marketing, 133
insight generation, 36
intelligent assistants, 34
intelligent machines (see also Athena Prime)
   benefits of, 27-30
   build versus buy
      analysis of, 64-66
      combined approaches, 69
      Machine Learning as a Service (MLaaS), 69
      product requirements document, 63
      recommendations for, 70
      risks of building, 66-68
      risks of buying, 68
      stakeholder involvement, 64
   in digital marketing, 31-37, 158
   framework of
      audience selection, 56
      basic elements, 45
      diagram of, 56
      exploration and optimization, 58
      final steps, 62
      importance of data, 54-56
      IMVU customer journey, 58-61
      message placement, 58
      ML for marketing, 46-48
      supervised learning algorithms, 49-50
      supervised or unsupervised algorithms, 51-53
      unsupervised learning algorithms, 50
   versus human interventions, 29, 173
interactions, defined, 100
internationalization, 144
internet users, number of, 15
iterative testing, 59

J
jobs
   fear of loss due to automation, 177, 197
   opportunities created by AI, 178, 183

K
K-factor, 134
k-means algorithm, 50
k-nearest neighbor (k-NN), 50
key performance indicators (KPIs), 27, 29, 73, 181
KISS (Keep it Simple, Stupid), 87

L
lapsed purchasers, 61
last-touch attribution model, 93
Lean AI
   AI + growth marketing
      assessing maturity of autonomous marketing, 21

smart marketing, 20
artificial intelligence
   defined, 12
   hype and reality of, 11, 159
defined, 1
key drivers of artificial intelligence
   algorithms, 16
   computing power, 15
   data availability, 15
Lean Startup movement defined, 13
machine learning, 12
trends for AI marketing, 17-20
Lean AI approach, 202
Lean AI movement, 206
Lean Startup movement
   central tenants of, 14
   defined, 13
   improving chances of success with, 14
   methodology for, 112
Lean Startup, The (Ries), 5, 202
Leanplum, 13, 55
learning
   competing on the rate of, 17, 19, 26
   machine learning, 31
   static versus dynamic, 25
life-cycle marketing, 137
Liftoff, 55-55, 83
linear attribution models, 94
linear regression, 49
liquidity events, 4
logistic regression, 49
lookalike audiences, 36, 57
loyalty, 86
LTV modeling, 127

M

machine learning (ML)
   versus artificial intelligence, 12
   concept underlying, 13, 31
   decision trees, 51
   deep learning, 20, 47
   defined, 12
   diagram of types, 48
   Naïve Bayes, 52
   random forest, 53
   reinforcement learning, 47
   semi-supervised, 47
   streamlining marketing processes with, 20
   supervised, 16, 46, 49-50
   unsupervised, 47, 50
   vectorized numerical operations needed for, 15
Machine Learning as a Service (MLaaS), 69
magical moments, creating, 76
market risks, reducing, 14, 14
   (see also risks)
marketing agencies, 7
Marketing AI Autonomy scale, 33
marketing attribution
   benefits of, 97
   defined, 92
   model selection, 95
   model types, 92
   people-based, 98-107
   tools for, 96
marketing orchestration, 33, 37
   (see also digital marketing)
MarTech vendors, 159
mass media techniques, 39
matching technologies
   deterministic, 101
   holistic matching, 102
   probabilistic, 101
McCarthy, John, 12
measurables, 161
media buying, automated, 33, 37
message placement, 58
messaging, in-app, 146
messenger platforms
   app streaming, 150
   chatbots, 150
   mobile DSPs and SSPs, 150
   opportunities created by, 149
metrics
   for creative performance, 81-90
      ad fatigue, 84
      creative best practices, 86
      creative campaign inputs, 82
      creative scheduling, 83
      future development and iteration, 89
      importance of creative assets, 81
      mobile ads best practices, 88

scaling customer acquisition, 85
using creating teams, 84
for cross-channel attribution, 91-107
    benefits of, 97
    defined, 91
    marketing attribution, defined, 92
    model selection, 95
    model types, 92
    people-based, 98-107
    tools for, 96
for startup growth, 73-80
    benefits of, 73
    beware of vanity metrics, 79
    conversion rate (CR), 78
    customer acquisition costs (CAC), 74
    customer lifetime value (LTV), 77
    retention rate, 74
    return on ad spend (ROAS), 77
selecting, 162, 181
micro-transactions, 142
Microsoft Azure, 32
minimum viable product, 4
mobile ads, best practices, 88
mobile DSPs and SSPs, 150
Mobile Growth Stack, 119
mobile marketing automation (MMA), 146
monetization, strategies for, 141
monthly active users (MAU), 28, 76, 124
Moore's law, 15
multi-touch attribution models, 93

N

Naïve Bayes, 52
Native Advertising Institute 2018 chart, 151
natural language generation, 36
Nectar9, 65
Net Promoter Score (NPS), 115, 125
neural networks, 20, 32, 167
neuro-linguistic programming (NLP), 32
new user experience (NUX), 136
notifications
    activity, 138
    push, 146

O

Open AI, 37
operational state, 161
orchestration, 33, 37
outcomes, focusing on, 161
over-the-top (OTT) interactions, 100
owned channels, 149

P

paid acquisition, 115
partnerships and integrations, 144
payment processing, 141
people-based attribution, 98-107
    approaches to
        private graphs, 103
        shared graphs, 102
    current state of, 100
    need for, 98
    recognizing users behind touchpoints, 101
    use cases for
        boosting ad efficiency, 105
        fraud prevention, 106
        improving customer journey, 107
        optimizing media mix and budget allocation, 104
        smarter retargeting, 105
performance marketing, 132
performance-centric influencer platforms, 133
person-centric approach, 92
personally identifiable information (PII), 57, 167, 169, 192, 194
Phiture, 119
platforms
    advantages of each, 28
    recommendations for managing, 28
post-purchase phase, 41
PR activity, 130
predictive modeling, 16
preimplementation evaluation, 161
pricing
    app store policies, 142
    bundling, 142
    discount coupons and sales, 143
    virtual currency, dynamic pricing, and mircotransactions, 142

print advertising, 149
privacy laws, 100, 169, 195-197
private databases, 103
probabilistic classifiers, 52
probabilistic matching, 101
product innovations, 117
product requirements document (PRD), 63
product updates, 166
product/market fit
    best way to achieve, 112
    defined, 4
programmatic ad networks, 27
purchase funnel, 38, 201
purchase phase, 40
push notifications, 146

Q

quantum computing, 15

R

radio advertising, 149
random forest, 53
rate of learning, competing on, 17, 19, 26
real-time customer analytics, 191
recurrent neural networks, 47
regulatory oversight, 169
reinforcement learning, 47
Reis, Eric, 5, 8, 112, 165, 202
retargeting, 105, 144
retention, 28
retention rate
    calculating, 75
    cohort analysis and, 75
    creating magical moments, 76
    defined, 74
    goals for, 75
    identifying behaviors affecting, 76
return on ad spend (ROAS)
    benefits of intelligent machines for, 28
    calculating, 77
    channel variations in, 29
    versus return on investment (ROI), 78
return on investment (ROI)
    achieving the best, 8
    calculating, 44
    improving, 159, 188

revenue model development, 140
risk reduction
    adaptability of ML models, 171
    benefits of AI for, 159
    biased algorithms, 168
    clear goals, 171
    compliance, 169
    data dependency, 166
    need for, 165
    transparency, 167
    with Lean Startup methodology, 14

S

Sankey diagram, 104
saturation, 84
scale
    defined, 25
    new dimensions for, 25-27
screenflow tracking, 126
search, 147
Segment, 187
segmentation development and management, 34-37
self-driving cars, 5, 21
semi-supervised learning, 47
sentiment tracking, 125
service requests, 35
shared databases, 102
silo-thinking, 184
Siri, 12
smart marketing, 20
SMS, 147
snackable content, 87
social networks, 148
social proof, 85
software development kits (SDKs), 162
startups (see also Lean Startup movement)
    balancing use of intelligent machines and human intelligence, 174
    challenges of privacy regulations, 197
    failure rates, 4, 201
    five approaches for AI models, 167
    focus on key performance indicators, 27
    goal of, 111, 203

growth team organizational structure, 183
key challenges to success, 4, 7, 31, 111, 193-195, 201
key metrics for growth, 73-80, 182
largest expense for, 8
leveraging third-party tools, 120
risks faced by, 165
two phases in, 112
strategic partnerships, 117
success
    focus on key performance indicators, 27
    improving chances of, 6, 13
    increased chance of with AI, 165
    key challenges to, 4, 111, 201
    key factors for achieving, 26, 118
    planning for, 181-192
    true secret to, 202
    winning together mindset, 202
supervised learning
    algorithms for, 49
    common principle underlying, 16
    uses for, 46
supply-side platforms (SSPs), 150
support systems
    AI and humans working together, 183-186
    CDP as the lifeblood of AI, 192
    data as the core of everything
        customer data platform, 187
        data structure and scope, 186
        data system, 189
        decision system, 191
        delivery system, 191
    data privacy and integrity, 192
    success goals and measurements, 181
support vector machines (SVMs), 50
sustainable growth, 76

T

target concept, 171
targeting, 34, 86
technical transparency, 167
television advertising, 149
Tensor Processing Unit (TPU), 15
time decay attribution model, 94
touchpoints, 92
transparency, 167
trust, 167, 194

U

U-Shaped attribution mode, 94
unique content, 116
unsupervised learning
    algorithms for, 50
    uses for, 47
updates, 166
upselling, 34, 38
user accounts, 136
user acquisition strategies (see also customer acquisition)
    concepts underlying, 111-113
    five key
        content, 116
        paid acquisition, 115
        product innovations, 117
        strategic partnerships, 117
        virality, 115
    three-step plan, 114
    user funnel stages, 113-115
user segmentation, 124 (see also customer segmentation; segmentation development and management)
user testing, 126

V

vanity metrics, 79
video prediction systems, 12, 16
video-powered mobile creatives, 88
viral coefficient, 116
virality, 115
virality loops, 134
virtual currency, 142
virtual marketing assistants, 34
voice-based interfaces, 34
Voronoi cells, 51

W

W-Shaped attribution model, 95
winning together mindset, 202

About the Author

Lomit Patel (*https://www.lomitpatel.com*) is the Vice President of Growth at IMVU, responsible for user acquisition, retention, and monetization. Prior to IMVU, Lomit managed growth at early-stage startups including Roku (IPO), TrustedID (acquired by Equifax), Texture (acquired by Apple), and EarthLink. Lomit is a public speaker, author, and advisor, and is recognized as a Mobile Hero by Liftoff.

"Mandatory reading for entrepreneurs."
—DAN HEATH, co-author of *Switch* and *Made to Stick*

THE NEW YORK TIMES BESTSELLER
THE LEAN STARTUP

How Today's Entrepreneurs Use Continuous Innovation to Create Radically Successful Businesses

ERIC RIES

"The essential template to understand the crucial leadership challenge of our time: initiating and managing growth!"
—WARREN BENNIS, Distinguished Professor of Business, University of Southern California

"Changes how we think about innovation and entrepreneurship."
—*THE FINANCIAL TIMES*

@LEANSTARTUP   FACEBOOK.COM/ERICRIES

THELEANSTARTUP.COM
LEARN MORE ABOUT HOW DROPBOX, WEALTHFRONT, AND OTHER SUCCESSFUL STARTUPS ARE BUILDING THEIR BUSINESSES.

CROWN BUSINESS